ROUTLEDGE LIBRARY EDITIONS: MANAGEMENT

Volume 25

ADMINISTRATIVE VITALITY

ADMINISTRATIVE VITALITY
The Conflict With Bureaucracy

MARSHALL E. DIMOCK

LONDON AND NEW YORK

First published in 1960 by Routledge & Kegan Paul Ltd.

This edition first published in 2018
by Routledge
2 Park Square, Milton Park, Abingdon, Oxon OX14 4RN

and by Routledge
711 Third Avenue, New York, NY 10017

Routledge is an imprint of the Taylor & Francis Group, an informa business

© 1959 Marshall E. Dimock

All rights reserved. No part of this book may be reprinted or reproduced or utilised in any form or by any electronic, mechanical, or other means, now known or hereafter invented, including photocopying and recording, or in any information storage or retrieval system, without permission in writing from the publishers.

Trademark notice: Product or corporate names may be trademarks or registered trademarks, and are used only for identification and explanation without intent to infringe.

British Library Cataloguing in Publication Data
A catalogue record for this book is available from the British Library

ISBN: 978-1-138-55938-7 (Set)
ISBN: 978-1-351-05538-3 (Set) (ebk)
ISBN: 978-0-8153-9211-8 (Volume 25) (hbk)
ISBN: 978-1-351-19991-9 (Volume 25) (ebk)

Publisher's Note
The publisher has gone to great lengths to ensure the quality of this reprint but points out that some imperfections in the original copies may be apparent.

Disclaimer
The publisher has made every effort to trace copyright holders and would welcome correspondence from those they have been unable to trace.

Administrative Vitality

Vitality

The Conflict With Bureaucracy

Marshall E. Dimock
Author of *A Philosophy of Administration,* etc.

Routledge and Kegan Paul
LONDON

First Published in England 1960
by Routledge & Kegan Paul Ltd.
Broadway House, 68-74 Carter Lane
London, E.C.4
Printed in Great Britain by
Lowe & Brydone (Printers) Ltd.
London, N.W.10
© *Marshall E. Dimock 1959*

No part of this book may be reproduced in any form without permission from the publisher, except for the quotation of brief passages in criticism.

To Louis Brandeis in partial fulfillment of a pledge made shortly before his death

Contents

		Introduction	ix
Chapter	1.	Vitality in Administration	1
Part	I:	Growth	
Chapter	2.	Pioneering in Big Business	11
Chapter	3.	Some Theories of Growth	32
Chapter	4.	Some Theories of Decay	45
Part	II:	Bureaucracy	
Chapter	5.	British Electricity	61
Chapter	6.	The Traditional Case for Bureaucracy	76
Chapter	7.	A New Look at Bureaucracy	86
Chapter	8.	The Pathologies of Bureaucracy	102

Contents   viii

Part III: Enterprise

Chapter 9.	Incentive and Idea	121
Chapter 10.	Person and Process	136
Chapter 11.	Marks and Spencer	153

Part IV: The Best of Both Worlds

Chapter 12.	Integrative Leadership	175
Chapter 13.	Decentralization	199
Chapter 14.	Responsibility and Response	218
Chapter 15.	Power and Security	241
Chapter 16.	A Vital Economy	261
	Notes	273
	Index	293

Introduction

A man heading a vigorous enterprise experiences the same thrill as a sailor with a spanking wind. And in each case the question lurking around the border of his consciousness is, "How long can it last?"

"I'd give a hundred thousand dollars," said a businessman to me some years ago, "if someone could tell me how to keep this corporation as hard-hitting as it's been in the past." He told me what he was worried about: promotions according to seniority instead of ability, the turning out of administrative specialists interested in patterns and procedures instead of businessmen interested in enterprise, the dilution of loyalty among executives and employees, the difficulty of stimulating that extra bit of drive that spells the difference between mere survival on the one hand and a rewarding profit on the other. "Today," he added, "people are more interested in their own security than they are in using their imagination and taking chances that might pay off."

This was in 1937. The discussion was part of a study I was making of bureaucracy and enterprise in large corporations, public and private. In a four-year period my assistants and I had interviewed some 250 corporation officials in a score of companies, and everywhere we heard the same complaint: Bureaucracy is inherent in large-scale organization; enterprise is harder to maintain than it used to be; what can be done about it?

This book is concerned with these central questions.

Some undertakings never seem to develop energy at all because they lack some vital ingredient such as incentive, or leadership, or the ability to discard a worn-out tradition. Others are full-sail for a while and soon slow down; indifference sets in, then inertia, and finally decay and they give way before a hardier competitor.

Why? What is the secret of vitality in administration? What ensures growth and prevents decay? What are the advantages and the disadvantages of bureaucracy and of its opposite pole, enterprise? What would happen if the best in each were identified and deliberately combined?

There is a paradox here that worries the American and British business leaders with whom I have talked: vitality in administration ensures growth, which often results in large size. With size comes a need for formalism in structure and method. But formalism breeds inflexibility, rigidity, sluggishness. An institution so affected may appear hale, but its weaknesses are apparent when some kind of stress occurs, such as the need to adjust to the conditions of war or depression, or a challenge presented by a more alert competitor.

Since I first studied the question of administrative vitality in the 1930's, the problem has become acute; and when William H. Whyte, Jr., wrote *The Organization Man* in 1956, most Americans had to admit that the unhappy situation he described was not overdrawn.

Some of the chapters in the present book are a discussion of bureaucracy and enterprise and how they are related and might be combined, and others are case studies of particular businesses in illustration. Most of these companies are large and all have been at least partially successful in solving some of the difficulties of administration that businessmen and government officials constantly encounter.

Of the five objectives of this book, the first is to show what is meant by vitality in institutions and their administration, and

Introduction xi

the second is to discover the causes of institutional growth and decay. The third is to take a new look at the concept of bureaucracy in an attempt to identify those aspects of it that are basic to all successful administration. The fourth is to take a similar look at the concept of enterprise. And the fifth is to show how the best aspects of both can be combined to form an amalgam that is vital administration.

Although all this is a large order, it is worth a try. I write not primarily for other scholars, but as an administrator-scholar concerned with the needs of executives in large organizations, both business and governmental. The studies I made during the 1930's were sponsored by the Laura Spelman Rockefeller Foundation while I was on the faculty of the University of Chicago. These studies centered on some of America's largest corporations, including American Telephone and Telegraph Company, General Motors, Pennsylvania Railroad, and Sears, Roebuck. The procedure was based on interviews, sometimes repeated, with officials at various levels from the president down to field supervisors. My assistants and I were also allowed to read confidential reports and administrative surveys and to watch bureaucratic situations in practice—a telephone exchange in operation, for example, or the processing department of a large insurance company.

Since that early work I have made similar studies of governmental programs, including public corporations in Britain and the United States, and state enterprises in Turkey and other so-called underdeveloped countries. I have also worked in old-line government agencies, such as the Department of Labor and the Justice Department, and in temporary agencies like the War Shipping Administration.

Then in 1958, with the support of the Alfred P. Sloan Foundation, I studied bureaucracy and enterprise in Great Britain, where most of this book was written. As in the initial period of the 1930's, the main concentration was on a group of business corporations, but also included were some nationalized industries and old-line government departments. In addition, I have benefited from two periods of observation at the Administrative Staff Col-

Introduction xii

lege at Henley-on-Thames, where men representing a cross section of the British economy come to grips with problems of administration, including the maintenance of administrative vitality.

Although the factors of bureaucracy and of enterprise appear everywhere the same, their emphases and combinations differ, depending on environment and the prevailing culture. Hence the advantage of studying vitality on a comparative basis as between countries and as between the programs of business and of government. In Britain, for example, administration is influenced by tradition and class structure, whereas in the United States it is fascinated by large size and tidiness of organization.

It seems equally clear that a study of vitality must draw from a number of different fields, including economic history, social psychology, and sociology, as well as from business administration and public administration, which normally are most closely related to the matter of institutional vitality. So diversified an approach runs the danger of giving less than satisfaction to the various academic specialists whose work is drawn upon, of course, and must be accompanied by apologies for any lack of sophistication that may appear.

The universal importance of administrative vitality has stimulated a number of books in recent years that deserve mention here. In addition to William H. Whyte, Jr., *The Organization Man*, there is a study by C. Wright Mills entitled *White Collar* that is directly pertinent. The Royal Institute of Public Administration in Great Britain has published two studies entitled *Large-Scale Organisation* and *Vitality in Administration*. E. N. Gladden has written *Civil Service or Bureaucracy?* and a Russian, Vladimir Dudintsev, a novel called *Not by Bread Alone*. Robert Merton has edited a book called *Reader in Bureaucracy*. The Harvard Research Center in Entrepreneurial History has brought out two symposia, *Change and the Entrepreneur* and *Entrepreneurship and Economic Growth*. Joseph A. Schumpeter wrote *Capitalism, Socialism, and Democracy*, and W. Arthur Lewis, *The Theory of Economic Growth*. And *Parkinson's Law*, by C.

Introduction xiii

Northcote Parkinson, says some sharp things under its spoofing approach.

Against this backdrop, the present book is an attempt to break new ground, to suggest some new syntheses, to seek some practical explanations, and to propose some practical solutions. It is but one of many, however, that will have to be written if the problem of administrative vitality is to be solved.

In preparing and writing this book over a period of years, I am deeply indebted to many people: not only to those authors whose works are mentioned here, but to others whose books and articles are cited in the footnotes; not only to those busy officials whose names are mentioned in the footnotes, but to scores of others who have taken the time to discuss my subject and their experience with me. I want especially to thank Mr. Arthur Page, former Vice-President of American Telephone and Telegraph Company, who arranged my entrees in the early studies; and Sir Henry Bunbury and Sir Noel Hall, who performed a similar service in connection with the British phases of my work. I would also acknowledge again the financial assistance of the Laura Spelman Rockefeller Foundation and the University of Chicago, and of the Alfred P. Sloan Foundation and New York University. My wife, Gladys Ogden Dimock, edited the final draft and counseled me at all stages of the study.

MARSHALL E. DIMOCK

Alderney
Channel Islands
September, 1958

Chapter *1* *Vitality in Administration*

A spirited enterprise appeals to the customer and hence has an edge over its competitors. But this spirit, which is vitality in administration, is hard to develop and harder to maintain. At present, too little is known about the causes of bureaucratic excesses, about the *mystique* of exceptional enterprise, or about the blend that is the best of both, to assure the maintenance of vitality either in individual programs or in the economy as a whole.

Bureaucracy is now a universal phenomenon in newly industrialized countries, as in the older ones. Nor is there any favoritism as between the affairs of business and those of government. Every industrialized nation has developed bureaucratic excesses that threaten to check its further advance. And even where industrialization is not a factor, there are traditional ways of doing things that encourage bureaucracy and discourage enterprise.[1] In either case, there is a dearth of administrative skills and managerial leadership, and especially of leadership that has found the key to vitality.

My thesis here is that bureaucracy is now in large supply and that enterprise is fading and needs to be restored; that the four main elements of bureaucracy are hierarchy, specialization, rules, and impersonality; and the four main ingredients of enterprise are incentive, idea, person, and process. Bureaucracy is formal and orderly and its strength is science and technology. Enterprise is personal and spontaneous and its strength is innovation and adaptation to change. The weaknesses of bureaucracy are self-centeredness, the avoidance of personal responsibility, and a quest for power, often in petty ways. The weaknesses of enterprise are confusion, lack of follow-through, and a disregard for system that approaches anarchy. Bureaucracy and enterprise complement each other at essential points.

The conditions requisite to vitalized administration are, first, a social environment that emphasizes responsibility and a broad approach to education, incentives that encourage competition and self-development, and institutional management under unified leadership, accompanied by delegations of authority to foster the maximum development of the potential abilities of administrators and employees throughout the program.

From infant industries to the councils of state, bureaucracy is in the news. So also is the search for its enterprise correctives and the secret of institutional vitality. Over a period of a few months in 1957 and 1958, for example, the following news stories were collected at random from various American and British newspapers:

President Eisenhower is trying to stop the infighting amongst the three professionalized services in the Pentagon.

Russia radically reforms her economic system, seeking regional and local decentralization so as to avoid the delay and cumbersomeness of centralized bureaucracy and to foster discretion and initiative.

The largest corporation in the United States announces that it is sending its top executives back to school; they need broadening and humanizing.

Reports out of Viet-Nam are that the dilemma there is "uniformity, deadly uniformity," and that a relaxation toward individualism is sought.

A congressional committee reports that one of the nation's leading labor unions is run by a self-perpetuating oligarchy more interested in its own welfare than in that of the rank and file. The railroads complain that they cannot compete because they are bureaucratized; government rules them with a heavy hand. Their competitors counter with the charge that the bureaucratic methods are of the carriers' own making.

Special committees in Great Britain report that under nationalization, the coal and electricity industries find it hard to be enterprising because the government withholds funds needed for capital investment and imposes too centralized a control; decentralization is said to be the remedy.

American motorcar manufacturers are losing their market to foreign competitors because they failed to anticipate consumer preferences correctly.

France's economy is said to be imperiled because too many "petty bureaucrats" are running things; a new method of producing administrators is sought.

Consumer cooperatives discover that when the business passes a certain size in membership and financial volume, member participation in management and educational affairs falls off sharply, placing an inappropriate responsibility on the paid staff.

Housewives contend that there are too few general practitioners and too many specialists; the old-fashioned doctor had better judgment because he understood the whole body better than the specialist.

Stockholders try, unsuccessfully, to displace the management of a corporation on the ground that it gives in too readily to labor and officer pressure and has too little regard for the owners' interests.

BUREAUCRACY AND ENTERPRISE

Bureaucracy is not necessarily a word of opprobrium, although it is often used that way. It is assumed in the present study that certain elements of bureaucracy are necessary to administrative efficiency and vitality. So the opprobrium is discounted here and the term is used in its positive sense. It is only the excesses of bureaucracy that are negative and objectionable.

Bureaucracy is the ordering of institutional management to secure the advantages of system. It is analogous to scientific management and to all "rational" method. Indeed, the argument for bureaucracy was summed up by Alexander Pope when he remarked that "Order is Heaven's first law." But bureaucracy in excess is logic carried to the point where executives and employees are more interested in tidiness than in people, as a fussy woman is concerned about the appearance of her sitting room.

An uncritical reverence for tradition is a constant invitation to rigidity and unresponsiveness in administration. So also is the large, hierarchical, specialized, impersonal organization associated with technology. These are the two factors which, singly or together, help to explain why institutional resistance is as much a problem in New York and London as it is in Ankara or Moscow, as different as these environments are in so many other ways.

The extent to which bureaucracy is found in any organization depends on both external and internal factors. Among the principal external factors are tradition, legalism, theocracy, concentrated economic and political power, technology, and a failure of inventiveness. The internal factors are the ingredients of administration that produce order and system: fixed targets, organization charts, procedure manuals, work plans, job classifications, control mechanisms, to mention only the more obvious ones. But not all of administration is of this formal character; much of it is informal and includes small groups that work near each other, the face-to-face relationships between administrators and employees, more or less tacit delegations of responsibility, and chance meetings at the water cooler or the cafeteria. Generally speaking, bureaucracy becomes necessary and important as direct, face-to-face relationships are superseded by remote, formal relationships; and when this element of vitality is lost, another element, which is system and power, is gained. The desirable objective is to retain both elements of strength in the same program.

In contrast to the stabilizing character of bureaucracy, enterprise is receptive to change. Enterprise is the expectation that innovation will occur and that progress is continual. It is a willingness to take chances, a welcoming of new ideas and methods, a readiness to part with the old if the new seems better, an incentive to efficiency, to reduce waste and to increase profits by means that are not necessarily tried and true. Enterprise is a strong desire to create and to be one's own boss, a driving energy prepared to overcome all opposition, a resiliency that makes quick adaptation possible, an ability to decide and to act without delay, and to carry others along on the new course. Enterprise is the encouragement of initiative, responsiveness, and orientation toward the consumer and his desires. It is an incentive, an idea, a person, and a process.

Both bureaucracy and enterprise contain a large element of rationality because both are concerned with the calculation and the achievement of a goal. They are alike also in being essentially neutral concepts, neither good nor bad in the customary or moral sense. Both inhere in all administration, furthermore, and it is the balance between them that determines the vitality or the lethargy with which institutions operate.

VITALITY

Vitality in administration is energy plus endurance, the ability to compete and the power to survive. Vitality is also a kind of graciousness that offers people satisfactions that are qualitative and subjective. A vital enterprise responds to people and to circumstances, and adapts to changing wants and conditions. Thus vitality combines the qualities of strength, drive, endurance, sensitivity, responsiveness, and adaptability in a synthesis called institutional management.

In a competitive field, where the margin of difference between mere survival on the one hand and an acceptable profit on the other is often infinitesimal, the firm that attracts and retains the customer is the vital one. It puts out the best product or service and makes improvements in them ahead of its rivals. It conducts research into methods as well as into materials. It consults consumer preferences and studies the advanced techniques of other producers. When technologies change, when war or depression occurs, when substitutes are found, when for any reason change takes place, the vital firm is the first to respond. It is managed by energetic and efficient executives and there are well-prepared plans for replacing them when they retire.

Of all its competitors, the vital firm has the clearest objectives and policies and an organization system most directly related to the achievement of these objectives. It does most to encourage and to reward independence, initiative, and invention. It makes use of all the incentives that are effective in a given society or that can be drawn from elsewhere, including the universal incentive which is the opportunity to develop selfhood. It has developed reliable means of measuring efficiency, administrative as well as financial, qualitative as well as quantitative. It is adept at planning and scheduling work aimed at reducing waste and securing economy of effort, but it never allows system, as system, to get the upper hand. And most of all, vital administration creates an environment in which everyone, employees and customers alike, is enthusiastic about the product, the reputation of the firm, and the atmosphere that permeates it.

"That extra 5 per cent!" How often have I heard that expression and that emphasis from business executives with whom I have discussed bureaucracy and enterprise. When one asks about it, that extra 5 per cent often turns out to consist of factors that are of a qualitative nature: the atmosphere of the shop or office, the personality of the sales clerk, the degree of individual attention accorded the customer, a feeling of belonging on the part of employees. These are all enterprise factors in administration, and the secret of the extra 5 per cent is the way they are combined with the useful factors of bureaucracy to produce a blend of efficiency and spirit that will please all parties of interest, and especially the consumer.

If vital administration is one that is able quickly to adapt to change, so also must it sometimes initiate change in order to avoid or to correct the excesses of bureaucracy.[2] For its part, bureaucracy is normally resistant to change and the result may be a kind of paralysis. Enterprise, on the other hand, is a principal cause of change, sometimes rapid change, as in technological innovation; and if administrators are not alert, disequilibriums attack them on another blind side and the resulting confusion causes a loss of morale and efficiency in all parts of the program.[3]

Vitality in administration applies not only to individual firms but also, I believe, to whole nations. In an economy where selling is combined with engineering, competition with quality of product, initiative with responsibility, and individualism with group effort, the extra 5 per cent is the sum of many small triumphs of technical and qualitative efficiency. It is a slightly greater inventiveness in the laboratory and in social organization, a keener perception of what people want and what will make them buy, a slightly higher level of morale pervading the nation and its institutions. Such a morale is sustained by many things, including culture, tradition, climate, economic prosperity, and patriotism.

But the same fatigue curve that operates in the individual operates also in institutions and in nations. Like people, nations are capable of periods of intense concentration, during which administrative efficiency and vitality are sustained at a high level. And if long continued, intensive work of this kind leads to physical and spiritual fatigue and then to listlessness, indifference, and decay.

Skillful administration will find ways to avoid this fatigue while maintaining a high level of performance, keeping incentives alive, and nurturing the qualitative factors that mark the difference between successful and unsuccessful competition. We in the West, because of our long experience with industry and urbanism, should be better able to keep our institutions vital than the peoples of nations that must still win their freedoms. But we must know what we are about and recognize the pitfalls of concentrated power and complacency, of excessive bureaucracy and depersonalized incentives. How foolish we would be, therefore, if, mistaking the smoothly operating excesses of bureaucracy for efficiency, we were to emphasize this concept to the neglect of enterprise, and find ourselves slowing down at a time when survival depends on an alert adaptation to the demands of a changing world.

Part *I* Growth

Vitality in institutions, as in all physical organisms, depends on how well the mechanism responds to the aging process and to environmental change.

We assume here that organization is an organic growth and that certain distinctive problems arise at various stages in this evolution. Generally speaking, enterprise comes easiest during the early growth period, when there is greater mobility and needs and opportunities are more readily appreciated. Bureaucratic problems appear with age, size, and complexity.

We shall turn to biology and to history for clues as to what happens in institutional growth, and to economic history and organizational case studies for illustrations.

A workable theory of growth and the reasons for decay will help to explain why bureaucracy and enterprise occur and how they might be combined to strengthen administrative vitality.

Chapter 2 *Pioneering in Big Business*

When a revolutionary new product or service appears on the scene, and at the same time a strong personality also appears, an empire is likely to be built in a short time. During this period a driving force is at work, apparently without much thought for proper methods of organization and administration, but successful nonetheless because the opportunity is so great. Then, when the corporate edifice has been created, sometimes so complicated as to defy understanding from the outside, the government and the public begin to be concerned about the power, political as well as economic, represented by the young giant.

At this point in the growth of the giant, the corporate administration consolidates its position. It gives more attention to organization and administration. It "institutionalizes," so to speak, dispersing authority internally instead of concentrating it in the hands of the entrepreneurs, as in the early days. A new type of administrator gains dominance: the careerist, the systems man, who takes the place of the first-generation "driver." The corporation develops a social conscience. It conducts research into new products, new fields, new methods. It begins to have the feeling that its good luck may not last indefinitely and that it will need more thought, more planning, and more careful study if it is to retain the position it has won so quickly.

Both figuratively and literally, the corporation also becomes more political, instinctively realizing that this is necessary to survival. Bureaucratic problems begin to appear, partly because of the rapid transition from the promotional to the stewardship stage of growth, but also because so little is known about what bureaucracy is, what causes its excesses, and what can be done about it that it gains a foothold before it is much noticed. The remedy for failures of system is thought to be more system, and hence experts are appointed to study the problems that for the most part have been created by other experts. Staff services multiply: the new type of scientific businessman needs scientific staff men to guide him. For one thing, this adds to his feeling of security, for his institution has begun to be attacked from the outside world and he is baffled by the changed attitude.

The rate of development slows down. Anxiety about enterprise now replaces the earlier concern with system. Corporations that have stuck to one line look around for new ones; they call it "diversification." This poses a new difficulty, a problem resembling that of political states: the corporation runs several, not merely one program, simultaneously, and it is hard to know at any one time what each part of the body is doing. Before, it was big in one direction; now it is big in many directions.

Nor is the outcome of all this evolution fully known, for we have been in the period of conglomerate enterprise too short a time to allow a sober assessment of either the problems or the consequences.

The history of no two corporations is identical, of course, and the environment of the age affects them all, but not in identical ways because some businesses are better able to chart an independent course and to adjust to change than others. Nevertheless, the biographies of businesses that are available[1] do seem to show striking resemblances between corporations and other forms of large-scale organization in the growth stages they pass through from birth to maturity, from simplicity to complexity. Enterprise comes easiest in the early stage, harder later on; and problems of bureaucracy become recognized at a certain point when they are already fairly well established, and seem to continue indefinitely thereafter unless corrective measures are taken.

Although corporate growth has been chosen for illustrative purposes here, the programs of government also, of course, are subject to constant change and modification. Indeed, there is more of this than is usually appreciated, as a look at government employment and expenditure figures will show quickly. Major departments are constantly being created, or renamed, or their work distributed, or their units rearranged. Partly this movement is in response to the needs of transitions between war and peace, and between prosperity and depression, mirroring changing community requirements. A second reason is the influence of strong personalities as these are brought to bear on administration through the political process; when strong men are assigned to a particular activity in government, the effects on it in terms of growth may be pronounced indeed, where the impact of a lesser personality may be imperceptible.

The case histories that follow relate to four firms that have pioneered in big business: an oil company, a milling company, a soap company, and a chemicals company. It is not supposed that four illustrations, or even forty, will wholly validate a thesis. The present ones were picked at random, however, and seem to offer instructive examples of what occurs in the actual growth of a big business from neophyte to bureaucracy.

STANDARD OIL

The history of Standard Oil from 1882 to 1911 is told by Professor Ralph W. Hidy and Mrs. Hidy in their book *Pioneering in Big Business;* the years from 1911 through 1927 are covered by George S. Gibb and Evelyn H. Knowlton in *The Resurgent Years.* These two books probably throw more light on the inside administrative history of a large company than any other study that has ever been made.[2]

The first volume picks up the story, not with the founding of the original companies by John D. Rockefeller and others, but with the beginnings of the combine twenty years later. "The roots of Standard Oil's policies," comment the Hidys, "went deep in . . . personalities,"[3] a statement that probably constitutes a valid generalization for most concerns that have sprung rapidly into prominence. Standard Oil was a combination of several preexisting companies, some of which were headed by strong men, and then there was Rockefeller himself. The initial problem, therefore, was how they were all to get along without friction. The answer was to set up a committee-type device and let each strong man pretty much run his own show, thus getting the best of both worlds: individual effort and collective enterprise.

This solution, which was adopted early in the 1870's, became the pattern of Standard Oil's operation almost down to the present day. The secret, say the Hidys, is that a group of vigorous executives worked closely together and almost dissociated from the members of the combine. And yet, "men and firms raced with each other in reducing costs, devising new techniques, developing products, improving their quality, and showing profits."[4]

Although there was competition and enterprise, however, there were also some of the characteristics of bureaucracy, notably organizational labyrinths and a protective wall of anonymity behind which the combine carried on without much interference. In discussing Standard Oil's administrative and organizational methods, the Hidys uncover the sinews of bureaucracy, emphasizing four things especially.

The first was decision making by consultation and agreement through committees of executives (hierarchy but with face-to-face relations). The second was the development of the staff function as a means of adding to the knowledge and thinking power of executives meeting in committees (a pooled service typical of bureaucracy). The third was the standardization of accounting, auditing, and statistics to facilitate common policies and to allow the widest possible delegation of authority to operating units (the control function combined with decentralization). And the fourth was an emphasis on innovation, not merely technical innovation such as new ways of splitting petroleum, but also administrative innovation relating to personnel systems, for example (enterprise promoted by competition). What these four factors added up to was efficiency at the center administered by a skillful bureaucracy, plus efficiency at the operating level administered by executives enjoying a high degree of freedom.

The pivot of these semiautonomous operations was a central brain exercising control through a headquarters office and a small staff. As might be expected, when size and complexity increased, administrative integration grew correspondingly important. Early in the life of the combine an eight-man committee was the focus for day-to-day management. "This informal, flexible committee was both policy committee and chief executive agency, long-range and routine."[5] Then as now, officials in this control group wore two hats: in the board room they made policy and outside of it they operated subsidiary companies or headed functional divisions. It was an unorthodox form of organization and defied all the principles of modern organization theory, but the plain fact is that it worked.

One of the first great administrators in Standard Oil's history was John D. Archbold, of whom the Hidys say that he never tried to restrict his subordinates' initiative and originality by imposing his own opinion on them; but he did expect detailed reports from them, especially in the field.[6] The policy was never to issue orders; administration was by suggestion and "requests," but there was rarely any doubt about compliance. "You gentlemen on the ground," said the elder Rockefeller on one occasion, "can judge better than we about the matter, but let us not drift into arrangements where we cannot control the policy." A system of unified policy making and decentralized operations had, of course, to be accompanied by a great deal of delegation, and the rule was: "He should be big enough to run the entire business subject to only general advice on policy. It is too big and complicated to be run at arm's length." In order to assure maximum efficiency in field operations—and this also was unorthodox—the executive committee often selected two men of complementary abilities.[7]

In this setup, where was the entrepreneurial function located? The Hidys answer this question clearly: "The entrepreneurial function was diffused throughout the organization. Though final approval of action resided in the top echelon, ideas originated all along the chain of command and were so modified that the identity of the actual parent was usually forever lost. . . . Although a few decisions appear to have been made by the directors with a minimum of suggestions from lower echelons, by far the majority of directorial acts appear to have resulted from specific recommendations from field men."[8]

Thus most of the money-making ideas, especially in this early period, moved from the bottom to the top. It was the field people, for example, who pressed the parent company into the *production* of petroleum products, which led to the "integrated business" and in 1911 resulted in the Supreme Court decision dissolving the trust. It was also the field people who insisted on the development of the natural gas business as a side line: "The decision of Standard Oil to go into the natural gas business," say the Hidys, "is an excellent example of a move initiated on the lower rungs of the managerial ladder. . . . Top management approved going into the natural gas industry but depended on the men in the field *both to carry out plans and to make suggestions for new steps.*"[9] In this developmental stage, "the usual competitive struggle was enlivened by the aggressiveness of individuals," which, incidentally, is a preliminary insight into what entrepreneurship involves.

There was also the element of power, a power which kept growing but which was also kept in reserve and brought forth when needed, subduing all opposition. Standard Oil was "an association of business houses united under one management in such a manner as to insure harmony of interests, and *a consolidation of capital adequate to any possible business emergency,* yet each retaining its individuality, and even competing sharply with each other."[10]

The shift toward neater institutionalization (bureaucracy) in Standard Oil occurred just after the turn of the century and before the Supreme Court's decision in 1911 dissolving the trust. There seem to have been two major considerations: the need for more orderly internal procedures, and the demand for a greater accountability to external factors, including public opinion and the threat of governmental interference.

In its early stages, say the Hidys, Standard Oil was controlled by less than twenty people. But when these retired a new form of control was necessary because by that time the combine had grown so large that it could no longer operate through a committee. The interests of the stockholders now became the guiding consideration. Standard Oil had become what Berle and Means call a semipublic corporation, meaning one in which ownership and management have become divorced and in which accountability is not to management-owners alone but also to the public. In short, "The interests of 3,500 minority stockholders had to be secured." The consequence was that where formerly the center of decision making in important matters was an informal committee of owner-managers, now the board of directors performed that function.[11] Already by 1899 there were sixteen members of the board of directors divided into three groups: big owners who played no other role, big owners who were active in management, and small owners who had special skills and qualifications. This was the transition point between owner-management operation and the greater public accountability emphasis that lay ahead.

As for the public accountability issue, the Hidys state the principle that operates here: "A large business unit has to live by more stringent rules than a small one does."[12] In its developmental stage, Standard Oil's secret weapon had been secrecy: get the jump on competitors but don't let them see how it is done; guard your power and don't let the public or the government know what you are doing. But such a policy could not be continued indefinitely. As might be expected, Standard Oil eventually paid a price for this extreme use of secrecy; for the more there was of it, the more vulnerable the holding company became to antitrust prosecution and to the attacks of social reformers, of whom Ida Tarbell was the outstanding example. In 1906, for the first time, say the Hidys, Standard Oil decided that it was "impolitic" to use "hidden" companies to cover up integration strategies, secure tax law advantages, escape labor regulations, and the like.[13]

With its enormous size and its dominance of the field, Standard Oil now found itself impaled on the horns of a dilemma: it was damned if it did and damned if it didn't. If it established uniform prices, it was accused of price fixing and monopoly; but if it allowed prices to remain flexible, its low prices in one locality were sure to be interpreted as a weapon to drive the independents out. Already, by the time the Hidys' account terminates in 1911, with so much at stake Standard Oil was deep in industrial politics.

The second phase of the Standard Oil story, as told by Gibb and Knowlton in their book *The Resurgent Years, 1911–1927*, shows how trends once started will continue, how traditions have a way of fixing themselves on institutions, and how problems of bureaucracy inevitably accompany large size. The resurgence mentioned in the title of this book refers to the Supreme Court decision of 1911 and the resulting problem of readjustment when the trust was dissolved. The parent company was split into several major companies, some on a territorial basis, but, paradoxically, the original New Jersey company was to continue to grow almost limitlessly on a world-wide scale.

The central problem throughout this period, say Gibb and Knowlton, was how a large corporation could be made to serve society and at the same time enjoy the freedom and flexibility needed for efficient operation and adaptation to the changing needs and opportunities of the economy.[14]

During the period traced by the Hidys, we have seen that the informal committee type of administration was gradually superseded by a board of directors. Now, in the following period of adjustment, company affairs were masterminded by a central oligarchy or a bureaucracy in the best sense of those terms. A year after the Supreme Court's decision, the initiative and responsibility formerly vested in a number of committees passed to the board of directors or to certain strong individuals in the top echelons of management. Headquarters (26 Broadway at that time) became in effect "a gigantic clearinghouse, directing the movement of millions of dollars daily here and there throughout the world wherever required by the shifting necessities of the oil business."[15] New factors were a centralized staff function, a centralized research activity, and the intensive application of scientific method as contrasted with the rule-of-thumb methods sufficing in the formative years.

The staff function, as we have seen, was present from the beginning, but after 1911 it became the nerve center of an integrated world-wide system. The Hidys have pointed out, for example, that already before 1911, "If persuasion was the avenue of team play, accounting was the prod. Every operation was expected to show a profit. In many instances finance was the real key to control."[16] Further, even before 1911, top management "gradually worked out an intelligence scheme to cover the entire United States."

After 1911 the main focus seems to have been on professionalizing management as speedily as possible. "The Jersey management," say Gibb and Knowlton, "which had become strongly professional in character by 1913 at the latest, became increasingly so thereafter, and the administration of company affairs was firmly in the hands of this small and self-perpetuating group of trustees." The authors hasten to add that with one brief exception this top brains trust was "neither oligarchic nor autocratic."[17]

Scientific management was emphasized. And scientific management, comment the authors, "was a drug concocted to cure grievous ailments in the American business system, but like all powerful drugs it was dangerous when misused,"[18] and the dangers, presumably, were those that attend excessive bureaucracy. In the period under review, however, the authors are persuaded that these hazards were largely avoided. "The affairs of the company were administered by a process of intimate and constant discussion. Each executive in a position of responsibility was backed by an assistant qualified for permanent succession, or at least able to carry out the duties of the office on a temporary basis. The tradition was management-in-depth."[19] In other words, there was hierarchy, professionalization, training, and careerism, all of them being institutional characteristics pertaining to bureaucracy.

As in the case of all bureaucracies, there was also a considerable stress on specialization. Thus, "As the size of the business increased, the administrative function itself was broken down into increasingly specialized divisions. Without exception, the Jersey board was composed of specialists. An increasing number of specialized staff departments served as the eyes and ears and hands of management. Each year the information-gathering process became more complex as new committees were formed to ease the crushing burdens which were being shouldered by existing administrative bodies."[20]

That the danger of mushrooming staff activities was recognized, however, is illustrated by the policy taken on basic scientific research. Whereas many other companies, including American Telephone and Telegraph and General Electric, have thought that the way to keep ahead is to be first in technical innovation, Standard Oil adopted a more conservative policy. A research department was established in 1919, but not as a center for basic work; the assumption was that new ideas and inventions would arise mainly from the outside and the job of the research unit was to uncover them, test them, and carry the useful ones forward to some practical end. If the Jersey laboratories happened to develop original ideas, so much the better, of course, but fostering creative research was not the main objective.[21]

The trend toward central staff activity continued to move forward, especially after 1927, for in that year the Jersey company ceased to be an operating company and was henceforth exclusively a holding company. Thereafter the board of directors and all the headquarters staff departments dealt with policy matters only, except that when certain individuals wore their executive hats they continued to move their chessmen around the world board to suit the interests of the company. "It is true," comment Gibb and Knowlton, "that the directors feared, for political reasons, to exert control over the affairs of many affiliated companies, and it is no less true that affiliated operations were guided, invisibly but decisively, by policies at 26 Broadway."[22]

What is the pattern of Standard Oil today? Scores of subsidiary corporations; a full-time board with directors continuing to serve in the dual capacity of policy maker and executive; a large and efficient staff activity, probably one of the best in the world; a great deal of freedom to operating officials; a reputation for pioneering in the field of personnel management; and a business that is shot through with politics—the politics of international oil—a seemingly inevitable factor if a company of this kind is to operate outside its homeland.[23]

GENERAL MILLS

General Mills is the story of a man, a man with drive and deep moral convictions, reminiscent of John D. Rockefeller. It is also the story of a management idea, of vertical integration and staff functions, and also of horizontal integration and a movement toward diversification.

James Gray has written *Business Without Boundaries: The Story of General Mills*.[24] The locale is the Twin Cities in Minnesota, heart of the milling industry in the United States. General Mills was a consolidation of four existing companies, one of which, Sperry of California, was already a hundred years old. The year was 1928, when the stock market boom and the merger movement were at their zenith.

The man was Cadwallader Washburn, a name picturesque enough to have been chosen by a Hollywood scriptwriter. He was a "universal genius of enterprise, the archetype of American entrepreneur," says Gray, a claim which seems to be borne out by the record. Gray also says of Washburn that every time he laid his hands on any project that could return him a profit, he did so with a "fastidiousness" that allowed the dictates of idealist and patriot to dominate those of the man of affairs. This sounds as though the characterization might be a little overdrawn, but the author explains that Washburn's fastidiousness was due to the fact that he never in any sense became a "practical" worker. He was an organizer, an energizer, an instigator; and although his approach was always "theoretical," it invariably proved to have an enormous practical advantage. "His mind was bound by no commitment to tradition," adds Gray, "and he used his capital freely to develop a better product than any that had existed before." Washburn was admittedly a "benevolent autocrat," but one who by championing new techniques transformed a "trade" into a "science." The science, incidentally, was based on the discovery of a country miller who, though neither fastidious nor scientist, changed the technology of grinding hard wheat.[25]

Gray refers to the boisterous twenties as a "time of opportunity and of risk when an administrator could not operate by a book of established rules but must improvise decisions to match each day's crisis.[26] This was even more true after the depression began in 1929, a year after the merger that created General Mills. Washburn introduced what the author calls a new technology: large-scale grinding, the linking of major wheat areas, a vertical integration of all Minneapolis millers. He formed a central holding company and with its stock purchased the assets of selected mills on the basis of ten times their average five years' earnings, the stock thus acquired being nontransferable.[27]

The three main elements of Washburn's management program were economy, efficiency, and organization. According to his principle of organization, the various operating units went on with the business of production while the central holding company integrated the processes of advertising and selling on a national scale. Also centralized were borrowing (at a cheaper rate than could be offered locally), taxes, financial transactions of all kinds, insurance, and financial records. A great deal of attention was also devoted to research, the slogan being "Think big and keep it simple."[28] The central staff, says Gray, did not "impose"

Washburn's ideas on the operating companies, but it did originate and offer ideas that could be accepted or rejected by them.[29]

The first phase of the corporate growth of General Mills extended from the time of the merger in 1928 to 1937, a period during which it was found that to centralize advertising and other functions at the top did not work well.[30] This might be called a lesson in overcentralization or, equally, a lesson in bureaucratic excesses. In 1937, therefore, General Mills abolished all subsidiaries and became an operating company.

The second stage of growth was from 1937 to the end of World War II, when the third stage began, but unfortunately the record here is too short to permit much to be said about it. There was an intensified program of research to discover new products and especially by-products of the grain business. There was also a diversification of the company to the point where it is now a conglomerate one, with side lines including even electrical appliances, such things as toasters for the morning breakfast routine.

At this third stage also, certain policies of management were considered somewhat distinctive. Thus it was felt that, today, what might be called the humanities of business are more important than its techniques. The relations of General Mills with its stockholders, for example, took on a kind of intimacy, with regional meetings of stockholders held to make them feel closer to the company. So far as internal management is concerned, there was a constant and thorough self-appraisal, for this, says Gray, is "the definitive mark of maturity." There was also a further decentralization of operations in the original companies.[31] Does this mean that bureaucracy was unwinding itself and that greater draughts of enterprise were being sought? The answer is not clear.

LEVER BROTHERS AND UNILEVER LIMITED

A third illustration of bureaucracy and managerial responses to it is the story of Unilever; it shows how influential and enduring are the historical factors giving rise to business enterprise and the role played by sheer accident of personality. But this case also shows how, with rational management, problems of this sort can be adjusted to and overcome.

Unilever operates in no less than fifty different countries and is engaged for the most part in the oil and fats business. Its wide variety of products, mainly to be used in the home, includes soaps, detergents, margarine, shortening, toilet preparations, and perfumes, plus fresh, canned, and frozen foods ranging from fish and meat to tea and strawberries. The company was formed by the joining of the Dutch family firms of Van den Berghs and Jurgens with the English Lever Brothers, each of which included a number of subsidiaries, the object being to seek diversity in unity under the combined name of Lever Brothers and Unilever Limited. None of the subsidiaries lost their separate identity, however, for as Sir Geoffrey Hayworth, a former chairman of Unilever, once remarked, "Running Atkinsons perfumery in South America obviously requires a very different technique from running a cattle-food business in Holland."[32]

The diversity of the business was partly deliberate, partly accidental. Thus, the reason the combine got into the retail fish business (now one of the largest in the United Kingdom) was that Lord Leverhulme had a private interest in helping the fishermen of the islands of Lewis and Harris, off the west coast of Scotland, and Mac Fisheries was started as a retail outlet for the catch. And to this line was added Wall's sausages, familiar to every English housewife, the reason being that sausages were once a "familiar sight on the fishmonger's counter."[33]

This is not a rational procedure in the usual connotation of that term and it does obviously complicate an already complicated business. And it should be said that most additions to the combine are effected in a different way. Thus, after drawing up its annual capital expenditure budget, Unilever decides to acquire a business only "if that were considered the most economical method of bringing about a desired development."[34] In other words, instead of building, merge.

With the possible exception of Du Pont, which also started as a family concern, there is probably no more diversified empire, operating on a world-wide basis, than Unilever. How can it organize, operate, decentralize, control, and motivate on so vast a scale? It is, in fact, a gigantic test of bureaucratic functioning. The methods used are a little like those of a federal government, and a little like those of Standard Oil and another British mammoth, Imperial Chemicals, in the use these companies make of the committee as a plural-headed executive constituting the nerve center of organization. In a highly diversified business the committee system is almost a necessity if the many different parts are to work together. In the case of Unilever the problem of integration is further complicated by the different national origins of the two parent groups in the combine. This gulf has been bridged by the device of having two holding companies, one Dutch and one British, but with identical boards of directors, which incidentally also shows how useful a corporate fiction may sometimes be. The maximum number of directors is twenty-five, and since what is sought is a unified body irrespective of nationality, there is no determination of quotas on this score. All board members are full-time working directors with definite assignments as heads of functional units or whole companies or even groups of companies; they are primarily administrators and they are compensated as such.

Since the board is too large to be effective in certain matters, however, there is the somewhat novel device of a so-called Special Committee consisting of a few directors (three as of 1957) who are relieved of all supervisory duties in order to devote their full energies to grand strategy. This committee not only deals with broad policy but also coordinates the activities of other directors and directs the work of the headquarters and staff agencies.

Probably the key word in Unilever organization is "groups." The functions of higher management have been delegated not only to the Special Committee, but on a lower level to four other bodies. Three of these have responsibilities on a regional basis and the fourth operates a self-contained business in Africa, where the purchase of raw materials is a dominant consideration. These groups are called management or control groups and their members include directors and other executives from the headquarters or area levels. Accompanying this line organization is an extensive staff activity, organized into departments and dealing with the usual responsibilities: buying, audit, marketing, personnel, and the like. Finally, in most countries where Unilever operates, there is a so-called national executive or national manager, in whose office programs are unified so as to secure the greatest impact on local centers. This officer is responsible for *all* Unilever activities in his market area and hence at this point the group concept of management merges with that of the orthodox, single-headed manager.

Turning now to the methods used by Unilever to cope with problems of bureaucracy and size, Sir Geoffrey Hayworth has noted that during his tenure as chairman the three most important objectives of administration were speed of decision, quality of decision, and adaptation to change.[35] To these ends, a good deal of staff and executive attention was concentrated on drawing up so-called annual operating plans and annual capital expenditure budgets for the field agencies. This procedure operates like most systems of annual budgeting, either in private or public administration: the estimates are locally prepared, centrally reviewed, and jointly decided. Once the decisions have been made, the field operator is assured of a clear road ahead; it is up to him to produce and no one will be breathing down his neck. This does not mean, of course, that headquarters loses interest once the budget has been adopted. On the contrary, there is constant check-up in a two-way exchange of personal visits between headquarters and the field. "It is no use for all the people who travel," remarks Sir Geoffrey, "to be going one way."[36]

Another key to Unilever's administrative success is a mastery of the staff activity, and here the policy and technique are strikingly like those of Standard Oil. Staff people must confine themselves to study and suggestion. They are encouraged to mix closely with operating people to learn their problems at first hand, and are expected to "sell" their wares if need be. But they are not permitted to issue orders.

Another similarity to Standard Oil is that individual abilities are held to be a prime ingredient of administration, and hence there is a concentration on personnel policies. Sir Geoffrey has said that in Unilever's world empire, "There are some two hundred people who take on themselves the decisions which make or mar the success of the business as a whole." Accordingly, "The biggest job of top management is to ensure the quality of this two hundred."[37] They are trained, tested, promoted, moved about through different parts of the company to gain experience, and an accurate inventory is secured of their strengths and weaknesses. In Sir Geoffrey's view, the most important executive traits are character, ability, and the will to cooperate, in that order of importance.[38] He believes, furthermore, that if just the right man is not available for a particular vacancy, it is invariably better to leave the job open, or to secure a temporary fill-in, than to make the mistake of promoting the wrong man.

Unilever tries to keep men alert and to avoid the deadening effect of large size by encouraging self-examination. By means of what the company calls internal personnel audits, individuals receive constructive criticism aimed at encouraging self-assessment and improving performance. A similar technique is used in group conferences on organization and method, apparently with worth-while results.[39] Unilever realizes that, like people, institutions also, especially if large, are likely to get into a rut in their personnel and organizational methods.

Two final observations by Sir Geoffrey Hayworth on bureaucracy will serve to round out this account. The first is that if an operating official is to be given his head and empowered with authority to achieve results in his own way, then headquarters has no business prescribing his organization and methods for him. Hence, says Sir Geoffrey, "we do not spend much time drawing up functional charts or writing definitions of duties. We believe that *undue precision and definition can be—and often are—the* enemy of flexibility, liveliness and effectiveness."[40] Experts may disagree on this point, but no one who has seen bureaucracy at first hand will deny that this is a major problem area in administration.

Sir Geoffrey's second observation is equally challenging. "We believe," he said, "that we should keep the fences between compartments of the business low, so that people can jump over them; in fact, we encourage them to do so. If you have picked the right people and they have developed confidence in each other, any friction that arises should be easily manageable and will be more than compensated for by the extra effectiveness and liveliness of the whole organization."[41] If, as seems likely, self-centeredness and segmentation are among the excesses of bureaucracy, then Unilever rightly chooses this problem area, also, for a major emphasis.

IMPERIAL CHEMICAL INDUSTRIES LIMITED

Against the backdrop of the foregoing illustrations, a brief account of the arrangements adopted by Britain's largest chemical combine will show another attempt to organize a complex business. ICI, as it is familiarly known, produces no less than 10,000 different items in the field of chemicals, including dyestuffs, nonferrous metals, explosives, paints, plastics, lime, and salt, among others.[42]

When Lord Melchett put ICI together in the 1920's, says *The Economist*, rationalization and size were the catchwords of the era. Mere size, it was claimed, bred efficiency. The best way to get the edge over competitors was simply to employ the best and therefore the most expensive management, the best technicians, accountants, and tax experts, and to spread their activities over the largest possible area, thus reducing unit costs and achieving maximum efficiencies. "But today," notes *The Economist*, "the doctrine of the late twenties no longer seems an eternal truth, because it has been shown that the small owner-managed business holds its own in many fields, and the problems of big business increase with each decade."[43]

Following the merger of 1926, a number of different administrative devices were tried and ICI underwent four distinct organizational transformations during the next thirty years. First there was centralization under a unified management. In 1931, however, a policy of decentralization was undertaken by means of a committee system somewhat similar to that of Standard Oil. Then in 1938 the single executive system, which had been retained along with the committees, was abolished and divisions became the center of operation. And finally, in 1944, under the pressure of continuing growth, the committees were abolished and since then the work of administration has been more closely centered in the divisions.

Today the company operates under a central board of directors, and manufacturing operations are split into fourteen divisions, each of which enjoys a good deal of administrative and financial autonomy. The divisions are responsible for all technical production activities in their respective fields and each has its own board of directors, which, however, is a board only in an organizational and not in a legal sense. Within the fourteen divisions are roughly a hundred separate plants or works, as they are called.

Thus the three layers of organization are top board, divisions, and works, representing an arithmetical magnitude, says the board chairman, of 1-14-100. By this simple means a worker in a plant or an executive in a division knows just where he stands relative to every other part of the company, and communications upward and downward are facilitated."[44]

At the top board level are three types of directors: lay directors are elder statesmen with no executive responsibilities; functional directors are in charge of the seven main functions into which the work of ICI is divided, these being finance, commerce, research, development, technical change, personnel, and overseas operations; and finally, group directors are in charge of the fourteen divisions. With the exception of the elder statesmen, therefore, company directors are all executives as well as policy officials.

In 1926, ICI was a £56 million merger; today its assets total more than £439 million and it employs more than 107,000 people in Great Britain alone. In a recent year the company earned a trading profit of £35 million and "decided to keep the troops happy" with a profit-sharing scheme. In an undertaking of such magnitude and complexity one may be permitted to conjecture that "keeping the troops happy" is a device prompted at least as much by the difficulty of solving certain morale and other problems of bureaucracy as it is by a desire to share profits.

CONCLUDING OBSERVATIONS

A study of these and similar case illustrations shows that, generally speaking, every institution has a kind of personality of its own and that it undergoes certain changes with each stage in its evolution. Calendar age is not the sole, nor is it even the most important, factor that operates here. Even more important are variables such as market demand for product or service, executive personality and leadership, efficiency of methods, adaptation to opportunity and to change, and the tradition and myth shared by the members of the work group.

As a rule also, when energies are still abundant and opportunities continue to be recognized, institutions keep on growing and subdividing until top management decides that a limit has been reached or until the undertaking becomes so large and sluggish that vigorous young competitors, smaller and enjoying greater maneuverability, are able to reduce the giant to size once more. What we do not know, and what causes thoughtful people much concern, is what happens to growth when the supply of individualistic and energetic leadership dries up. Will innovation cease and can mere knowledge suffice without the spark of energy?

To summarize the distinctive phases in the growth periods of institutions that come to be called bureaucracies, in the founding era the emphasis is on promotional activities: acquiring capital, picking key men, creating a rough kind of organization, supplying the personal drive to compensate for the lack of efficient organization and method.

As soon as these problems of management have been overcome, a second type of situation occurs: the technical and organizational side of the institution operates smoothly and the men who threw their energies into it at the outset have often grown more effective under responsibilities, so that during this stage the highest peak of efficiency and effectiveness is often attained.

But the smooth grooving of organization and process lays the foundation for a third stage: now the balance between organization and personality tends to tip adversely to the latter. People tend to slow down, they are not quite so lively, they fall into habits of complacency, they feel the big battles have been won and that it is time to enjoy an easier life.

At this point yet another stage sets in: the pioneers of the business are replaced by career men, skilled at system and smooth operation, men who tend to say, "Well, if it's a good show, let's keep it that way." These men are the true bureaucrats. They seem to believe that if they can keep on reproducing their own kind through the same preparatory schools, the same colleges, the same clubs, and the same suburbia, their institutions will continue to prosper and to grow bigger and better.

But such men overlook two things. First, they have a tendency to undertake more scope than their pioneer predecessors, but with less human drive to go on. And secondly, they often lack the qualities of innovation and enterprise. In fact, size and scope in any undertaking demand an increasing amount of energy, but, paradoxically, the effect of size and scope is to reduce energy. This is the problem of all institutions in their mature period.

Chapter 3 *Some Theories of Growth*

What are the main aspects of growth in institutions? In the field of management that question has not yet been given much thought. Are there any principles of growth developed in other fields of knowledge, therefore, that might be helpful in an understanding of vitality in administration? I am not sufficiently expert to deal with all of the theories of growth that might be examined, but some of them that relate to biology, sociology, and economics do seem to bear on the present inquiry and a brief look at them—approaching the subject from different angles, as they do—may prove useful.

BIOLOGICAL THEORY

In the animal world, specialization is the means of overcoming competition from the environment and assuring survival. The life of a large institution is also characterized by specialization. But an excess of specialization leads to inflexibility, which is self-defeating. The organism must continually adjust to its environment or die; adjustment requires coordination; and coordination must be accompanied by the creative element, which is enterprise. One of the most interesting theoretical problems in biology, therefore, is how the rival needs of specialization and coordina-

Some Theories of Growth   33

tion are reconciled as animals increase in size and adapt to their environment.[1]

In the nature of living things, say Worth and Enders, specialization is the usual means by which a species of animal overcomes competition from the inimical features of the environment. Thus most animals display some sort of physical modification relative to eating, for example, or defense, or reproduction.[2] Hence, animals vary according to species and the variations tend to become increasingly pronounced.

Variation is the basis of the difference between man and the other animals. Man has acquired a larger brain, making possible a more elaborate language, more abstract thought, more highly developed customs and mores, a greater accumulation of knowledge and its transmission to future generations, and the communication of feeling and fact, as well as of habit.

Moreover, in the human animal there is a longer period of care of the offspring, a longer period of development of the brain. Thus humans and their institutions are capable of a greater complexity and of appreciating a greater variety of values. Basically, however, "All living things have a certain sameness, and one does not have to scratch far below the surface to see this. We can learn some of the basic principles of life from animal societies, from the single cell, or from a multicellular organism."[3]

Since animals are a combination of habit, or specialized ways of doing things (bureaucracy), and of adaptation (enterprise), the two must operate in a harmonious relationship. Because these factors are so essential to survival and to well-being, "during the course of evolution those variations or adaptations which tend to give the group a unity will have an advantage, and the offspring of those groups may tend to become more numerous than less well-organized groups."[4] Thus a successful species is one that has developed coordination internally among the faculties of the individual, and externally between the individual and the group. Animals learn to integrate and to communicate; they reach out toward new combinations in behavior and in thought processes; they even reach out toward intelligence, a characteristic once thought to be the exclusive possession of mankind.

Biologists are less sure about how coordination takes place. Most of them apparently agree with Bonner that there is no law on the subject; that there seem to be many ways and no one can yet be called "right" for all purposes and all situations. But *failure* to adapt and to coordinate results in a static condition which may lead to decline, because "Life is motion . . . the world is always a new place."[5] Thus life can never rest on dead center; it is necessary constantly to pour in fresh supplies of energy because the motor is never quiet except in death.

A little reflection on these theories shows an interesting similarity between growth in living organisms and in complicated human institutions. Both largely rely on organization and habit; both specialize and must adapt in order to survive in their own environment; both must beware of Spencerian social statics. Accordingly, coordination—which means conscious thought concerning goals, methods, and values—must occur if further advances are to be realized.

Coordination calls for more organization, but of a kind that respects and even promotes individual variations in people (they also must adapt to their environment) as well as in institutional arrangements. The wrong kind of coordination might prove as inflexible as specialization at its worst; therefore what is needed is a type of organization that will foster a free flow of energies, experimentation, variation, and teamwork. To allow for both individualism and for the strength of the group comes close to defining the kind of coordination that is required if both bureaucracy and enterprise are to play their essential roles in an administration characterized by vitality.

SOCIAL THEORY

According to sociology, the simpler the relationship, the more informal is it likely to be and the easier are the means of communication. In a small group, and even more when only two people are together, sentiments as well as knowledge and understandings are, as a rule, readily communicated. This is especially true in a stable, cohesive group where there is little movement into or out of it.. The two main kinds of groups are the primary and the secondary. The primary group is small and usually social in character, while the secondary group is large and often official. Although the small group may be plagued with cliques and personal antagonisms, it is essentially a we-group, if only because a lack of mobility allows for no alternative. Being inherently cohesive, there is a feeling of social identity. My home is in a small town in Vermont, for example, and when my house burned down, my wife and I had half a dozen invitations to stay temporarily with neighbors, although at that time we had lived in the community for only a few months. Care for the family that has been "burned out" is the tradition in that neighborhood and it was automatically extended to newcomers who, owning property, were considered as "belonging."

The differences between primary and secondary groups are not absolute, of course, because the development of a group is gradual and evolutionary and there is no particular point at which it is possible to say that during the past this group was a primary one and now, having become large and formal, it is a secondary one. Groups are characterized more by process than by absolute category. In contrast to the primary group, for example, a secondary group is formal, highly organized, makes rules for itself, needs more leadership, finds communication difficult, and tends toward impersonality. But all of these elements are also found in a lesser degree in the simplest of situations. Less prominent, less traditional, and less often expressed, they become increasingly visible as the simple group gains size.

Although we associate certain characteristics with the primary group and others with the formal group, therefore, actually the difference is an academic distinction. The pattern of the primary group is a simple one, and as growth occurs it becomes larger and more complex. But these changes are in degree and in combination and not in kind. The elements remain the same: individuals, communications, attitudes, traditions, organization, management.

If I seem to stress the obvious, it is to drive home the point that since all groups include the same elements in varying degree and combination, if it seems desirable to change the aspect of a particular group, it is only necessary to discover what the various elements and combinations are in order to guide them to a desired end. Thus it is possible in a corporation, for example, to accentuate either the formal or the informal, the impersonal or the human, aspects of the institution. If the group cannot be kept small and yet the rigors of size and bureaucracy would be avoided, then a deliberate study of the elements of the group and the exercise of leadership according to a deliberate policy will promote the desired result. If animals, human and otherwise, have inborn qualities plus the ability to learn new responses, so also have groups.

Are there any other possible implications of social theory that might apply to the complex of bureaucracy, enterprise, and vitality? There is, for example, the human aspect of the matter: people are more comfortable in primary groups than in secondary ones because less adjustment is needed; there is a greater feeling of contentment and more opportunity to enjoy the inertia that seems to characterize most human animals unless conditioned otherwise. The larger and more formal the group becomes, the harder it is for its members to communicate with one another. Written communications increasingly take the place of communication by word of mouth, and a feeling of impersonality appears, bringing with it a feeling of isolation.

A chain of consequences then sets in: no longer held together by a common communications system, the original group splinters into subgroups that become rivals rather than partners. The members of these smaller groups lose interest in the larger objectives of the larger group and form lesser or alternative loyalties and attachments that are more easily understood and more satisfying. And finally, as bewilderment, uncertainty, and a sense of insecurity increase, people turn against what they cannot understand and make it more difficult for the leaders of a program to win consent than when relationships were primary and informal. But the winning of consent is indispensable to the success of any undertaking in which people are involved, which includes most businesses, most of society, and all of government. At this point it may be suggested that the factors that operate within the group have a bearing on the question of institutional size. Some people have argued that large size is almost always an advantage, while others contend that there is a point beyond which mere size is too costly in terms of the adjustments required of the individual and of the institution itself. There must be effective communication in order to produce efficient results, and although the point at which communication breaks down is never a fixed one, it is nonetheless an ascertainable one that the alert administrator will look for and recognize when he sees it. By various devices he may be able to move that point of diminishing returns forward, but not beyond certain limits. That hard-to-define thing, the inner life or continuum of the group, which is compounded of habit, tradition, inertia, prejudice, intolerance, and many other factors, defeats rationality time after time and hence acts as an automatic brake on growth and adjustment.

ECONOMIC THEORY

Professor W. Arthur Lewis of the University of Manchester in England deals in two of his books with economic growth in underdeveloped countries and also in those that have reached industrial maturity.[6] All economic growth, says Lewis, tends to be logistic in character: it starts slowly, accelerates, and then slows down again, the reason being that each stimulus to growth eventually wears itself out and there must be a recharging of energy before there can be a resurgence of growth. Once economic growth has begun, furthermore, institutions change continually in directions favorable to it, and hence strengthen the forces of growth at a cumulative rate. There is an energetic introduction of new ideas concerning technology, forms of organization, administrative procedures, commodities, services, and the like.

But when the stimulus to growth wears itself out, then the rate of advance begins to decline and the institutional changes that occur gradually become less favorable to growth.[7] It might almost be said that the multiplier operates on the upgrade, the accelerator on the downgrade.

Lewis' studies indicate that economic growth demands a willingness to experiment accompanied by a belief in rationality; that through experimentation, technology improves and needed changes occur in social attitudes and relations. Two additional necessary conditions are a high degree of freedom and stimulating incentives. An institution must have the freedom to maneuver, and the incentives must be such as will inspire employees and promote enterprise.

Among the checks to economic growth is an overemphasis on planning, which is rational design, which is an aspect of bureaucracy. Planning by direction, says Lewis, is inevitably inflexible because the standardization that simplifies the work of central planners results in a Procrustean tendency that binds the speed at which improvements can be introduced.[8]

Where people are concerned, the real problem is not to get them to work harder but to work more effectively. Here the key is trade-union leadership, which in the past has been largely restrictive. The worker will give of his best only if he identifies himself with the working unit and develops a sense of pride and loyalty. The assumption that bureaucracy has "infinite ability," says Lewis, is pragmatically without foundation.[9]

In no society, of course, is it possible for everyone to be adventurous, but in every society some people must be enterprising or there will be no innovation. Innovation is largely the result of the rewards and prestige that are possible, and in every society there are some individuals whose natural bent is to experiment in defiance of established opinions or vested interests. "Some societies," concludes Lewis, "admire and encourage such people, while others regard them as buccaneers to be suppressed, but economic growth depends very largely on the extent to which

Some Theories of Growth 39

the social atmosphere nourishes such people, and gives them scope."[10]

When growth results in a tendency toward concentration of economic power, the reason, says Lewis, is that competition is more acceptable in a rapidly expanding community than in a static one, and in addition newly developing economies must rely at the outset on monopoly because the supply of managerial talent is limited and often concentrated in government agencies. Monopoly is acceptable when it promotes growth and is objectionable when it restricts growth, but in the end the continuous expansion of large-scale organization seems likely to depend on the availability of entrepreneurial and managerial skills.[11]

Finally, Lewis believes that great entrepreneurs are born, not made; that they are stimulated by the desire for social success, big profits, or fear of failure; that city dwellers contribute more to change than country people do; that economic growth results from the actions of governments as well as from the maneuvers of individuals; and that the ultimate benefit of economic growth is not necessarily to promote happiness but to widen the range of choice.[12]

Another Professor Lewis, the American economist Ben W. Lewis, also has studied the subject of economic growth,[13] with special emphasis on the problems of mature, largely monopolistic industries in which growth is more difficult than in newer and more competitive undertakings.

The problems of growth, says Ben Lewis, are the problems posed by bureaucracy: how to prevent overcentralization and overstaffing, how to secure a commercial outlook, how to avoid too many layers of organization, and how to blend efficiency, responsibility, and politics. Speaking of hospital administration under the national health program in Great Britain, for example, Lewis remarks that "The elaborate superstructure of boards, committees and subcommittees, with the inevitable conflicts of jurisdiction, interests and personalities has aroused some criticism; and the general tripartite structure that was adopted in order to blend central control with local autonomy has produced difficult problems of its own."[14]

In this study, Lewis concludes that there is much in the British situation that is disheartening and much in British policy that is hard to defend; that the basic difficulties are due to cartelization and restrictions in the private sector of the economy; and that whether Britain succeeds in forging ahead economically will depend fully as much on the temper and attitudes of the British people themselves as on the political hue of the government that happens to be in office.[15]

SOME APPLICATIONS OF GROWTH THEORIES

A brief look into the world of large enterprise will provide some additional insights into the problems of orderly institutional growth.

Five hundred corporations in the United States, says Adolf Berle, control two-thirds of the nonfarm economy of the nation, and among these five hundred units a still smaller group exercises the ultimate decision-making power. Why has this occurred?

It was once assumed that a corporation should own only a limited amount of property, but today, through diversification, those limits seem to have disappeared. It was once believed that a corporation should engage in only one type of business, but now they "rove the country, if not the world," and engage in any type of economic activity they wish. It was once believed that a corporation should not last longer than a certain definite period of time—twenty or thirty years or so—but today a corporation has a perpetual life and its assets are allowed to pile up without limit except as they are voluntarily distributed through the payment of dividends.[16]

The effect on people of this evolution in the size and influence of the corporation in modern society has been marked indeed. Most people now work for an institution instead of for themselves, and the entrepreneur has been superseded by the Organization Man, with all that that development implies in personal maladjustments and social irresponsibility.

For the corporation itself, it is now management instead of owners, says Berle, who are responsible for directing and creating. Stockholders constitute the "passive receptive" side of the business and are, in effect, functionless. In most large corporations power rests in the board of directors, and in some cases the board consists entirely of officers and no outside interest is represented. Joined to the control bloc of the larger investors, the board is virtually autonomous. Indeed, the control of large corporations by management to the virtual exclusion of owners is now in most cases an accomplished fact, says Berle, unless, of course—and here he is apparently thinking of the current trend toward diversification—there is outside control by a higher oligarchy owning enough shares in the corporation to dominate the situation at all times.

As an outstanding authority on corporations in the United States, Berle is not being swept away by his own eloquence when he says that the large contemporary corporation is the "true collectivism" and that there is seemingly no way of avoiding accumulations of power, so rapidly has power been shifted from the periphery to the center and concentrated there. Such rapid growth is also the reason that bureaucracy has sprung into sudden prominence.

I wonder if Berle is right in his conclusion that growth cannot be controlled so as to avoid excessive concentrations of power. And if he is right, then are the excesses of bureaucracy equally inevitable? How rapidly can people adjust to social change, and are there limits beyond which it does not pay to adjust? Equally disturbing is the possibility that there may be bounds to both specialization and coordination. "As civilization becomes more complex and more dependent on the machine," says a British management expert, "it is likely that a limit will be reached determined by the shortage of well trained managers, for in any society only a certain proportion is suitable for leadership."[17]

The situation in corporate management is paralleled by corresponding developments in the big labor unions, as Clark Kerr, Chancellor of the University of California, has made clear in a recent study.[18] In the United States the unions now claim some eighteen million members. They negotiate thousands of contracts a year covering the working rules that govern important aspects of the life of businessmen in nearly every trade and industry and in nearly every town. The unions can close down, says Kerr, even the giants, firms such as General Motors and United States Steel. Income, leisure, job security, retirement, place of work, job opportunities, discipline—all these areas of modern economic life are affected by unions participating in the bureaucratic process.

Kerr also makes the point about the inertia of individuals in groups. "Union members," he said, "are traditionally apathetic except in some crisis, and very little can be done about it."[19] Like Berle, he refers to an oligarchy of managers controlling, in this case, the big unions. Furthermore, their work has become more routine as pattern-following and grievance precedents have become established. The worker is subject to a web of rules that becomes more thickly woven as the influence of the big union increases.

The dilemma of the individual in both big business and big unions, says Kerr, is that he needs some kind of defense against control by an oligarchy, and such a defense can be guaranteed only by the political state. Thus the role of government relative to big institutions, whether of business or of labor, is increasing, with layers of control added one on top of the other. Growth also constantly adds to the levels of organization and to the infinite variety of their cross-referencing in institutional management. Every step in institutional growth, therefore, contributes to the problems of bureaucracy and enterprise and affects the staying power of the economy.

In his book, *White Collar*,[20] C. Wright Mills argues that technology and bigness have upset the nineteenth-century assumption that society is divided between entrepreneurs and wage earners. A new middle class of bureaucrats has appeared, consisting of managers, technicians, paper-pushers, professionals. The problems of morale resulting from bureaucracy, he says, are serious and steadily growing worse. Work within narrow, set limits at the office leaves executives and employees restless and dissatisfied both there and at home; employees are conditioned by rules and regulations to stereotype their relations with the customer so that even "personal attention" follows a prescription; whenever there is a transfer of control over one's employment from one corporation to another, for a price, the change takes place in a personality market that is artificial and phony, and hence a man's personality becomes the instrument of an alien purpose. The result, says Mills, is the "systematic creation and maintenance of estrangement from society and from selfhood" of every man and woman caught up in the bureaucratic vortex.[21]

How can this be? Does growth have a limiting as well as a releasing function? Does it cramp the individual as it expands the institution? There will be much more to say about this in later chapters.[22]

CONCLUSION

Whether one starts with the theories of the biologists, the sociologists, or the economists, there seems to be a considerable agreement concerning the conditions under which growth occurs and continues: life is motion; institutions grow from the simple to the complex; their need is to adjust to environment and to change; the larger the institution becomes, the more clearly must it define its goals and its methods.

Specialization is an attempt to adjust to environment. Some people are more enterprising than others, having a better native endowment and a higher motivation. They communicate more effectively and are more rational and adaptable. The integrations they effect tend toward social solidarity and heightened morale. Their choices of goals and values are also conducive to vitality and survival.

When large size is attained, growth adjustments become more difficult. There may be too many layers of organization; decision and action are slowed down; formal relations displace personal relations; segmentation hinders over-all cooperation; growth becomes excessive when it causes a concentration of power that restricts freedom, experimentation, and deviation; thereafter, groups within the institution vie with each other instead of pooling their energies in a common effort; people lose their resourcefulness and their initiative; accumulated traditions and prejudices have a wider scope; and the institution develops a life of its own to which newcomers are expected to conform.

Growth is gradual and evolutionary rather than by categories. The elements in simple and complex situations differ more in degree and combination than they do in kind. Nevertheless, the variations may be such as to create totally different environments, depending on the extent to which they are rule-ridden and formal, or spontaneous and informal.

Bureaucracy and enterprise play out their respective roles in these varying degrees of complexity. The key to their combination in a kind of balance is the quality of the coordination that is provided. Undue emphasis on order encourages efficiency to the point of stagnation, and undue emphasis on flexibility sacrifices the efficiencies of a smooth operation. In this situation, the quality of coordination one can effect becomes the test of managerial talent. From many sources—biological, sociological, and economic—comes the suggestion that continuous, beneficial growth is to be found somewhere within this complex of factors.

Chapter 4 *Some Theories of Decay*

If life is motion for institutions as for living organisms, so also is decay, because that process also is incapable of standing still. But where life starts quickly and gradually slows down, decay starts slowly and gathers speed. Hence the administrator who would keep his business alive must be alert to recognize the first signs of decay. What are these signs, and what are the main issues involved in institutional decline?

Most of the factors that affect growth, when taken in reverse, so to speak, also affect decay. In addition, both growth and decay are influenced by external factors in the environment, and frequently the same one will affect institutional vitality favorably or unfavorably according to the way in which the institution receives it. Most government policies, for example, are external factors of this kind. And finally, there is a large area of internal administration in which growth or decay depend pretty largely on how well management does its job, and here also the factors should be capable of being spotted and explained to the satisfaction of the practical administrator.

ADMINISTRATOR'S CHECK LIST

When sales begin to fall off, when customers hesitate and then go elsewhere, when employees show signs of lethargy, department heads are intent only on their own work, and everyone seems to sense that something is wrong, then the enterprise is clearly headed for trouble. When things have got just a little worse, there is a sudden realization in some quarters, at least, that the trouble has been reached. The problem of most managers is how to detect the onset of diminished vitality soon enough to arrest the trend and to apply specific remedies before it is too late.

The following check list covers some of the areas of institutional management in which signs of decay often appear, illustrated by the typical comments of an administrator blind to the fact that decay has set in. It is not a complete list, nor are solutions suggested, because most of that will come in Part IV. The present purpose is to show how numerous are the elements of decay in the management of individual programs, how all of these elements are interrelated, and how the neglect of some of the more important ones, such as consumer orientation or technological change, might in themselves be enough to defeat the enterprise even if others did not contribute to the same end. These illustrations assume a business concern, but most of them would be equally appropriate in the case of a government agency or any other large-scale enterprise.

Famous Last Words of Administrators

Technology: A better product by my competitor would cause my business to slip away.

Innovation: If my competitor invents a cheaper method, I am finished.

Suppliers: I can hold up my end all right, but my suppliers let me down.

Location: My rival's new site has caused my workers to move away and my transportation costs to be higher.

Contracts: My contract with a big distributor is about to expire; if he will not renew it, I will be forced to the wall.

Subsidiary: If I become part of a larger concern, there would be more security all around.

Taxes: That company's lower taxes are the margin of difference in its favor.

Unions: A prolonged strike would close me down for good.
Tariffs: Razing tariff walls may be good for the consumer, but it would be fatal to me.
Style: People are fickle; they go for my product this year and boycott it the next.
Costs: Institutional resistances make it impossible for me to bring my costs down as low as those of my competitor.
Method: The most efficient organization is the one that has everything reduced to System.
Decision making: Most of administration is routine and in these areas decision making is automatic.
Centralization: Everything should be decentralized except policy formation.
Inertia: My executives are living on past reputations; our product has a name but no future.
Seniority: Youth has the new viewpoint that might save the business, but I dare not violate seniority promotions.
Specialists: I never hire anyone but a specialist if I can help it.
Machines: Our equipment is outmoded, but it still runs.
Organization: The organization creaks, but we have good men.
Planning: I'm too busy doing things today to think about tomorrow.
Policies: Policies are too much like planning; they are socialistic.
Teamwork: A top executive is a relic of the past; several men are better than one.
Staff: My executives are not as good as they used to be, so I will simply expand the staff activities.
Delegation: Why delegate when I'm paid more than anyone else to do what they can't do?
Rules: There ought to be a rule for every situation, nothing left to chance.
Coordination: If department heads cannot take care of themselves, they have no business being in this outfit.
Control: As long as we make a profit, why worry about how we do it?
Public relations: If we do a good job, it will be appreciated all right.
Incentives: The only thing the average man is interested in is profits for himself.
Salaries: We pay as much as the average.
Morale: As long as employees work eight hours a day, they can think what they like about me and the business.

Accounts: The only reason for keeping accounts is to satisfy the auditors.
Renewal: As long as profits are good, there is no need to worry too much about depreciation and reserves.
Size: This business *must* be efficient because it is so big.

Some people will disagree over what is implied or suggested in these statements, which no doubt do reveal some of my own points of view and prejudices. Nevertheless, most administrators have said or thought something of the kind on one or more of these points at some time in their experience, and what they did after that was the test of their ability. Taken together, furthermore, these points underscore the complex nature of the causes of decay, and hence the need for sophistication in matters of institutional morphology.

Against this background, here is a series of intellectual issues, the discussion of which might help the administrator to recognize the danger signals of decay. These four issues are the nature of decay, the equilibriums that seem to be involved, the leadership factor, and the question of homogeneity.

THE NATURE OF DECAY

Is decay inevitable, or is it controllable? Once started, must decay continue its downward course, or can it be arrested and the trend turned back toward growth?

There are a number of variations on the theme of inevitability. Plato, for example, believed that everything that has a genesis is foredoomed to disintegration, which seems like a fair guess. But when he adds that retrogression is connected with periodic rhythms that exist in nature and is apparently inevitable, he pushes the theory beyond proof. Plato's inevitability thesis was handed down through Hegel, Marx, Spengler, Weber, and Schumpeter, among others, but today many people reject the principle of an inherent life span for institutions and even for individuals, nor are they willing to accept the thesis of inherent factors beyond men's control. Rather, the rational, realistic position holds that retrogression is due to determinable causes, complicated but susceptible of analysis, intelligible if not measurable; and that if enough were known about these causes, much could be done to check a trend toward decline and even to reverse it. An incomplete appreciation of the factors and consequences of decline, plus inertia, are largely responsible for much of the past neglect of this subject. But now that evidences of institutional decline are becoming more prominent as our economic institutions, especially, grow larger and older and more complex, and the Organization Man offers so drab a prospect, it seems likely that institutional morphology will become a widely studied area of the social sciences. Today the inevitability theory seems about ready to give way to a more optimistic belief in the rational and deliberate control of institutional vitality.

A convincing confirmation of this view is offered by H. G. Barnett in his book *Innovation*.[1] Barnett is an anthropologist and his interpretations are based on data extending over long periods of history. Societies and institutions, he believes, have their ups and downs and there may be several instances of each phase. In Africa, for example, a certain society once excelled in administrative skills but later lost them and is now having to regain them. Barnett also believes that all governing skills are learned, and that if a society standing high in administrative skills is determined to hold on to them, and if other societies that once had such skills wish to regain them, in both cases the remedy is first to discover the causes of growth, and then to find out why the skills were lost.

Arnold Toynbee supports the inevitability theory of decline up to a certain point, but allows for possible exceptions.[2] Thus he asserts that growth continues until energy is exhausted, following which a downward trend leads to disintegration. Theoretically, says Toynbee, this downward plunge could be stopped and even reversed; but in the twenty-one civilizations he has studied, this has not happened. If it were to happen, it would be due to the sudden ability of a dominant minority to respond to challenges which previously, on the downward grade, it had been unable to meet.

The reference, of course, is to whole civilizations, whereas we are concerned at present with the more immediate question of institutions within those civilizations. The question is, does Toynbee's theory offer any insights here? If so, then there is some hope that with the proper incentives and challenges, administrators can, in fact, reverse a downward trend and turn institutions upward once more.

Toynbee's discussion of the role of what he calls the gifted minority in society, one that is constantly refreshed from below, is especially interesting to the administrator who would safeguard the life of his business. Thus growth and decay depend on the outcome of a series of challenges and responses. Although generally speaking the greater the challenge, the greater the response, a challenge may be so severe that a successful response is impossible.[3] All of the areas included in the check list discussed above offer challenges to the administrator, and it is doubtful whether any of them is so severe as to defeat a successful response.

Certain individuals constitute the mainstay of the creative minority that succeeds in meeting repeated challenges. In a growing society, a creative personality takes the lead in responding successfully to a challenge that confronts his group. But in an already disintegrating society, the same creative personality must be content merely to try to come to the rescue when response has failed.[4]

The distinctive quality of the human mind, continues Toynbee, is its adaptability, its inventiveness, its contriving ability. But the very success of adaptation decreases the chances of future adaptability. This seeming paradox is explained by the fact that with sustained success over a period of time, the respondent becomes fat and complacent, specialized and stereotyped, the victim of inertia and moral disintegration. Neither the group nor the individual can withstand the enervating effects of repeated success. When this loss of potency attacks the creative individuals of the gifted minority, they retain their position and their power, but now they can no longer respond as they once did.[5]

When the response is no longer equal to the challenge, then, says Toynbee, most people succumb outright; some just manage to survive, but the wear and tear is such that they are not good for much; others follow the leaders but are not particularly strengthened thereby; and a few are able to put forth a satisfactory response and are strengthened and prepared to meet the next challenge that comes along.[6] Political scientists call this process the circulation of elites, meaning the replacement of leaders who have become inadequate by others who are more resourceful.

The two kinds of challenge, says Toynbee, are the external and the internal, and the internal is the more important. Growth in the personality, or in the group, or in the society means that the active agent determines its own environment and becomes its own challenger. In other words, the criterion of growth and its safeguard against decay is self-determination. The gifted individual is able to harmonize all the diverse elements of his environment into an effective whole and to redirect energies that are in conflict with that harmony.[7] It takes only a moment's reflection to realize that this is precisely what administrators are almost constantly called upon to do.

EQUILIBRIUM FACTORS

Equilibrium, says Toynbee, is never a static condition. Rather, there is a constant tipping of a condition or a situation this way and that as different forces impinge on it, so that adjustments are constantly being made and the point of equilibrium is repeatedly encountered, passed, and re-encountered. This process constitutes balance. And some of the factors necessary to balance have a direct bearing on the problem of institutional life and decay.

First, there is the principle of compensation. When a living organism, for example, is handicapped by the loss of a particular organ or faculty, it is apt to respond to this challenge by specializing in the use of another one until the organism has secured an advantage over its fellows in this second field of activity to offset the handicap in the first one. In economics this is called mobility, and in administration it is flexibility.

There is also the matter of the uses and abuses of mechanization. The breakdown of a society, says Toynbee, is caused less often by attack from the outside than by a kind of internal conditioning that might have been avoided. One aspect of this conditioning is the crystallization of habit and custom at points where they reach a state of rest. The greatest danger here is mechanization.[8] Mechanical techniques are easy to isolate and to communicate, and hence they are dangerous to the human spirit unless they can be counterbalanced by factors of a spiritual nature. If the tasks of production, for example, were ever to be wholly assigned to an impersonal collective man, says Toynbee, production and growth would come to a standstill.[9]

In the history of societies, standardization also is a major aspect of disintegration. If differentiation is the natural outcome of a series of successful responses to challenge, then standardization is no less the natural outcome of a series of unsuccessful responses. Initiative and imagination are lacking, the same solution is tried over and over again irrespective of the circumstances, and the effect is retrogression and decay. Here Toynbee seems to confirm C. Wright Mills when he says that human nature's reaction against factory and office routine has reached the point where freedom from an excessive pressure of work now often counts for more than remuneration.[10]

Finally, from his wide historical survey Toynbee has found reason to believe that large size is an element of weakness and the prelude to disintegration. In the last stage of decline but one, he says, a society sometimes tries to purchase reprieve by submitting to forcible unification with a larger entity; it merges or combines. A vigorous society stands by itself and grows slowly but steadily as repeated challenges are met and overcome. Magnitude, on the other hand, is a pathological effort to find some alternative means of self-expression in lieu of a lost creative power.[11]

If this theory of size is to be applied to institutions, then a distinction should probably be made between a merger, on the one hand, where the separate parts are under the absolute control of the new institution, and, on the other hand, a federation, as in the case of the United States, or an affiliation, as when sovereign nations combine for certain purposes in a United Nations. Some of the world's greatest political philosophers since the time of Dante and Aquinas have held that greater benefits are to be found in federation than in an excessive splintering of units. Whether this applies equally to business associations is, of course, another matter. I believe that the goal of policy should be optimum size, neither more nor less, a theme that will be developed in a later chapter.[12] Toynbee's theory of equilibrium would seem to support this solution of the problem of size.

ROLE OF LEADERSHIP

Decay sets in, says Toynbee, when the gifted minority that has provided the leadership of a society loses its energies and fails to respond to the repeated challenges presented by the environment. In its growth stages, the minority has an *élan* which is what administrators call morale or atmosphere. The most important factor in producing morale, continues Toynbee, is the number of inspired individuals that the group includes. He suggests, in effect, that the administrator who can rise above his daily tasks and see his institution with a fresh eye is the one capable of providing energy and drive and of preventing the onset of decline. Unfortunately, many administrators are limited to trouble shooting, to the settling of immediate and often petty crises, and to keeping their noses to the grindstone; as a result, they have no time or energies left over to devote to questions of morale, inspiration, and vitality.

A number of possible solutions to this situation have been proposed from time to time. One is to have a committee of elder statesmen issue orders to younger men, but this is merely shifting the responsibility. Another is to supplement an executive's effectiveness by an expanded staff activity, but this merely adds to the number of people who must share the administrator's attention. The better way is to have men in executive positions who can combine knowledge with power in their administrative relations and who can keep sufficiently fresh and alert themselves to be able to communicate these qualities to their organization.

Toynbee's studies show how, in the past, men developed this freshness and alertness by a process that he calls withdrawal and return. Thus if an individual who has exhausted himself in his work withdraws from it for a time and recharges his energies, so to speak, during a period of seclusion which may last for months or even years, then when he returns to active work he finds that his creative powers have been increased and a transformation for the better has occurred in his personality and his effectiveness. The return, however, is an essential factor in this process; not to return leaves it only half completed. Nor does withdrawal mean idleness; indeed, it may include more work than before, but of a different and refreshing kind.[13]

On this theory, no administrator or political leader should stay so close to pressing events for so long that he loses perspective and the ability to innovate and to inspire, and becomes tired and sluggish. A period of reflection that broadens horizons and restores energies might do more in the long run to meet the needs of modern executives than all the courses on executive development that are so much emphasized today.[14]

This discussion of energies ties in with a recent finding that as psychology develops, there is a decreasing tendency to discard assertions of individual superiority—such as Toynbee's gifted minority—as so much snobbery or capitalist propaganda. In a recent study of the psychological aspects of management, for example, Chris Argyris argues that personality is a form of energy, that degrees of energy differ in different people, and that psychology is beginning to understand what stimulates or discourages energy in the individual.[15]

The two principal forms of energy are the physiological and the psychological, the latter consisting of mental and emotional states that determine physical fatigue, endurance, and effectiveness. The degree of psychological energy varies with a person's condition or his emotional state. Psychological energy is challenged by the need to use it, being greatest when the challenge is

Some Theories of Decay

greatest and reserves of energy must be drawn on. The most important psychological need is for "self-actualization," and when this need is frustrated, then defense mechanisms start to operate, from which stem various forms of regression. If all this is true, then one may deduce that in institutions also the onset of decline is due in part, at least, to a failure to develop the potentials of human psychology among administrators and employees, with the result that energies that might be put to good use are frustrated and lost.

Where spiritual decay is concerned, Toynbee believes that perfectionists and martinets, whether in administration or elsewhere, are frequently the cause. The vice of the perfectionist is his attempt to make rules that apply indiscriminately to all possible situations, thus narrowing the range of the individual's choice and of independent action. For when legalism is carried to excess it achieves its results at the "odious" price of treating people as so much brick and mortar rather than as sensitive human material with feelings, needs, and psychological reactions.[16] By contrast, the successful administrator relies on communications, not power, for power must eventually be abused. Indeed, says Toynbee, when an administrator finds that he *must* rely on power, it is a sign that his leadership has failed.[17]

HOMOGENEITY

This brings us to the last of the four areas earlier announced, the subject of homogeneity in administration.

Toynbee fears the onset of uniformity and conformity as evidences of decline, but, somewhat paradoxically, he distrusts innovation if it comes from the outside. By a series of logical steps he concludes that borrowing is harmful. Institutions are kept alive by means of internalized responses to challenge. Like individuals, institutions and whole cultures also must develop a personality, because the radiation of a strong personality offsets the corrosive effects of decay. Personality involves selfhood, integrity, self-determination. Hence what sociologists and anthropologists call cross-acculturation, or what in simple terms is called borrowing from others, is a de-energizing factor insofar as it dilutes the personality.

In the growth stage, continues Toynbee, all of the elements of a society cohere to constitute an indivisible whole. The society (or institution?) "radiates abroad,"[18] but apparently it must not pick up any influences from abroad lest it weaken its integrity. One man's meat, he reminds us, is another man's poison, and so it is with cultures.[19] The difficulties I find with this argument are, first, his assumption that borrowing once started must necessarily be carried to excess, and, secondly, that a synthesis involving outside components is radically different from a synthesis of innate components. But if borrowing is done with a sense of discrimination, neither of these assumptions is necessarily true. I cannot see why a society or an institution would not, in fact, be stronger if, as a result of borrowing where it needs buttressing, it succeeded in effecting a better synthesis.

To justify Toynbee's position one would have to suppose, first, that there is some peculiar genius which a society or a group possesses for its exclusive use; and secondly, that any addition to this genius from the outside would inevitably weaken it. Although Shakespeare's rule, "To thine own self be true," is surely a valid one and homogeneity helps to maintain balance, nevertheless an excessive self-containment is frequently a manifestation of ossification and decay. As competition is a major stimulus to efficiency, so also discriminating borrowing from outside sources will enrich a heritage. This is a device commonly relied on, for example, in successful mercantile concerns, such as Marks and Spencer in Britain, which will be dealt with in a later chapter.[20]

So while it seems plain that coherence and integrity are necessary to institutional survival, it does not seem reasonable to conclude that all borrowing from outside sources is subversive. There must, of course, be discrimination according to criteria that are freshly examined from time to time, but under these safeguards the institutions of business and government do, in fact, borrow effectively all the time, and a constant stream of experts passes through every industrialized nation to learn from the experience of others.

CONCLUSION

Decay is inherent in living organisms and in institutions. But in institutions, which are less delicate than living organisms, decay can be arrested and reversed and the institutions renewed. Thus the energy age of an institution may be either greater or less than its calendar age.

Most of the causes of decay are found in the factors of growth, but in a reverse way, as when the impetus to growth is not sufficiently maintained or some of its elements are carried to excess while others are neglected. Since growth is a balanced process, loss of balance is a major cause of retrogression. The sources of decay may be internal or external, and in either case they constitute a challenge to the administrator, who must respond successfully if the institution is to survive.

Challenges from the outside may stem from competition with other institutions, from conflict with them, and from comparisons with them. Competition usually strengthens both sides. Conflict may, in extreme form, cause the death of one of them. Comparison may result in a mutual borrowing or in splendid isolation. If borrowing takes place, it must be discriminating and at a pace that will assure absorption by the borrower.

Internal challenges stem from all the elements in the complex we call administration, and the survival of the institution depends on the kind of response that is forthcoming. Even external challenges must be settled internally within the institution. The leaders of institutions are most likely to forestall decay if they meet challenges halfway instead of waiting until they are in battle array and it is too late to act effectively. Appearing too late with too little gives the advantage to a competitor, whereas successful anticipation keeps an administrator in control, poised, resourceful, and capable of maneuvering from strength instead of being on the defensive.

A main resource of any institution that would survive, therefore, is the high quality of its leadership, offered by men able to act creatively and to anticipate institutional and administrative needs. All things are sudden to those who are unprepared.

No inexorable life span determines the death of institutions, nor is their decline the result of some occult process or the attachment of particular labels to politico-economic systems. Rather, in institutions, certain elements produce a better or a worse performance depending on which are most prominent. A challenge to institutional management, therefore, is to discover the rules of change and to develop a check list of vital areas of work that must be watched for signs of decay. If the symptoms are known in advance, they will be more quickly recognized when they appear. And most of these symptoms are in some way related to the complex called bureaucracy.

Part II Bureaucracy

The term bureaucracy is a respectable one that has fallen on evil days. Properly describing a process—the how of administration—it has frequently been used as a word of contempt, an epithet to be hurled at government when it "interferes" with business or costs too much. When so used, the term applies to the what of administration and not to the how.

As institutions grow they tend to become increasingly formal and to have fixed ways of doing things, and it is this general process of formalization that is properly called bureaucracy. When an organization is said to be bureaucratic, meaning that it has become bound up in red tape, concerned with masses of paper work, and dedicated to rigid rules of operation, the term applies as much to a department store or a manufacturing corporation as it does to the much-abused public services. It is this operational aspect of bureaucracy that the present study would get at. If an excess of bureaucracy interferes with efficiency and vitality, then we must discover the reason.

In addition, however, bureaucracy may also be used in an ideal sense to describe an organization that has attained the highest possible efficiency. But in this use of the term, the most efficient organization is by definition the most rational one; and since bureaucracy is held to be the most rational, it must also be the most efficient of all forms of organization. I think that most practical administrators would agree that these assumptions lead to false conclusions. In this second part of the book the attempt will be, first, to try to discover why some authorities have thought so highly of bureaucracy in the ideal sense; secondly, to develop an indipendent theory of bureaucracy that will explain both its efficiencies and its pitfalls; and thirdly, to identify the pathological elements of bureaucracy as well as those capable of being combined with the factors of enterprise to form a new synthesis, which is vitality in administration.

Chapter 5 British Electricity

An account of a bureaucracy in action will help to illustrate the kinds of problems that arise when an institution becomes hierarchical, specialized, and subject to overhead rules and policies. This is the story of Britain's electricity monopoly as told by the Herbert Committee which reported to Parliament and the nation in 1956.[1] The fact that the subject is a public enterprise is not particularly significant because all large undertakings have common problems and opportunities as they grow in age and size.

SIZE AND ORGANIZATION

Britain's electricity supply industry is one of the largest in the nation, the result of an amalgamation in 1948 of 560 separate supply undertakings into one national electricity scheme. Involved were 300 power stations, £900 million in capital assets, and a staff of some 150,000 engineers, administrators, and other workers of all kinds. The capital stake alone is truly impressive, with £200 million needed each year to keep pace with Britain's industrial development. This sum represents about 8 per cent of the total gross investment of the nation for all purposes, and 19 per cent of all investment in the industrial sector alone. And in personnel, already by 1955 the total was 179,171 employees and increases were at the rate of from two to four thousand a year.

How to combine more than 500 previously separate agencies so as to operate on a nationwide basis, how to administer a £900 million enterprise, absorb annually 8 per cent of the nation's gross investable capital, direct a staff of over 180,000 persons, carry on a centralized purchasing program, conduct labor relations, and train almost 8,000 employees at any one time—these are some of the more obvious dimensions that meet the eye. But how to do all this and at the same time prevent an excess of centralization and bureaucracy as well as supply the needed amounts of enterprise and vitality—this is the far more difficult problem.

At the outset in Great Britain, electricity supply was undertaken by local companies authorized under the Electric Lighting Act of 1882 for particular areas and supplying local customers situated within a few miles of the source of power. But by 1919 something more was needed to send industrial power over longer distances at less cost, and in that year Parliament established under the Electricity (Supply) Act a supervisory body known as the Electricity Commissioners. As a first step toward an integrated supply system, the act merely provided for voluntary agreement among producers. Hence by 1925 there were still 541 separate authorized undertakings drawing supplies from 494 generating stations of varying size and efficiency.

In 1926 another Electricity (Supply) Act created the Central Electricity Board to supplement the regulatory work of the Electricity Commissioners. One of Britain's first public corporations, the board was authorized to control generation without owning the stations and, with the exception of the north of Scotland, to build an interconnecting grid system of main transmission lines. The entire output of this system was sold to the board, which in turn fixed the resale price to distributors. Moreover, although the board did not actually own the generating stations, any new stations or extensions of facilities had to be planned in cooperation with the board and approved by the Electricity Commissioners.

By the time Britain entered World War II in 1939, the country had been divided into six operational areas, each with its own control center and with London as the National Load Center. Despite the divided authority, this centralized control of generation led to a more effective pooling of plant and to increased efficiency of operation, a condition that was immediately reflected during the war period.

Then in 1947 came the Electricity Act which nationalized and consolidated the entire electricity industry. Both the Electricity Commissioners and the Central Electricity Board were abolished, and the generation, transmission, and distribution of electricity were transferred to public ownership. In place of the old structure, two layers of public corporations now covered the nation. At the top, a public body called the Central Authority was in command of the industry, and beneath it twelve Area Electricity Boards were responsible for a unified business within their respective areas. Then in addition, and in line with nationalization policies favored at the time, each area board was advised by an Electricity Consultative Council set up to represent the consumer interest and viewpoint and to act as a counterpoise to centralization and bureaucracy.

The over-all function of the Central Authority was to develop and maintain an efficient and economical system of electricity supply; to provide bulk power to the area boards for distribution; to coordinate distribution and exercise general control over the policies and finances of the boards; to conduct research and development; to extend supply to rural areas; to promote simplification and standardization of methods; and to promote the welfare, health, and safety of employees. For their part, the area boards then purchased the bulk supply of current; fixed and published schedules; cooperated with the Central Authority in such matters as rural electrification and standardization; and carried on the retail end of the business in their respective areas.

The division of financial responsibility between the Central Authority and the area boards became important. With the approval of the Minister of Fuel and Supply and the Treasury, area boards might borrow temporarily to discharge their functions, but the issue of stock for the whole industry was reserved to the Central Authority. Moreover, the area boards were obliged to contribute as required to the Central Reserve Fund for the industry, but they might also establish their own reserve funds and retain their own surplus revenues, if the Central Authority approved.

The organization of the Central Authority and the area boards followed the usual pattern of the private corporation, with a board of directors (the chairman being full time and the others part time), and executive duties entrusted to a paid staff operating through functional departments. Board members were appointed by the Minister of Fuel and Supply, executive officials by the respective boards, and all were exempt from the civil service laws. The 1947 legislation made it clear, moreover, that actual administrative arrangements and the internal organization of the boards were matters to be left entirely to the industry to determine.

Thus things stood at the time of the Herbert Committee report in 1956. A year later, acting on the committee's recommendations but rejecting some of them, Parliament fixed the organization of the electricity industry as follows:

1. Twelve area operating boards, as before, but with the central reserve fund to be divided and thereafter retained by each board that earns it.
2. A single generating board, acting as supplier to the twelve distribution systems.
3. To replace the former Central Authority, a new Electricity Council consisting of representatives of the twelve regional boards and the generating board, headed by an independent chairman and two deputy chairmen, and employing a relatively small central staff.

The Electricity Council's responsibilities are similar to those of a holding company and include five main functions: labor relations and industry-wide bargaining; research, much of which is farmed out, however, or undertaken by the operating boards;

approval of proposed rates and tariffs—something that has become fairly automatic since the Council also has a "judicial" review power over board finances; approval of proposed capital budgets; and relations with the Minister of Fuel and Supply, a purpose here being to reduce the Minister's direct responsibility by increasing the Council's role as his alter ego.

There are now three ways by which the generating board and the twelve area retail boards can get their capital funds: by Treasury advances, by borrowing with a guarantee, or by borrowing on the open market in the manner of a private business. So far, however (1958), only the first of these methods has actually been authorized by the government.[2]

HIERARCHY AND COORDINATION

Although the Herbert Committee found progress in the electricity industry between 1947 and 1956 to be a cause for general congratulation, no one familiar with the problems of bureaucracy will be surprised to learn that many troubles relating to size and organization were uncovered.

As in any large organization, the committee found that right relations between levels of coordination are a constant difficulty and hence management constantly seeks a better arrangement. Neglect at the center causes over-all planning and finance to suffer, but overstress at the center produces delay and red tape. "The formal structure of the industry," said the Herbert report, "is not conducive to the highest efficiency; what sufficed during the installation period will not do for the long haul; friction and duplication must be avoided; the top must emphasize planning, the field be free to exercise initiative." The committee therefore recommended—and this was by all odds the most important recommendation in its report—that a new top agency (since called the Electricity Council) should become the planning, financing, high-policy "brain" for the industry.[3]

Delays resulting from intricate clearances are the consequence of inadequate hierarchical articulations. Why, asked the committee, can the Americans build a power station in little over half the time needed in Britain? True, there had been materials and manpower shortages which would explain some of the difficulty. But that did not explain why it took some two and a half years in technical discussion before final approval was given for a proposed power station, or why another five years were then required to build and prepare it for operation.

The committee thought that, over and above materials and manpower shortages, the necessity for clearances from "the many ministries and semi-public groups . . . accounts for the biggest delay," and that in addition, in Britain there is now "almost complete lack of competition between plant manufacturers," a criticism obviously directed at the private sector of the economy.[4] It would not be enough, therefore, merely to improve communications and to simplify clearances among the levels of the hierarchy; there would have to be organization changes in the industry, increased competition, and a greater freedom to administrators to exercise initiative. Accordingly, the committee recommended that the area boards should be given a wider authority to proceed without advance clearances.

Interspersed throughout the Herbert report are frequent references to the danger of exceeding the point of size where efficiency is greatest. Thus, "No organization should be larger than is necessary to achieve the major economies of scale. The larger an organization is the greater the problems in running it." If there are to be substantial gains from size, these problems must be faced; otherwise, growth in size must be cut off at a certain point.[5] Indeed, the committee thought that already the area boards had reached the optimum size for best results; that they should now assume a more "personal" and direct responsibility for the raising and spending of capital; and that the level below the area board should be given more freedom under a manager responsible for all aspects of the work.

SPECIALIZATION AND PROFESSIONALIZATION

How to make a bureaucracy businesslike and hard-hitting, and then to keep it that way, is a universal problem of large-scale organization. "This is not in any reasonable sense of the term an inefficient industry," commented the Herbert Committee. Rather, it is an efficient industry that could be improved and it is in danger of losing efficiency partly for reasons beyond its control.

Up to that time (1956) the *esprit de corps* in the industry had been high. There were inevitable difficulties and problems, as in any large undertaking, but they were tackled and solved. The business leadership had been taken over from numerous smaller undertakings and these men ran the industry. But what would happen when they were gone and replacements were needed? "We are concerned," said the Herbert Committee, "that this morale . . . be maintained in the younger men who in future will have had experience only in the unified industry."[6]

This is "the second-generation problem," as someone has called it, and it is an ominous aspect of the whole bureaucratic trend for private as for public endeavor. Men would have to be brought in from the universities and the technical schools to fill anticipated vacancies, of course, but where would they get practical, competitive business experience? The committee had to remain silent on this point.

The question of technical personnel presented no problem because already by 1956 the nationalized industry was training men at the rate of about 8,000 a year. Candidates were recruited from the schools and then trained for four to five years. Graduate trainees needed two years more for an engineering degree or a higher national certificate. Bureaucracies are among the best customers of a nation's schools and they are also rivals, because bureaucracies must train if they are to solve their leadership problem, especially in the area of business management and coordination.

The Herbert Committee found, however, that although the industry stressed training, it gave too little attention to research and development, which are equally needed when planning for the future. In 1954–55, for example, expenditures for research amounted to less than 0.2 per cent of annual revenue. The industry should therefore lean less heavily on research by outside organizations and do more itself.

So far as finances were concerned, the committee found that the area boards had generally managed to achieve moderate surpluses from the outset and that in no sense could their activities be called subsidized. The industry was self-supporting, as Parliament had insisted it should be. During the seven years of operation, the twelve area boards had connected nearly three million new consumers and had increased the units of power sold per annum by about 76 per cent. In addition, the rate of rural electrification was some two and a half times greater than in 1938, the last full year before World War II. In the important matter of thermal efficiency of generation, there had been a rise from 20.52 to 23.83 per cent between 1938 and 1954, the comparable rate for the United States being 28.7 per cent as of the latter date.

The committee several times noted that the work habits of different nations are a factor in individual enterprise efficiency. Thus, if Britain were to adopt the American pattern of work by shifts, then periods of effective demand for electricity would be spread instead of concentrated; this would greatly improve the load factor, which in 1954–55 stood at 46.8.

As the Herbert Committee also noted, a bureaucracy needs promotion and development in the technical sphere, fresh viewpoints in management, more effective incentives throughout, and the kind of drive and acumen more often found in competitive industries. But as the committee remarked, "Electricity supply is a monopoly industry which has a constantly growing demand for its product. These facts expose it to two serious risks, either of which could, in our view, sap its efficiency." In the first place, "the industry could, without financial embarrassment, jog along comfortably without much effort," but also without much enterprise. And secondly, there is the danger that the industry might be used, in effect, as a tax collector for the government. To avoid both of these hazards the industry must be run on strictly business lines and the boundary between government and the industry must be clear for all to see.[7]

Furthermore, if the regional units of the industry could be made to compete among themselves by means of comparisons within the system, this would be helpful because even under nationalization, said the committee, competition is a spur to efficiency and an enterprising spirit.

The committee complimented the industry on its growth, but was concerned about overstaffing. Thus, "The passive attitude adopted by the Central Authority has, in our opinion, caused management at all levels to be disinclined to seek out redundancy when ascertained. In consequence we find that work study, operational research and investigations into restrictive practices are undertaken without enthusiasm, if they are undertaken at all." Thus the effective deployment of manpower is hampered and there may be hidden pockets of underemployment which undermine the morale not only of those directly concerned but also of their colleagues who are working at "full stretch."[8]

Another thorny problem concerns promotions. Although the electricity supply industry is not under civil service, the committee noted a tendency to imitate that system too closely. "We fully understand the Authority's preoccupaion with the need in a public utility industry to avoid charges of favouritism, but this particular nettle must be grasped as the industry depends for its efficiency and progress on the quality of its leadership." Although to mark certain men for particular jobs might be "invidious," and to give them special educational opportunities might lead to jealousy, nevertheless, said the committee, these methods of progressive industry should be adopted.[9]

INCENTIVES

Where incentives are concerned, competition has a special importance. Although self-aggrandizement is often a principal characteristic of bureaucracy, the Herbert Committee apparently believed that an urge for wider scope is a useful incentive. The incursion of the electricity boards into the retail sale of electrical appliances, for example, was approved. So long as it was fair, it did no injustice to private dealers and was to be encouraged as a stimulus to competition.

In the matter of salaries, the committee favored rates equal to the best in private industry. The public should realize that the talent required to run the electricity boards was in considerable demand. Hence salaries should not be depressed through false analogies, nor should political considerations, such as the jealousies of higher civil servants and union officials, be allowed to prevail. Even the top salaries of £8,500 a year should be raised, and part-time board members earning only £500 a year deserved substantial increases because their compensation was out of line with their responsibilities. Indeed, board members have a special importance because it is they who largely supply the freshness and the outside viewpoint that large organizations especially need.

The strongest incentive, however, should be a desire to excel, and hence the tendency to standardization and rigidity should be stopped. The Herbert Committee reiterated this principle many times but in no case more strongly, perhaps, than as applied to collective labor agreements. Thus, "The all-embracing nature of the national agreements leaves them [the board managements] no opportunity of recognizing individual prowess or special efficiency by such means as the award of merit pay." An antidote to bureaucracy is differentiation.[10]

ACCOUNTABILITY AND MANAGERIAL FREEDOM

Where bureaucracy is legalistic and venerates rules and regulations, enterprise often scores its greatest successes when on the borderline of illegality.

The main difference between public corporations and the giants of the private world is that responsibility to the legislature and to the public is greater in the case of the public bodies. One result is a mass of rules and regulations to ensure accountability. The Herbert Committee thought, however, that in the electricity supply industry the problem of accountability was pretty well in hand. The board managements acted responsibly and control from the government was maintained at a proper distance. The Minister realized that if he started giving orders directly to the boards, he would soon be increasingly involved in day-to-day administration which would, of course, only add to his worries. Hence he was content to consult informally with management— and then only on large matters, such as finances—instead of issuing commands.

But enormous problems remained in a bureaucratic structure of the magnitude of the electricity industry. In the relations between the boards and the government, the Herbert Committee favored these principles: First, no administrative duties should be discharged centrally unless it was clear that they could be better performed there than in the area boards. Secondly, in central planning and decision making there should be a firm touch but also a light one; central management should seek to create a reputation for being at once judicious and stimulating. And thirdly, the head office should inspire and lead, and in consultation with field officials should cause them to feel responsible and encouraged rather than frustrated.

Growth capital was another problem in this relationship. At the time of the Herbert report, the Minister was expected to advise Parliament on the raising of growth capital, but had, of course, to rely largely on the industry's own assessment of its needs. To ease this burden the committee recommended (and this has since been done) that the newly created Electricity Council should assume a larger share of the responsibility and that the Central Reserve Fund should be distributed among the generation board and the area boards so as to extend their control of growth funds. To allow the boards to compete for capital funds in the open market and without Treasury guarantees, said the committee, would make them more autonomous.

In addition to these changes, long-term budgets now cover a three-year period and facilitate planning; standard accounts for the whole system have been developed; and organization and methods sections in the area boards review all major items of expense with a view to suggesting improved performance.

A year after the Herbert Committee had reported, another body, the Select Committee on Nationalised Industries, looked into the affairs of eight nationalized boards, electricity included. Among other things, this group concluded that Treasury control over borrowing, executive compensation, and the like "has in no way unduly hampered or is hampering the initiative of the Boards." It was then noted that "If any Board was able to find all its capital from internal resources without borrowing, the Treasury's influence would be very much diminished."[11] And so it would, since financial freedoms are the basis of all other managerial freedoms and fiscal policy and business policy can never wholly coincide.

On the basic issue of accountability versus managerial freedoms, however, the Herbert Committee was convinced that a nationalized industry *must* be in the hands of a Minister responsible to Parliament and that his authority to give directions to the industry must be retained. His foremost power is that of appointing board members; he must satisfy himself through periodic reports that the industry is being run efficiently on a commercial basis, or, if it is to be subsidized, then he must issue specific orders to that effect; he should continue to have the power to authorize the amount and terms of capital to be raised; and he should be free to give or to withhold his consent to "the issue of directions" by the top administrative echelon in the industry.[12]

CONCLUSION

This illustration of the electricity industry in Britain shows clearly the pitfalls that beset all large bureaucratic institutions. Such pitfalls include multiple levels of organization; the difficulty of combining planning and coordination; the dispersion of financial responsibilities; the magnitude and professionalization of staffs; the possible neglect of pretraining and in-service training; delays due to long chains of command; the necessity of intricate clearances; the tendency to exceed optimum size; an insistence on seniority promotions; the difficulty of assuring business acumen and of emphasizing commercial growth; the problem of securing optimum technical efficiency; the weakness of intramural competition; the danger of overstaffing and redundancy; the depressing effect on incentive of "civil service conditions"; the possible neglect of sources of commercial revenue; the false economy of inadequate salaries; the danger of standardization, especially in wage agreements; the de-energizing effect of an overemphasis on legal accountability at the expense of indispensable managerial freedoms; the confusion of authority and the inertia that result from uncertain jurisdictions; the debilitating effect of overcentralization; the imposition of artificial limitations on the supply of growth capital; the danger of restricting initiative because of outside control; the neglect of modern methods of accountancy, long-range planning, and scientific method; the inability to borrow without Treasury guarantee; and the difficulties of coordination in any undertaking that has become exceedingly large.

All of these difficulties were found, for example, and many of them in aggravated form, by the Fleck Committee that studied the British coal industry and reported in 1955.[13] The coal industry is much older than the electricity supply industry, of course, and hence it is more complicated and its bureaucratic problems are greater. Another interesting illustration of the universal character of bureaucracy is revealed in an intensive study of hospital administration in Britain made by the Acton Trust Society, which in 1958 had published four volumes of a projected six-volume work.

Several comments in this study are especially apt. Thus, it is noted that "public accountability implies central authority; central authority, where a large, complex and widely diffused system like the Hospital Service is concerned, implies *a long chain of command raising, at every stage, the perennial question of devolution and initiative. . . .*" The main complaint against a nationwide hospital service, said the report, is that it involves too many authorities, too many committees, too many administrators, and in consequence authority has become diffuse and uncertain, decisions slow and cumbersome. Moreover, there is too much interference with the day-to-day administration of individual hospitals. Thus, a hospital that had formerly been independent complained of "bureaucratisation, impersonality, and loss of independence." The staff felt uncomfortable in a situation involving extensive relations with many people rather than more intensive relations with a smaller group.[14] Difficulties such as these are due more to the inherent characteristics of bureaucracy than they are to the private or public nature of the undertaking.

With his doctrinaire notions of efficiency, Max Weber might argue that the complexities of bureaucracy, though many, are relatively unimportant; or he might say that if sufficient draughts of logic and order were supplied to their solution, they might be overcome. But men of practical experience know that this is not so. Business management is a frame of mind for which there is no substitute, even in public undertakings.

Ben W. Lewis, who studied these problems broadly in his book, *British Planning and Nationalization*,[15] identifies the same bureaucratic difficulties noted here. The government, he says, is well aware of the problems involved in trying to combine efficiency of operation with responsibility to the public. Going beyond a "bureaucratic thirst for power," the complexities of bureaucracy are inherent in institutional administration everywhere. The main problem in railway management, for example, is overcentralization, overstaffing, and lack of a commercial outlook. In all large enterprises there are too many layers of organization. Monopoly takes the place of competition; an entire industry becomes a single unit; problems of the firm, the industry, and of the economy as a whole merge, with "final, almost terrifying economic responsibility" resting on a small group of policy officials.[16]

Lewis also agrees that labels are unimportant. The issue is not one of private individual enterprise versus public ownership or state socialism. Rather, it is monopoly versus competition, bureaucracy versus flexibility. What Britain needs (and this might be said equally of the United States) "is an industrial and commercial rebirth—inventiveness, mechanization, daring, and drive." The leaders of British thought know this, he adds, but so far the efforts to solve the nation's problems of bureaucracy and enterprise have been more successful in achieving organization for responsibility than reorganization for efficiency.[17]

Chapter 6 The Traditional Case for Bureaucracy

Many social scientists believe that the only type of management that is superior to bureaucracy at its best is capitalist entrepreneurship, but many would add that the day of the individual entrepreneur is almost past. Consequently, administrators must now increasingly turn to bureaucracy as a guide to institutional management.

The idea that bureaucracy is the most efficient form of administration has best been expressed in Germany. British administrators, on the other hand, have long resisted bureaucracy and all other theories that stress logic to the exclusion of counterbalancing, human factors. But in the United States, despite a skepticism inherited from Britain, bureaucracy has come to have a rather wide appeal in recent decades, especially in big business.

There are a number of reasons for this changed attitude. Thus, as Whyte so convincingly shows in *The Organization Man*,[1] businessmen are looking for beliefs that will legitimatize large size and inherent bureaucratic procedures and assumptions. Economists are no longer sure that market forces alone can do the whole job of decision making, and hence they have turned their attention to the hierarchies of business where administrative decisions are made. Joseph A. Schumpeter of Harvard has even argued that the success of the American economic system is due to big-business bureaucracy and that when socialism succeeds capitalism, as seemed likely, this same bureaucratic element would assure a continuing economic progress; in fact, he even talked about enterprise itself becoming "routine."[2]

Among the younger social scientists, whose influence is greater than is sometimes supposed, there is often a tendency to regard bureaucracy with favor because it is "rational," and how else, they ask, can a "real" science of society be developed if not by means of "rigorous" rationality?[3] Sociologists especially are apt to accept bureaucracy as potentially the most effective form of institutional management. Although few claim to know much about efficient management from the practical standpoint, they follow the lead of their great theorizer and categorizer, Max Weber, a German scholar whose books appeared in the mid-1920's.[4]

MAX WEBER'S THESIS

Max Weber was thoroughly modern in his assumption that trends in organization and management in the dominant institutions of society affect all other institutions. Thus the progressive bureaucratization of the institutions of business and industry are exerting a marked influence on military organization, church organization, governmental organization, and all other forms of large-scale enterprise. The age of the entrepreneur, which Weber dealt with so brilliantly in his book, *The Protestant Ethic and the Spirit of Capitalism*,[5] is being superseded, he said, by a universal bureaucracy controlled by managers who are professionalized and disciplined. His discussion of this subject in *Wirtschaft und Gesellschaft*,[6] which appeared in 1925, was the forerunner of later studies, such as Burnham's *The Managerial Revolution*, Berle's *The Twentieth Century Capitalist Revolution*, and Whyte's *The Organization Man*, all of which have tended to confirm Weber in his sociological prognostications.[7]

Weber's method was both historical and analytical. Historically, he found the prototypes of modern bureaucracies in the earliest civilizations and deduced that there must be some innate social necessity for the appearance of this form of organization. Analytically, he calls bureaucracy the "ideal-typical" form of administration to distinguish it from others, the "patrimonial" and the "charismatic," for example, the latter being one that stresses the role of the gifted individual. He then sets out to prove that bureaucracy is a modern form of organization, at once typical and ideal, and that it will become dominant because modern educational systems have produced factors such as technology, the rationalization of economic processes, and the specialization and professionalization of occupations. Weber does not offer empirical proof of these assumptions; being a grand theorizer, he is content merely to announce them.

Although Weber believed bureaucracy to be inherent in all formal organization, he also assumed that since Western society lives under a regime of law which applies to all institutions, bureaucracy is a legal as well as an administrative concept, and from this he drew a number of important inferences. Every organization, he said, includes a few policy officials and many operating officials, who are the bureaucrats. These men are subject to the law and to the authority of policy officials and hence might be supposed to occupy a subordinate position in the hierarchy of power. And in a formal sense, so they do. But in addition, since bureaucrats are so numerous and so expert in institutional management, it is they who exercise the real power when it comes to the actual conduct of affairs.

A bureaucrat holds an office which is part of a much larger framework of organization that is hierarchical and laid out with as much scientific precision as possible. A bureaucrat's authority is therefore attached to the position he occupies in the hierarchy and is not independent of it. This being the case, he has a professional and a legal duty to conform to what is expected of him; his only responsibility is to comply with authority and to do his duty without fear or favor.

Offices are filled by merit and merit is determined by educational requirements and the granting of formal degrees. Hence there is no room for amateurs and nonprofessionals. A knowledge of the special rules of his office constitutes the special learning that sets a bureaucrat apart from and makes him superior to other men. In the modern world, this special knowledge is basically technical.

A bureaucrat, continues Weber, is expected to devote his whole attention to his office and to have no other source of employment or influence outside of the organization, because that would destroy the symmetry and discipline of the system. Moreover, since he is a career man, his employment will be continuous and he will be protected from arbitrary dismissal. And since he is a specialist and a professional, his duty is to confine himself to his assigned area and not to encroach on the authority of others. An office, moreover, is a continuum. Once the principle of jurisdictional competency is established, an office becomes permanent and is held by later incumbents with little change in its character. This theory resembles some of our modern civil service assumptions and helps to explain why popular attacks on bureaucracy emphasize the tenaciousness of officialdom, once its power has been established.

Weber's ideal-typical system also stresses the importance of rules, for, he thought, if law is to regulate every official action, there must be rules for every such action. Thus he stated specifically that the management of the modern office is based on *written* rules; that all administrative acts, decisions, and rules are to be formulated and recorded even in cases where oral discussion is involved. Administration presupposes an expert training in rules and a knowledge of them as precise and cumulative as possible. It is this knowledge that constitutes the special technical learning which is the most priceless possession of the bureaucrat.

In sum, the essential attributes of Weber's ideal and efficient administrative system are law and rules throughout, hierarchy, precise jurisdiction, specialization, professionalization, impersonality of attitude and procedure, and continuity of office and function. Nothing must be left to chance or to discretion, which are not needed when organization and procedure have been logically constructed. Make the *system* efficient, said Weber, and then merely find the men to fit the indicated slots. But the men who fit these slots, being numerous and expert, are collectively in a position to exercise the real power in the organization, no matter how much formal power may reside among policy officials at the top.

THE CLAIMED ADVANTAGES OF BUREAUCRACY

Max Weber had definite ideas about what kind of society was desirable and he justified his advocacy of a bureaucratic system of organization on grounds of efficiency in achieving that society. Experience universally shows, he said, that the "purely" bureaucratic type of administration is "capable of attaining the highest degree of efficiency and is in this sense formally the most rationally known means of carrying out imperative control of human beings." The only real choice in administration, he said, is between bureaucracy on the one hand and what he called dilettantism on the other. Moreover, it makes little difference whether the economic system is organized on a capitalist or on a socialist basis, although in some ways capitalism is the more rational of the two because its profit objectives are so clear.[8]

The chief advantage of bureaucracy over other forms of organization, thought Weber, is its reliance on technical knowledge and technical efficiency. Whether a system is capitalist or socialist, or something else, is less important than its sophistication in technical matters. Bureaucracy is to other forms of organization as machine production is to hand production. Hence if one believes in technology, one must also believe in bureaucracy. The technical virtues of bureaucracy are precision, predictability, technical know-how, continuity, coherence, strict subordination in a set hierarchy, and the reduction of friction and of material and personnel costs—all these raised to the optimum point. Indeed, as Weber warms to his subject, he seems to be describing a sort of technocracy.

Administration, according to Weber, is analogous to the self-operating market of the classical economists: it is impersonal and automatic. Impersonality is deliberately created by the adoption of certain known rules designed to rid administration of love, hatred, and all other personal, irrational, and emotional factors that cannot be predicted. The more perfectly administration is depersonalized, the more predictable and automatic it becomes. Quality of performance and attainment of objective are assured, once the proper method has been set in motion.

Weber notes only briefly the effect of bureaucracy on enterprise, freedom, resourcefulness—that whole complex of positive factors in administration—brushing these considerations aside on the ground that they belong in another category. "The bearing of this thesis may be disregarded here," he says with some certainty. Rationality cannot tolerate a regime in which freedom, arbitrary action, personality factors, and favor and preferences are to be found; such elements are subjective and valuational and hence are out of place in administration.

Being dedicated to logic, Weber supported the leveling out of individual differences and social and economic differences of all kinds. This, however, will result in higher government costs and higher taxation because, despite increased efficiency, it is to be expected that once privilege has been destroyed, the masses would demand more services for themselves at public expense. He also opposed benevolence in employers in favor of treatment according to the strict rights of employees. We must trust the expert, he said, not *noblesse oblige*. He thought that England, where family, traditions of service and charity, and sentiments of public duty are so strong, would be the last nation to become bureaucratized, and he considered this a great handicap to her progress. As the first nation to develop a modern capitalist system, she might be expected to combine efficiency and technology really effectively if she could bring herself to discard her ideas of morality and propriety and become rational instead.[9]

Weber did not have much to say about the role of the individual in society, but in a bureaucracy his role is clear. Although collectively it is the bureaucrat who has the power, he cannot expect to "squirm out" of the apparatus in which he is harnessed; he is chained to his work by his entire material and "ideal" existence; he is a single cog in an ever-moving machine which is directed from the top. As part of this machine he is carried along a fixed route of march; he is entrusted with specialized tasks to be discharged by means of an unvarying routine; he is forged to a community of functionairies having a common interest in the continuing progress of the system. In fact, if the system is thoroughly rational it will carry on even after an enemy has occupied the state, because all he need do is change the top officials. But it may be noted here that it was in Germany itself, whose administrative traditions Weber was mirroring, that the Nazis were to prove this last assumption wrong.[10]

Another advantage of bureaucracy, said Weber, is its ability to develop an inner life of its own. Indeed, the dearest wish of a bureaucracy is to be left alone to generate its own momentum, thus guaranteeing permanence, purity of motive, impartiality, faithfulness to routine, and all the rest. Bureaucracy dislikes cabinets as being too personal and favors instead the use of committees because of their matter-of-factness and objectivity. Urbanism also is desirable because it means "the complete depersonalization of administrative management."[11]

Every bureaucracy, continues Weber, seeks to increase the superiority of its professional elite by keeping its knowledge and intentions secret. Whenever the power interests of the elite are at stake, there one will find secrecy. The concept of the official secret is the invention of bureaucracy and applies as much to political parties, churches, foreign powers, and economic competitors as it does to government agencies or corporate boards of directors. By means of secrecy, routine, discipline, specialized knowledge, and technical perfection, an organization develops a power that not even an absolute monarch can wholly overthrow. Such power stems from the cohesion of many small units into a collective whole that is able to undertake or to resist pretty much what it wants to.

COMMENTARY ON THE WEBERIAN THESIS

When I have interviewed businessmen and public officials on

the subject of bureaucracy, I have often asked whether in their opinion Weber's thesis was a correct one, whether bureaucracy is in fact the most efficient form of administration, and the reaction to this question tends to follow a pattern. Before offering an answer there will be the query, "What did Weber mean by 'rational'?" I would reply that apparently he meant a logical progression toward predetermined institutional objectives. The person being interviewed would then ask, "What did he mean by efficiency?" and I would say that I thought he meant the greatest amount of production for the least expenditure of energy, but I could not be sure about it because Weber apparently assumed efficiency and rationality to mean the same thing and used the two terms interchangeably.

At this point the usual comments from business and government officials alike would be these: first, my observation is that people, whether in groups or acting separately, are never wholly rational; secondly, efficiency appears to be something more than rationality even as Weber uses that term; thirdly, there is a wide range of choice between bureaucracy as Weber defined it and what he called "dilettantism"; and fourthly, if all of Weber's assumptions and objectives are considered, the system he recommends would prove far more congenial under socialistic than under capitalistic conditions of enterprise.

Having said these things, however, my informants would then comment on what they thought was valid and what was objectionable in the Weberian thesis, and here also there was a fairly general pattern. Thus, carefully defined objectives, organization, technologies, and procedures are necessary in large-scale undertakings. But impersonality and a strict adherence to rules are not desirable because they militate against a sales approach in the business and detract from consumer and employee satisfactions. Also, Weber's thesis overlooks the role of leadership, the need to coordinate and to inspire effort. Actually, an excessive routine is an evil that the progressive administrator must constantly do battle with if his organization is to remain flexible enough to change when change is needed.

So much for the practical side. From the academic standpoint, Professor Carl J. Friedrich of Harvard has, I think, pointed up the main weakness in the Weberian thesis when he comments that Weber's genius overshot the mark by proliferating what would seem to social scientists as merely working hypotheses in the form of "ideal types," which he did not pause "to test against empirical data; yet he himself would have been the first to concede the importance of doing so."[12]

On the basis of both empirical evidence and academic criticism, therefore, it appears that Weber's analysis of the factors of bureaucracy is probably a correct one, but that his "model" of administration is not likely to produce the results he predicted for it. His methodology is classificatory and static rather than evolutionary and organic. A formal classifier may be able to differentiate the major elements of a process, but he cannot describe a complete process, much less the fluidity and subtleties of the administrative process. Furthermore, Weber was a dualist, addicted to the either/or approach, and this also is invariably a source of distortion where process is concerned.

But perhaps the greatest objection to Weber's thesis is his assumption that bureaucracy is a distinct form with a separate identity and character of its own. On the contrary, it seems more likely that all the elements of bureaucracy inhere in varying degree in all forms of social organization, from the simplest to the most complex.

Joseph A. Schumpeter, the late Harvard Professor and follower of Weber, also made a careful study of bureaucracy.[13] Schumpeter's conclusion was a curious one: bureaucracy, he said, is the main reason for the latter-day success of capitalism, but an excess of bureaucracy will cause capitalism eventually to give way to socialism; and when socialism has been established, bureaucracy will then produce efficient results. His reasons for this belief are equally curious: unit efficiency under socialism would probably be lower than it is at present under capitalist competition, but, on the other hand, quantity production and worker morale would be higher and hence total efficiency also would be higher. As a

The Traditional Case for Bureaucracy

socialist dogma, however, bureaucracy is losing its appeal, as shown by the efforts of the U.S.S.R. and the Communist regime in China to eliminate the bureaucratic inertias that plague them. The British, long chided for their empiricism and their suspicion of too rigorous a logic, are probably nearer right on this fateful issue than any other people. So great is the British aversion to the concept of bureaucracy that even in the matter of pronunciation, Fowler's *Modern English Usage* says of it, "The formation is so barbarous that all attempt at self-respect in pronunciation may perhaps as well be abandoned," and the sophisticated *Oxford English Dictionary* defines bureaucrat as "An official who endeavours to concentrate administrative powers in his own bureau." Nevertheless, this attitude does not prevent the British from recognizing that certain aspects of bureaucracy, and especially scientific management and technology, are essential to institutional survival and economic growth.

The problem, of course, is to find an acceptable middle ground somewhere between Weber's ideal and the other extreme of dilettantism. That this middle ground has not yet been found is made abundantly clear by the editor of a book entitled *Reader in Bureaucracy*, who in 1952 collected some of the best thought on the subject. "The study of bureaucracy," said this editor, "has not hardened into categories of analysis beyond dispute, nor has it developed a single theory that supersedes all others. . . . It would be premature to refer to 'the theory of bureaucracy,' as though there existed a single, well-defined conceptual scheme adequate for understanding this form of organization."[14]

I shall not try to harden theories, to establish categories that are beyond dispute, nor to offer a theory to supersede all others. Mine is the more modest task of trying to suggest to administrators certain aspects of bureaucracy that may be usefully combined with factors of enterprise to produce a better and more viable institution.

Chapter 7 A New Look at Bureaucracy

The Weberian theory of bureaucracy seems to be inadequate in terms of both efficiency and human relations, for it is people, after all, who are the motive power of organization. Orthodox bureaucracy carries impersonality to the point of inhumanity, rules to the point where individuality and initiative are neutralized, and automatic processes to the point where motivation is excluded. We need, therefore, a new theory to suggest what is proper in bureaucracy and what is pathological, and how to stimulate the first and control the second.

The formalism of bureaucracy is largely intentional, based as it is on deliberately constructed laws, rules, organization charts, administrative manuals, and the like. But bureaucracy is more than conscious logic; it is also the tenacity of tradition in the society of which an institution is a part. At its best, bureaucracy is science, technology, and scientific management; at its worst, it is tradition that has long since lost its reason for being. When bureaucratic traits are carried to excess or are not balanced by the countervailing factors of enterprise, then the results can only be pathologies that hamper administration. It is these excesses that the administrator must watch for and then discourage, correct, or combine with other factors to produce a desired synthesis.

The way to understand bureaucracy is to discover as much as possible about the administrative and cultural factors, the relationships, and the cause-and-effect sequences that occur within and among organizations. Administrators themselves are best able to observe these intricate and sometimes exceedingly subtle changes that occur in the administrative process. They know what Chester Barnard has pointed out so well, that the higher one goes in executive work, the greater is the importance of the nonlogical, qualitative, policy, and personality factors of administration.[1] Moreover, administrators are used to thinking in terms of syntheses and balances rather than, as the logician does, in terms of rigid classifications and polarities, and hence the administrator's integrative approach, which is also that of the sociologist and the anthropologist, seems most likely to offer a practical solution to problems confronting practical men.[2]

The factors of bureaucracy converge on administration from four different sources: the external, the internal, the dimensional, and the personal. The external source is the cultural setting and includes the legal, public policy, and traditional belief systems, for example, that press in upon an administrative program. The internal source is the administrative process itself, centered on organization, direction, coordination, and the like. The dimensional source consists of factors such as the age and size of the institution. And the personal source is, of course, the human factor and especially the leadership and work-relationship aspects of it. The limited purpose in what follows is to try to communicate a sense of the influence and interrelationships of these sources and factors in administration.

EXTERNAL SOURCES

The external factors that influence the growth of bureaucracy are social and cultural and consist of traditions, habits, mores— all the accustomed ways of acting together that have grown up in a social community. *Custom, being repetitive and hard to change,* has the same routinizing effect as legislation or administrative rules. In both cases there is inflexibility, lack of responsiveness, and resistance to change. Thus society itself is as much a source of bureaucracy as the so-called rational arrangement within its institutions. What the administrator can do to change the influence of such factors on his institution varies greatly, of course, but in no case is he entirely helpless.

The main cultural sources of bureaucracy are these:

Religion. If a religion is formalistic, authoritative, and traditional, and if it promulgates strict rules to which the faithful are expected undeviatingly to adhere, it leaves little room for freedom of individual conscience or decision and constitutes a powerful conditioning influence in favor of bureaucracy. Moreover, where there is a union of church and state (theocracy), the influence on institutional management is even more direct and presumably more effective than where separation is the case. Weber and others have argued that it was a relaxation of religious dogma that triggered the growth of capitalism; if so, then a further relaxation of certain traditions and dogmas might trigger the further growth of enterprise by permitting a freer examination of the bureaucratic traits of capitalism.

The Military. Military administration is often taken as the model for bureaucratic organizations of all kinds. "The larger a business becomes," remarked a former president of Sears, Roebuck, "the more it resembles the Army: hierarchical divisions, unified authority, line-and-staff, precise subordinations, undeviating compliance with authority."[3] The military frame, uncritically accepted, has had a long influence on administration, in both business and government.

Legalism. The single most important cause of bureaucracy, said John Dickinson, is legalism, the making of uniform policies and regulations, hence producing inflexibilities characteristic of government. Legalism is becoming more common in American business because of increasing government regulation, pressures from stockholders and unions, and the long-range policies of management seeking consistency, certainty, and favorable public relations.[4] In some other countries legalism has been carried even further, as in Turkey, for example, where it is a composite of theocratic and political inheritances, a religious belief in the subordination of the individual, and a long tradition of administrative centralization.[5]

Education. An educational system based on excessive discipline may have the effect of discouraging initiative in the individual and dampening the spark of creativity. With too great a sense of obedience there is a tendency uncritically to accept the pattern that is offered. But an educational system that brings out the qualities of independence in the student will cause him to scrutinize what is offered, reject it if he wishes, or change it if he can.

Family. Either overprotection or excessive discipline in the family may cause a person to remain dependent even after reaching adulthood, and the effect is to contribute to administrative bureaucracy. A greater freedom during childhood encourages the independence that administrators need.

The Economy. An economic structure characterized by the concentration of ownership in land and in industry is likely to beget hierarchy, social status, and rules and sanctions for "keeping people in their place." These characteristics might also appear in an economy dominated by a labor minority.

Government. The spreading influence of government regulation, in the community and in business, limits managerial freedoms and encourages the dependence of people and of institutions on government. In both cases the result is to strengthen bureaucracy.

Labor Unions. Labor unions that divide the responsibility of management, that insist on reducing every aspect of labor relations to written rule, and that stand in the way of skill coordinations contribute directly to administrative bureaucracy.

Public Policy. Legislation and other expressions of public policy relating to competition, labor relations, monopoly, and the like possibly spread or check the incidence of bureaucracy as much as any other single factor.[6] Fortunately, public policy is a dynamic aspect of society and is more easily changed than is the influence of religion or family life, for example.

Perhaps this is enough to show that some of the deepest causes of bureaucracy are external and flow from the basic institutions, traditions, and beliefs of the community; that most of them are interacting and all impinge on administration. In a later chapter it will be shown how administrators can do far more in a positive way about most of these factors than is commonly supposed, because, for better or for worse, ours is a managerial civilization.[7]

Nor should the point be overlooked that cultural factors influence institutional administration favorably as well as adversely. France, for example, has a strong legalistic tradition which in many cases has produced an excess of bureaucracy by emphasizing rules to the neglect of initiative. But the French are an individualistic and resourceful people and the recent surge of energy in the French economy has been largely due to the fact that French industrialists and even some government officials have operated *outside* the formal structure (but still within the law) in order to achieve many of their economic triumphs, such as new industries, the free European market, and the expansion of export trade and engineering industries. Thus, just as informal arrangements are a necessary part of formal organization, so also are the individualistic forces that operate alongside the French paper bureaucracy necessary to achieve these triumphs of enterprise.[8]

INTERNAL SOURCES

There is the closest kind of reciprocal relationship between the external sources of the factors of bureaucracy, dealt with above, and the administrative process itself which is the main internal source. The formal ingredients of this process may either strengthen or weaken the influence of tradition and uniformity. For example:

Planning. Precision planning may open up wider areas of individual freedom to administrators or, what is more likely, confine administrators to narrow roles.

Organization. Administration requires a hierarchical arrangement of functions and personnel, and according to the method used the result will be to release energies or to restrict them. But the natural tendency of hierarchical organization is toward inflexibility.

Budgeting. Once approved, plans for raising and spending money tend to enforce a conformity to approved ways of doing things.

Position Classification. After a person's position in the organization has been classified and he knows what he is expected to do, he may feel that he cannot be called on to assume additional duties even in an emergency.

Specialization. To confine his interest to a particular field narrows the individual just as hierarchy restricts his freedom in his job.

Professions and Unions. As the member of an organized profession or a labor union, an employee's status may become the most important part of his working life and his response to his group may be greater than to his employer.

Direction. There are many ways of giving directions, one of them being to take advantage of an opportunity to make one's power felt. The exercise of power in petty ways is a symptom of advanced bureaucratic excesses.

Supervision. Checking on the work of others may also be approached in different ways, ranging from something akin to the teaching function to the giving of minute orders covering every aspect of the work and leaving nothing to individual initiative.

Control. When the emphasis is on the means of control rather than on its results, the effect may be a proliferation of paper work. A British study, for example, showed that after nationalization, 37 per cent of the time of hospital administrators at the higher level was spent on paper work, while only 8 per cent was spent on the running of the hospitals themselves.[9]

Now I grant that in all of these illustrations there are alternative ways of doing things that will discourage rather than encourage the excesses of bureaucracy. But it is equally true that all of the elements of the administrative process tend toward order, routine, predictability, and conformity; and the larger the program becomes, the more are these factors accentuated. Hence the preponderance of influence from internal sources is toward a greater degree of bureaucracy.

DIMENSIONAL SOURCES

Of all the variables that influence institutional management, size is probably the most prolific source of difficulty. Size increases the influence of every factor in administration that contributes to bureaucratic excesses. With size, additional layers of organization and echelons of executives are needed. Communications must travel further and are harder to control. Delegation is hazardous because so much harm can be done when supervision is spread thinly from the top, and coordination is correspondingly difficult. Primary relations and informal contacts tend to be relegated to the water cooler. Standard practices are invited and then retained after their usefulness is over because few people are in a position to see the whole picture. Names are too numerous to remember, and top executives must rely on something roughly equivalent to assigned numbers. But of all of these consequences of large size, the one I would underscore as possibly the most important is the necessity for rules and regulations because these are what cabin and confine men more than anything else. But precise rules are difficult to avoid when size contributes to impersonality and men hesitate to place trust in people whom they do not know well.

The role that age plays in administration is not so clear. The logical assumption would be that, other things being equal, the greater the age of an institution, the greater the possibility that it will be precedent- and rule-ridden. But this is not necessarily so, because quite young institutions may rapidly become bureaucratic and some that are old have discovered the secret of maintaining vitality. It seems likely that the chief factor here is the influence of the right kind of leadership.

The nationalization of the British coal industry shows how the factors of size and age may operate to create resistance to change. The age and traditions of the industry enormously increased the difficulties of integrating a thousand pits and 800 previously separate undertakings widely scattered over most of the country and employing over 700,000 workers. To accomplish this in a matter of a few months, said the Fleck Committee, which studied the matter, in an industry which "by its nature" is slow to adapt to change, made it a bureaucratic problem unparalleled in any other industry.[10] A new leadership in an old institution may use the new-broom technique or, more subtly and hence more effectively, it may have had enough experience in bringing about change so that it knows how to handle "gaited" employees and traditional ways of doing things.[11] An administrator sophisticated in the ways of bureaucracy can bring about quite remarkable transformations in old institutions without disrupting them.

A third variable is geographical extent, which is the areal aspect of size and sufficiently important to be considered separately. As distance is obliterated and institutions spread their activities over increasingly larger areas, the problem of areal coordination becomes a focal point of research into bureaucracy. Thus a common difficulty of the United Nations and its specialized agencies, of a nation's foreign service, of the large oil companies, and of a firm such as Unilever or General Motors is how to combine product and area, headquarters and periphery control, under a unified management capable of producing both consistency and managerial freedom.

If not offset by skillful management, geographical magnitudes encourage centralization, uniformity, insufficient discretion, standardization, failures of coordination—all the faults associated with improper bureaucratic functioning. It is still an open question, I think, whether there are not limits to the geographical extent to which institutions may attain before they become objectionably bureaucratic. It is possible that when the highest efficiency has been reached, it is better to create new organisms rather than to go on expanding the old one to the point where it becomes hard to manage.

PERSONAL SOURCES

The traits of leaders and the way these traits are synthesized have much to do with the quality of bureaucratic situations. Even the defect of excessive rules can be minimized if self-confident men are willing to entrust responsibilities to others. And when such men predominate in an organization, it is in a position to renew itself in a way that no other can.

That there is in fact a type of personality that may be called bureaucratic seems unquestionably true.[12] Some men are figure-minded, some are authoritarian, some are innovators of ideas, and others excel at patiently piling fact on fact; some men are enterprisers or entrepreneurs, and some are bureaucratic. Indeed, so distinct are the qualities involved that some of these personality types have been studied and their behavior analyzed. In one case, for example, a successful British bureaucrat was described in these terms:

> This success was due to his comprehensive understanding of the working of the administrative machine. He has learned to attach importance, once policy has been settled, to clear and unequivocal rules being worked out by appropriate officers at all levels for the guidance of executive and clerical staff. He believes that the discretionary powers and the delegated authority at each level must be clearly defined so that there is no disparity of treatment. The extent of discretion must be compatible with the intellectual attainments of the staff to whom the respective duties are delegated. Too much latitude must not be allowed, as otherwise the rules may become so loose that there is the risk of the procedures as laid down leaving too much scope for argument in favour of exceptional treatment. It is not possible to allow all and sundry to have access to any administrative level as this can lead to the danger of getting wires crossed.

This bureaucrat concedes that exceptions to rules may have to be made occasionally, but he believes that this is "bad" administration and should be avoided as far as possible; that little allowance should be made for employees' idiosyncrasies, "especially if he does not know them personally."[13]

That whole societies may correctly be labeled as bureaucratic or enterprising seems open to more doubt. There are, of course, degrees and patterns in such matters, but absolute labeling is a

A New Look at Bureaucracy

dubious procedure. Nevertheless, certain generalizations may be offered. Thus, although certain conditioning factors may influence the character and spirit of whole cultures, within all of them there will always be found some notable exceptions amongst individuals. Further, anthropologists and psychologists have come to believe that individual personalities are largely created by the dominant expectations of the group or the society, and hence the viewpoints of managers have a wide effect.

As prominent members of the community, managers have a considerable influence, for example, on traditions and folklore; equally, on a nation's educational system and whether it promotes conformity or independence; equally, on whether age will be allowed to ossify institutions or simply cause executives to become more ingenious in coping with that problem. Managers are capable, if they will, of exercising a considerable degree of free will in determining whether the best elements of bureaucracy will produce efficiency and order, or whether the worst ones will produce stagnation and decay. Almost literally, the better a sociologist today's business leader can be, the better executive is he likely to become when bureaucratic problems press in on him.

The hierarchical aspect of bureaucracy will serve to illustrate this point. When a small program becomes part of a large undertaking and loses its independence, the effect on the behavior and morale of its personnel is hard to realize unless one has experienced it. Here, for example, is a British hospital that had always been a voluntary (private) institution in which the relations between board and paid staff and amongst the members of the staff themselves had been simple and intimate. But after nationalization, all this was changed. The institution was now one of a group of hospitals and its policies and decisions were made at a higher level and communicated down the line. Functional heads at the higher level largely superseded the unified authority formerly exercised by the head of the hospital, and that official himself was replaced by a former subordinate whose duties were more circumscribed. Communications which previously had been from the head of the hospital to his functional subordinates were now for the most part from functional officials at the higher level direct to functional officials at the hospital level. The determination of the hospital's policies and procedures, its supplies, finances, employment activities, and even its board meetings, were transferred to the higher level.

The result, of course, was stratification and remote control. Former directing officials felt that they had lost authority and prestige and so did the medical staff. There was a general feeling of resentment against "unnecessary intervention" in the internal affairs of the hospital. In situations such as these the qualities of the sociologist not only provide the administrator with a sense of perspective but they also help him to recognize and deal with the symptoms of social maladjustment that appear on every hand. An interesting footnote to this particular case is that hospitals in the same group that had always been public institutions did not feel the adjustment and the subordination nearly so much as those that had been private, because they were conditioned to control by a higher public agency.[14]

As Weber noted, a bureaucracy, being continuous, comes to have a life of its own. Men are born, so to speak, into General Motors, U.S. Steel, or any other large bureaucracy, just as they are born into society, because their personality fits in with that of the institution. A corporation would continue to operate even if all of its top leadership were to die on the same day, because it has a momentum compounded of tradition, accepted ways of doing things, the prejudices and aspirations of its members, and attitudes toward all kinds of things that help to determine its social milieu and even the group personality it presents to the public. Newcomers are expected to "fit in," sometimes by means of a more or less formal course in which they learn institutional prejudices and attitudes along with rules of organization and procedure. With advancing bureaucracy, all this folklore and protocol become increasingly compulsive: we do this and we don't do that. People who are pliable conform with alacrity; some do it slowly; a few not at all. A man who fails to conform either succeeds the boss or he goes somewhere else.

A New Look at Bureaucracy

The principal way of changing a traditional, rule-ridden institution is either through strong leadership with a mind of its own or through some kind of challenge that shakes people out of their lethargy and causes them to modify their values and behavior patterns in certain respects. And since a sufficient challenge may be more harmful than the ailment, determined leadership is the more effective method. The study of British hospital administration will again illustrate some of these points. It was found, for example, that when as a policy of nationalization the head of a formerly independent hospital was replaced by his immediate subordinate, that official had to move into the former head's office in order to exercise real as well as paper authority. Tradition was so strong that authority attached not only to a particular person and office but even to a particular desk. It was also found that the effect of centralization and bureaucracy was to multiply directing authority. Where formerly there had been a single executive, after nationalization the triumvirate—secretary, finance, and supply officer—became the pattern. The stratification of administrative procedures unaccompanied by a unifying leadership turned out to be costly in terms of efficiency and public satisfaction. In many cases it was almost impossible to determine clear lines of authority, and responsibility was equally diffused at the point where the work was done. These difficulties were reflected in long waiting lists for admission, unorganized out-patient clinics, inefficiency in the case of emergencies and casualty treatment, the waste of X-ray film, and uncertainty as to where specialists, such as physiotherapists, should report.[15]

Almost by definition, an administrator is a purposeful and principled person, not a chameleon changing color with his surroundings. If administration were as legalistic and as automatic as Weber seemed to think, a chameleon might do well enough; but the more need there is for a vigorous and efficient undertaking free from bureaucratic excesses, the more purposeful must its top leadership be.

It is sometimes argued that if the mood of the majority is easygoing or even slothful, top management should conform to those preferences in order to maintain "a happy ship." But such an orientation invariably leads to retrogression and loss of efficiency. A happy ship may be a very slow one and find it hard to stand up to the storm.[16] Leadership is a dynamic effort to combat the forces of stagnation, and hence honest conflict denotes a healthy institution; where friction is wholly lacking it is a sign that the institution is becoming moribund. This is one of the frightening things about the Organization Man—he is a yes man.

TWO CASE STUDIES

The emphasis here on the free will and responsibility of the administrator in determining the vitality of his institution is confirmed by two case studies by sociologists who used factual, observational methods. These studies also show the importance of the environment in which administration is carried on.

The first study was written by Peter M. Blau and is entitled *The Dynamics of Bureaucracy*.[17] His subject was a state employment agency and a federal law enforcement agency, both therefore governmental. Although he makes it clear that his findings cannot necessarily be considered a representative picture of American bureaucracy, nevertheless they are of more than limited interest. The most important ones for present purposes are these:

1. Strict hierarchical control may have been the most efficient method of bureaucratic operation in the Germany of Weber's day, but in the United States, with a different social setting, it seems more efficient to allow junior officials a considerable degree of discretion in discharging their duties.

2. Impersonality does not appeal to American employees. Where Weber believed that bureaucratic officials should approach the public in a spirit of formalistic impersonality, Blau discovered that in the American environment, at any rate, this was not so. Thus, the workers in an employment agency derived satisfaction from contacts with their clients, appreciated their clients' gratitude, and some even kept letter files of such testimonials; in addition, ten out of fifteen interviewers said that they made

special efforts for clients who were personable and seemed highly motivated.

3. The degree to which rigid rules are followed seems to depend on the type of leadership involved. Paradoxically, the day-to-day activities of the federal agency were less standardized than those of a state agency in the same field, and the difference was due to the type of supervisory method used. Thus, in the state agency the supervisor adopted precise legal standards and results were checked twice, first by the supervisor and then by a review section. In the federal agency, on the other hand, the supervisor *stressed accomplishment more than strict conformity to procedures,* allowing discretion and encouraging a professional orientation rather than a clerkish mentality.

4. The formal and informal parts of an official's life in the institution tend to supplement each other. To the extent that officials derive satisfactions out of their informal relations with colleagues, they tend to set high standards of official performance.

5. Rationality is something more than routine and conformity. It will be recalled that Weber's conception of rationality was that everyone must conform to the expectations of the group without deviation or independence of thought. Deviation was an invitation to chaos and the undermining of "logic." Not so, says Blau; at least, not in the American environment. Rather, if all the members of a complex administrative situation are trained to seek results and to use their own intelligence, it may become possible to secure spontaneous and cooperative effort with a minimum of standardization.

The second study was written by Roy G. Francis and Robert C. Stone and is entitled *Service and Procedure in Bureaucracy*.[18] Their subject was the Louisiana Division of Employment Security and their most interesting conclusions are these:

1. In the American environment employees are apparently more interested in service than in formal procedures. Although there are "degrees of indifference" ranging all the way from the dully routine to the fully spontaneous, most employees seem to be interested in the goals of the organization.

2. Rules and regulations have their uses, but these vary. When employees want action, they de-emphasize rules; but when they want to "throw the book" at a client, they rarely have any trouble in finding the book. The morale of an organization is influenced by the quality of management and supervision, which has much to do with the way employees behave.

3. Like judges, bureaucrats also often seem to get the results they intuitively want. For example, certain officials, deciding whether a man was entitled to unemployment compensation, admitted frankly that they "were not dedicated exclusively either to the agency's procedural system or to the interests of the agency's clients." Rather, "the orientation of agency interviewers seemed to stem from a moral attitude about the dispensing of money."[19]

4. Emphasis on procedure is strongest when related to the keeping of files, weakest when related to the making of policy decisions. Even when top management stresses rules, regulations, and strict procedures, employees down the line often humanize them as they face their clients. If there is a conflict between rules and service, service generally prevails.

5. Employees want objectivity in official dealings, but at the same time they also want a "well-knit system of personal obligations." They object to remote, impersonal controls that they cannot influence or avoid.

This study, conclude Francis and Stone, shows that "bureaucracy and a system of personal relations can constitute parts of the same social system" and that the norm of service in a measure counteracts the tendency for rules and impersonality to become ends in themselves.[20]

CONCLUSION

To draw together the various parts of the analysis in this chapter, bureaucracy is a formal pattern of administration that can be deliberately created, as Max Weber favored doing, but more generally it is something that appears spontaneously and is found in some degree in all institutions. External cultural factors may limit or assist the executive in coping with the excesses of bureaucracy, and hence he must understand the impact on internal administration of various forms of social conditioning, including the effect of public policy decisions.

The processes of internal administration, such as organization, planning, and control, all tend toward tradition and set ways of doing things. Whether to reinforce or to diminish the influence of these factors depends on what top management is trying to accomplish. If it wants a sales approach, consumer orientation, competition, adjustment to change, resiliency, and highly motivated executives and employees, then it will be necessary to check the bureaucratic factors in order to avoid harmful excesses.

The dimensional sources of bureaucracy relate to size, age, and area, all of which influence internal administration. The administrator has a measure of control in all of these matters, however, once he knows what to look for and what norms and methods to apply. Generally speaking, the problems of bureaucracy increase along with the dimensional factors, and if the administrator is to apply remedies, his own recourse may be to limit size or to seek fresh leadership.

Finally, the personality factor is decisive because the philosophy of the administrator helps to determine whether his program will be excessively bureaucratic or balanced and forward-looking. Only strong and self-reliant leadership can keep up with change.

Chapter 8 The Pathologies of Bureaucracy

The pathologies of bureaucracy are the excesses of group behavior that prevent an enterprise from being consumer-oriented and responsive to need and change. The result is loss of efficiency.

Efficiency is the relation between what is accomplished and what might be accomplished. Where most definitions of efficiency neglect the qualitative aspects of the subject, this one by Harrington Emerson, one of America's early efficiency experts, emphasizes the *potential* in the efficiency complex, not only in the use of markets, processes, and technology, but also in the matter of employee morale and what might be called the spirit of the enterprise.[1]

The most frequent criticisms of the inefficiencies of bureaucracy are these:

Excessive red tape created by complicated and often obsolete rules and regulations

The "run-around" when jurisdictions are confused

Buck-passing because of failure to delegate decision making far enough down the line

Indifference and abruptness to customers seeking explanations, because of low employee motivation and a feeling of security in a situation devoid of challenges

The Pathologies of Bureaucracy

Impersonality stemming from a lack of sales motivation
Delay in decision making when channels of communication are overextended through many echelons of authority
Duplication of services in a large undertaking in which the various parts act more or less independently
Encroachment of staff services on the unified command of the line organization because responsibilities have not been clearly determined
Lack of resiliency and responsiveness stemming from group introversion
Lack of sales motive when competition is restricted
Inflexibility caused by a martinet insistence on perfection
Routinism imposed by a seedy tradition
Complacency and inertia resulting from a long period of success
Discoordinations resulting from excessive stratification
Timidity due to an urge to play it safe
Officiousness because of low morale or uncompensated ego desires
Self-aggrandizement stimulated by a feeling of personal and group insecurity
Mediocrity resulting from a belief that leveling is the best policy
Waste and carelessness due to lack of employee interest
Lack of ambition because of grooving
Featherbedding encouraged by a feeling of insecurity or a sense of real or imagined injustice
Conformity for fear of being considered ambitious, overaggressive, and a threat to the group norm
Secrecy emphasized for the feeling of power it offers to the group or the individual
Egotism regarding skill or status resulting from inadequate normal outlets
Obeisance in small things, disloyalty in large ones stimulated by a feeling of inferiority
Group resistance and heel-dragging following feigned acquiescence, because of a desire to keep to the old ways of doing things

These evidences of bureaucratic behavior sooner or later appear in most organized groups, to be sure, but they are likely to be more common and to repeat themselves more often when the group is large, formal, and impersonal. In no case, however, are they inevitable. Although they inhere in administration itself, they are controllable by the executive who recognizes the signs of their onset and takes the necessary measures to correct them. And to recognize the symptoms, it is necessary to understand the situations that give rise to them.

THE RATIONALE OF BUREAUCRATIC BEHAVIOR

A close look at bureaucracy suggests that pathological behavior is due to an imbalance between the role of the individual and that of the group in administration, and that people tend to react to this imbalance in three ways.

First, people working in large organizations are apt to become self-centered. Their personality has been submerged in an impersonal environment and they try to compensate by emphasizing the exclusiveness, status, and belongingness that are to be found in smaller group affiliations. This also partly explains the animosities that commonly arise along class, professional, and skill lines. The trend is toward the solidarity, autonomy, insulation, and parochialism of the small group and constitutes the first pathological characteristic of bureaucracy.

Secondly, people working in large organizations tend to avoid responsibility if they can. The size, complexity, and regimentation of work relationships gradually chill people's interest and self-confidence, and they become either listless or frustrated and tense. When employees' lives are ordered to the point where rules are easier to understand than the objectives of the program, which seem far off and unreal, then the energy needed to accept responsibility spontaneously is simply not there.[2]

Thirdly, people working in large organizations try to compensate for declining individual status by taking advantage of opportunities to exert their power, often in petty ways. When self-expression is artificially limited by the work environment and superior effort makes no difference,[3] people tend to develop split personalities, one being recessive and insecure, and the other aggressive and inclined to make others in the organization, including the higher-ups, feel their power.

The common factor in all three of these types of behavior is the loss of personal identification and self-fulfillment. Every individual, says Ordway Tead in *The Art of Administration*, has two main interests. The first is integrity or selfhood, and the second is to achieve an effective relationship to his surroundings. A man wants to be considered a success in his own eyes and in those of people whose approval he values. Hence the individual and the group are inseparable. To the extent that a man succeeds in combining his two main interests to his own satisfaction, to that extent will he be likely to behave normally rather than neurotically.[4]

The man who feels lost and swallowed up in a large impersonal organization instinctively embraces whatever will make him feel more secure and important. He will cherish his own particular skill as clerk, checker, lawyer, or teacher. Or he will seek the power and confidence that come from membership in a trade union or a professional association, where the narcissism of the group compensates for the loss of personal influence. He also seeks personal, face-to-face relationships in the informal, social aspects of the formal organization that offer companionship, status, and a recognition of human dignity. At a higher level, a division or a department develops a kind of personality with which the individual can identify himself, sharing in its successes and protecting it in its failures. By all of these means the individual seeks security and self-expression, and the organization develops the pathological traits of bureaucracy.

Additional psychological clues to the conflict between bureaucracy and the individual are offered by Chris Argyris in his book, *Personality and Organization*. Thus, institutions are made up of individuals and the formal organization. The effect of organization is to stratify and depersonalize, causing the individual to focus on the *parts* of the program rather than on the whole of it. The result is a conflict between the instinct of the individual for self-integration and the formal demands of the organization on his employment. As a person must increasingly adapt to an uncongenial environment, the chances of a mental and emotional disturbance also increase.[5] A partial remedy is to emphasize informal organization which mitigates feelings of dependence and submissiveness, narrows the opportunity for arbitrary, unilateral action, offers a release for pent-up feelings, and creates a kind of "psychological shelter."[6] The escape into bureaucratic introversion may be avoided through the encouragement of normal self-expression in informal relationships within the formal framework.

Let us now take a closer look at each of the three main types of bureaucratic excess.

SELF-CENTEREDNESS AND STRATIFICATION

At lunch one day in London I tried out this group-behavior explanation of bureaucracy on an official of one of Britain's largest industrial combines. He thought for a moment and then said, "There may be something in this thesis. In our company, divisions fight for their autonomy more than for anything else." Each division, he said, was more critical of other divisions than it was of outside programs. Everybody had his own compartment; men wore blinders and never turned sideways. They were parochial in their outlook. "One way we try to get people over their narrowness and exclusiveness," he continued, "is to send them out occasionally to see what is being done with the products they help to make."

One of the first to develop the thesis of self-centeredness in relation to bureaucracy was Joseph M. Juran, an outstanding student of scientific management and equally experienced in business and in government. In his book, *Bureaucracy: A Challenge to Better Management*,[7] Juran notes that all groups—not merely those of business and government—seek self-sufficiency, and hence he defines bureaucracy as any large organization whose affairs are conducted through more or less autonomous groups. In Britain, the Fleck Committee found self-centeredness and autonomy to be a main characteristic of the coal industry, which, said the committee, has always tended to regard itself as "different and separate from its fellows." And once it became a nationalized monopoly, its self-centeredness became even more pronounced.[8]

Stratification results from many levels of clearance in an

organization where strict rules are in force. Men at the foot of the hierarchy are robbed of discretion and initiative; they find themselves on the treadmill of routine; they are not permitted to make exceptions in their dealings with customers; conformity becomes an obsession. When stratification reaches the point where an agency's internal rules are sacred and error must be avoided at all costs, then many other things are neglected, including consumer interests, response to change, and cooperation with other agencies.

Another factor in bureaucratic stratification is suggested by Friedrich, who identifies the desire for secrecy as one of the six main traits of a developing bureaucracy.[9] By means of secrecy bureaucrats try to protect their own specialized knowledge of rules and techniques from envious or competitive eyes, government bureaus try to escape legislative probings, and businesses try to protect their trade secrets. And on all sides there is a desire to be left alone, to find a quiet corner in which to hide, instead of risking the feeling of being lost in an organizational maze.

To counteract these tendencies of bureaucracy, experienced executives hold that a bit of spice is necessary in any program and that if top management is unwilling to take chances it can expect nothing better than paralysis of initiative.[10] Owen D. Young, former head of General Electric, once told me that counterbalancing factors to excessive bureaucracy are attractive policies and energetic leadership; that insofar as the younger generation of business executives is lacking in "convictions" and self-assurance, enterprise will decline and the mediocrity of bureaucracy will fasten itself on all the governing institutions of society, big business included.[11]

A few case illustrations will show how the myopia caused by stratification and self-centeredness may spread throughout an organization:

1. Lucius Eastman, president of a successful wholesale grocery concern, once related how he had tried to organize his business "so scientifically" that it would "run itself," but he soon discovered that he had courted disaster. The fatal defects of large-

scale concerns are these: executives become too specialized; each man has his own department and loses his perspective on the undertaking as a whole; even the top executive loses touch. Thus, "One of my high-paid executives failed to show me a communication and it cost us hundreds of thousands of dollars worth of business." Overspecialization limits people to the point where eventually the traits of the executive, which must be broad, are no longer available. "You can't find men able to integrate their work," Eastman concluded, "because they themselves aren't integrated. A specialist is no good in a competitive business."[12]

2. In his book on Russian bureaucracy, *Not By Bread Alone,* Dudintsev illustrates how a bureaucrat tends to wall himself off from others, especially as he ascends the administrative hierarchy, and how social distance reinforces hierarchical distance. Even learned men, teamed together in organization, build walls around their exclusive lore so as to discourage intruders. The skilled bureaucrat develops affectations designed to magnify the importance of his position and to keep others in their place. A key to bureaucracy is its exclusive language and hence, if one is to cope successfully with entrenched bureaucrats, methods of communication must be used which they understand.[13]

3. Summarizing their case studies of American business bureaucracies, the authors of *Executive Action* make these points: People who have worked in the same environment for a long time come to wear blinders. They see new things in the light of past experience, and hence if new methods and ideas are to be accepted, they must be compatible with what has gone before, what is already understood. Again, specialists are apt to be impervious to the needs of others, so intent are they on their own specialty; in large technical organizations, people who are thing-minded, so to speak, are usually insensitive in human relations. Finally, the staff activity may grow to objectionable lengths because of executive loneliness at the top.[14]

4. In a study of military bureaucracy, Arthur K. Davis has noted that bureaucratic behavior tends to become automatic: "The essence of any military organization is its structure of

authority, the ultimate source of which is the enormous file of written regulations. Military groups carry the normal bureaucratic stress on authority to its extreme development."[15]

5. Yet another study shows that the effect of routine on an institution is similar to the chronic use of sedatives. Routine makes thinking unnecessary and thus finally impossible; it emphasizes the means so much that the ends are progressively lost to sight.[16]

6. The frustration that comes from impersonal relations is exhausting, says C. Wright Mills in *White Collar*. "The grey walls of work and the stereotype of permitted initiatives" alienates a man from the product of his labor, and hence after years of paper work he is "bored at work and restless at play, and this terrible alternation wears him out."[17]

A psychological insight into the causes of grooving and stratification is, of course, a first step in understanding, but it means more when combined with a knowledge of what institutional management contributes to the malaise. In what follows there are suggested some of the crucial areas to be watched:

Fuzzily defined objectives that make it easy to overlook the onset of change

An organization structure that comes to be regarded as an end instead of a means to an end

Policies that are not clearly understood either by those who administer them or by the users of the service

The tendency of employees, and especially of specialists, to insulate their work

A multiplication of rules and procedures that contribute psychologically to the feeling of exclusiveness of knowledge and status, and a feeling of security

An internal administration that is impersonally conducted and which, when seen from the outside, seems even more impersonal

A tendency to play it safe and to become involved only when it cannot be avoided

A preoccupation with creature comforts, status, and administrative convenience

On this last point, one of Parkinson's "laws" is instructive: ". . . Perfection of planned layout is achieved only by institutions on the point of collapse. . . . During a period of exciting discovery or progress there is no time to plan the perfect headquarters. . . . The time for that comes later, when all the important work is done. Perfection, we know, is finality; and finality is death."[18]

AVOIDANCE OF RESPONSIBILITY

That the desire to escape responsibility may be a prominent characteristic of pathological bureaucracy is suggested by the late Harold J. Laski. In his article on bureaucracy in *The Encyclopedia of the Social Sciences* he argues that bureaucrats dislike experimentation; there is a constant pressure toward caution; an excessive number of clearances multiplies *paperasserie* and slows down the work. Rules may not be changed, routine becomes a passion, and flexibility is impossible. So stupefying a preoccupation with procedure makes it easy to avoid coming to grips with responsibilities that might require some deviation from accepted ways of doing things.

The fact is that bureaucrats are conditioned by their environment to regard the assumption of responsibility as of secondary importance. In addition to a preoccupation with procedure, there is also a philosophy of do-the-least. A functionary's responsibility invariably exceeds his control and hence responsibility is buckpassed. This not only relieves an employee of responsibility but also of work. As a former military officer explains, "the bureaucrat tends to pass responsibility upward and work downward."[19]

Another conditioning factor of bureaucracy is thinking that has become institutionalized. Herbert Simon makes the point that a "rational" person must be organized and "institutionalized." If the "severe" limits imposed by human psychology on deliberation are to be overcome, he says, then individual decisions must be subject to the influence of the organized group.[20] What he does not add is that diffused responsibility is frequently no responsibility at all.

With the "institutionalized" person (bureaucrat), habit becomes a substitute for thinking. Habit, says Simon, permits similar stimuli or situations to be met with similar responses or reactions, and thus "conscious rethinking" is obviated or minimized. The artificial counterpart of habit is organizational routine. Simon concludes therefore that insofar as the handling of recurring questions is covered by organization practice, it no longer requires conscious thought.[21] This, of course, is true; but it is also true that only insofar as people can be encouraged to think are they likely to be alert and responsive to new situations.

Bureaucrats characteristically pay more attention to minor matters than to those of greater consequence. Parkinson calls this the Law of Triviality: "The time spent on any item of the agenda will be in inverse proportion to the sum involved."[22] Then, as Dudintsev explains, "business as usual" is often the excuse for not taking up more important matters out of their normal order; it interrupts the established routine. Responsibility is blandly put off while administration takes its course.[23] In addition, among accomplished bureaucrats the techniques of resistance become a kind of second nature and are invaluable when responsibility is to be avoided. Among the old-timers in an organization the communications system is so subtle and effective that an executive wishing to identify responsibility comes to feel that he is boxing with shadow men. Thus employees may resist at will whatever programs they dislike and the executive is powerless to do anything about it.

A rule-run organization is easily surprised by the unexpected. An old illustration makes a familiar point: a century or so ago in London the first cargo of ice was brought in from Norway on a cold day in March. Duty had to be determined, but no one was sure what the rule was. So the ice was stacked on the dock alongside the customhouse while conferences were held between Customs, Treasury, the Board of Trade, and other officials, but no one claimed jurisdiction. Finally after some five months of delay it was decided that ice should be classed as dry goods and taxed accordingly, but by that time the cargo had settled the matter by melting and running into the river.[24]

In bureaucracy, the old judges the new, often with a jaundiced eye. In another case a Russian inventor had had his invention turned down by a Communist bureaucrat. The explanation was that "All this is according to rule. You produce something new, and this new thing is sent for an opinion to the old."[25] Moreover, there is the dogma that collective activity is superior to individual effort; that in administration, "building ants" are more useful than "geniuses." In Dudintsev's book, one of his characters remarks that "The collective is superior to any individual genius"; slow-but-sure is the course of steady advance and the assurance of success. Not only that, but by means of collectivism "we shall reach the required decisions gradually, without panic, at the required time, even at the required hour."[26] All that is needed is to believe in the theory of collective activity—the group instead of the man.

Added to these factors in the life of the bureaucrat that make it easy for him to avoid responsibility, the following dangers may be noted:

Creating new levels of coordination instead of deciding issues oneself or delegating authority commensurate with responsibility
Adding functions, staff, and activity that may or may not be related to sound organic growth, in order to increase the feeling of security and the importance of the we-group
Failure to be direct and forthright in dealings with organized labor, management, investors, customers, and the government
Fostering the forms of accountability rather than its substance
Allowing unnecessary controls to invade managerial freedoms because submissiveness and routine are the easier path

These factors also add to the insulation surrounding the bureaucrat and encourage him to pass responsibility on to someone else, it hardly matters who. But as Peter Drucker has quite simply remarked, "managers must manage." All authority not expressly reserved to higher management is granted to lower management; managers on the firing line have the basic jobs;

and every manager's job should be given the broadest possible scope and authority.[27]

POWER AND STATUS

The belief that an urge to acquire power and status is a symptom of bureaucracy has a wide support, but it comes largely from those who concentrate their criticisms on government, overlooking the fact that *all* institutions seek to aggrandize themselves in certain ways. In other words, this is the political or propagandist use of the term bureaucracy, and although people will doubtless continue to employ it as a whip and government as a whipping boy, most studies of this aspect of bureaucracy are largely irrelevant to the present inquiry.[28]

Actually, of course, in the propagandist argument it is a little hard to reconcile the complaint, on the one hand, that government is too aggressive, and, on the other, that it is slothful and inefficient and cannot do anything well. This double standard is effectively discussed by Friedrich and Cole in their book, *Responsible Bureaucracy*, in which they argue that a bureaucracy "lusty for power" is preferable to one that is content to grow fat and slothful. Indeed, the fierce enthusiasm of the government functionary for his office and the official for his power is often regarded with a certain satisfaction, if not envy.[29] Hence it is necessary to distinguish between energy in administration and a neurotic desire to make one's power felt, to exercise power for its own sake. It is this latter aspect of power that constitutes the problem of pathological bureaucracy.

When people are sadistically inclined, says Carl Dreyfuss, a bureaucracy provides them with almost limitless opportunities to work off their aggressions. This opportunity applies right down to the lowest levels of organization at which employees may issue orders, even if it is only to apprentices, office boys, and messengers. "Sadistic impulses, especially when coupled with a strong craving for power," says Dreyfuss, "often render an employee a very undesirable coworker or superior, as he is always anxious to exercise and to overreach his power of command and to torture and harass his coworkers."[30] Anyone who has worked in a large organization will unhappily be able to recall illustrations of this point.

In his study of military bureaucracy, Davis found a state of chronic status anxiety to be typical. "Everyone focusses on his superior, whose slightest display of pleasure or displeasure is magnified and distorted downward. The mildest criticism from a superior is often viewed as a crushing attack." Under these conditions, ceremonialism becomes an end in itself, frequently at the expense of efficiency.[31]

Social distance is an ancillary factor in the power complex of the bureaucrat. The authors of *Executive Action* show how size contributes to social remoteness, how the head of a small business is more likely to be in close touch with the social factors of his organization than is the executive of a large corporation, how piling up layers of authority distorts communication, and how the effect of anonymity on most people is to stimulate a neurotic thirst for power.[32]

In Britain, the chairman of Imperial Chemicals, one of the nation's largest industrial concerns, regards social distance as a decisive factor in the nature of management at different levels within large organizations. The factory manager, for example, is generally well known to many workers in the lower ranges of the program, but at each higher level relations become more impersonal and bureaucracy takes hold as atmosphere declines. The impersonality of power relations is therefore a serious threat to administration.[33]

Oligarchy is another factor in the structure of bureaucratic power. In his study of *The 20th Century Capitalist Revolution*, Berle refers to "tiny self-perpetuating oligarchies" that guide America's largest corporations.[34] Another interesting statement of this thesis is by Robert Michels, who refers to the "aristocratic tendency" found in all large organizations, and whose "iron law" of oligarchy asserts that there comes to be a division between "a minority of directors and a majority of directed."[35]

In a bureaucracy, says Mills, status becomes as important as function because the position of the individual depends first on the degree of his participation in the program and secondly on his proximity to the wielders of power. In effect, therefore, the private secretary to the top man is often more powerful than the head of a division.[36]

Parkinson's Law of the Rising Pyramid asserts that size of staff has no necessary relation to the amount of work to be done. The reason is that every official desires to multiply the number of his assistants, not that of his rivals, and in addition officials instinctively know how to make work for each other. Thus if a man would prevent his appointees from becoming a threat to his own position, he merely appoints two officials where formerly there was one and divides the work between them, and they go on subdividing ad infinitum, like certain lower forms of vegetable life.[37] Although this "law" is suggestive, however, it is not the whole story, because the tendency to divide work rests also on other factors. In a formal organization, the salary and promotion system often depends on the number of people supervised by a particular official rather than on the skill required of him or the quality of results. Lack of motivation and failure of leadership are additional factors in proliferating staff. When motivation and leadership are dynamic, especially under conditions of competition and profit making, the tendency to redundancy is often checked. As a man can work off his fat by vigorous exercise, so also can an institution.

Over and above these considerations, however, there seems to be an inherent tendency for any large organization to gather more and more employees to itself, the motive being, apparently, that status and power accompany size even if the size is mostly fat. The result, of course, is wasted manpower and dissipated resources. Another, nonmodern, illustration will also make the point that the problem is one of long standing. Thus, on September 13, A.D. 288, Servaeus Africanus, a high official of the Roman administration in Egypt, found it necessary to write to the district governor of Middle Egypt to complain of the useless multiplicity of officials in the administration of the crown accounts:

> ... It is apparent from the accounts alone that a number of persons, wishing to batten on the estates of the Treasury, have invented titles for themselves, such as comptroller, secretary, or superintendent, whereby they procure no advantage to the Treasury but swallow up the profits. It has therefore become necessary for me to send you instructions to arrange a single superintendent of good standing to be chosen for each estate on the responsibility of the local municipal council, and to abolish all remaining offices, though the superintendent elected shall have power to choose two, or at most three, assistants. By this means the wasteful expenditure will be curtailed, and the estates of the Treasury receive proper attention. You will, of course, ensure that only such persons are appointed to assist the superintendents as can stand public scrutiny. Goodbye.[38]

The date on this letter is almost illusory because the difficulty complained of is a current one. Continual accretions to the size of a bureaucracy occur almost imperceptibly, and the administrator who puts a false value on status and power basks in the glory of his empire until someone more hardheaded tries to correct the situation. In the above illustration the corrective was the imposition of a unified command, and the remedy is still an effective one.

Undue emphasis on status and power reveals itself through many symptoms, including these:

A preoccupation with quantity instead of quality of output
The assumption that growth necessarily means size
Collusive practices within industry, labor unions, governments, or cartels, even though, if exposed, they would injure the reputation of the program
The assumption that expansion into several unrelated areas is safer than undivided attention to one
An attempt to buy favors, immunities, or privileges from government, although these practices also damage the reputation of the program
A feeling of complacency simply because the organization is so big

A toleration of redundancy either by management or by labor
The domination of the organization by men who are manipulators instead of responsible managers
A neglect of values that are broadly social and human
The assumption that materialistic incentives alone will produce vitality and enterprise, overlooking the fact that great bodies move slowly

CONCLUSION

The excesses of bureaucracy usually result from an overemphasis on size, impersonality, status, conformity, and routine. As people seek to escape from the anonymity, the social remoteness, and the impersonality that characterize bureaucracy, and to develop selfhood and a satisfying relationship to their environment, they concentrate in groups that are smaller and hence less overwhelming than the whole organization. Groups seek autonomy as the individual seeks selfhood, and in both cases the result is self-centeredness, stratification, and a desire to avoid responsibility.

When people who have been swallowed up in a large undertaking try to regain a feeling of importance, in addition to attaching themselves to a group they also seek power and status through various forms of aggrandizement that may be narcissistic, sadistic, or merely aggressive. This urge for power may be put to constructive uses or it may become so introverted that the whole group is neurotic.

The alert administrator will detect evidences of pathological bureaucracy in such factors as undue delay, officiousness, buckpassing, and the like. He will also find useful outlets for creative energies and for the natural desire for a feeling of self-importance that normal people have, and he will see that fair treatment and recognition are forthcoming. For employees who are concerned with the group but are not smothered by it are free to focus on the objectives of the program and on the public to be served.

Part *III* Enterprise

Enterprise is initiative applied to the innovation of ideas or adaptation to change; it is the spirit of an institution; and it is the re-energizing function of administration that attempts to offset the grooving caused by bureaucracy. No matter what a particular economic system may be called, it is enterprise that prevents stagnation and pushes death aside.

Bureaucracy emphasizes order, enterprise stresses change; one guards the neat arrangement of the old, the other is the initiative that responds to the new; one is conservative, the other adventurous; one consolidates gains, the other produces gains in the first place; one relies on logic, the other on acumen; one stresses accountability, the other artistry; one seeks prudence, the other new profits; one is basically a group quality, the other is more often an individual quality. Enterprise is harder to produce and to sustain than bureaucracy, and less is known about it.

There are four main components of enterprise. First, there must be an incentive to want to innovate and to accept new situations. Secondly, there must be an idea, something positive emerging from innovation. Thirdly, both of these developments depend on innovative people. And fourthly, the processes of administration must encourage rather than obstruct invention *and initiative. Thus the four elements of enterprise are incentive, idea, person, and process.*

The first two of these elements are discussed in the chapter that follows and the last two in the next one. But although each element gets the separate attention it needs for purposes of analysis, they are, of course, inseparable and it is only in balance that they are effective in combating the pathologies of bureaucracy.

Chapter 9 *Incentive and Idea*

Like bureaucracy, enterprise also is a complex of many factors. Enterprise is initiative, innovation, flexibility, empirical shrewdness; and of these, probably initiative is basic to all the others because without this self-starting proclivity there would be no urge to invent, no dare to gamble, no desire to take action outside of established routines. What, therefore, causes people to want to start something new, to take up a challenge, to respond to change? And how important is individual initiative compared to that of the group?

Enterprise is also the basis of technological advance, the means to new products and services and to securing a competitive advantage over rivals. In addition, enterprise relates to social invention, in the use of the modern corporation, for example, and how to get people to work harmoniously together without limiting their freedom and their individuality.

But again, like bureaucracy, enterprise also has its faults. Change may become change for its own sake and disrupt effective ways of doing things. A man may be a good starter but a poor finisher, full of brilliant ideas but unable to judge their practicality and to carry them out. A third danger is dilettantism, which is a sort of institutionalized inability to grow up. And finally, there is what might be called the side effects of enterprise: the social lag between invention and the ability of people to adjust to it, for example, or progressive elements in one part of a firm and stodgy ones in another, creating an imbalance that is more or less disruptive. Just as the pathological faults of bureaucracy are self-centeredness, sluggishness in assuming responsibility, and power neuroses, so those of enterprise reflect the opposite tendencies: exhibitionism, recklessness, and a devil-may-care attitude that may be arresting in a social gathering but deadly in an economic venture.

So while bureaucracy needs the counterbalancing factors of enterprise to control its pathologies, enterprise in turn needs the counterbalancing factors of bureaucracy to keep it from running wild. For enterprise as for bureaucracy, it takes the proper factors of the opposite concept, plus an understanding management, to open up the full possibilities of each. Fortunately, both are held together by much connective tissue, including a common reliance on technology, on logical method, on outstanding individuals, on skillful management, and on a favorable cultural setting.

When the initiative, the innovation, and responsiveness found in enterprise at its best are combined with the orderliness, the system, and the science found in bureaucracy at its best, the managerial blend produces flexibility along with efficiency, salesmanship along with a husbanding of resources. It is some such blend that progressive administrators everlastingly seek.

THE INCENTIVE IN ENTERPRISE

What is it that causes people in all kinds of endeavor—from the writing of poetry to the management of a giant corporation—to create, to invent, to innovate? Psychologists have recently turned their attention to this question and are developing a theory of enterprise that is grounded in human nature.

It has been found that people who are self-starters, discoverers, innovators, and capable of working without the prod of artificial stimulants have what is called an achievement motive. This pattern generally develops early in life and, with proper handling, is capable of considerable growth. The pattern is apparently influenced by both environment and individual personality, with the latter playing a major role. Though still a fairly new one, this theory of motivation has been validated by a number of clinical tests and seems to explain aspects of motivation that heretofore have been little understood.[1]

The findings of this research that are relevant to the present study show that an innovative person possessed of an achievement motive behaves in an especially energetic way, whether his objective be intellectual, physical, technical, managerial, or something else. How hard he works depends more on his own inner concerns and desires than on stimulation from the outside. Such people are independent and do not need specially constructed incentives. They like to take risks and are not discouraged by occasional failures or even by social disapproval. Civilizations grow when the number of such people is large, decline when it diminishes, thus confirming Toynbee's thesis of the gifted minority.

The achievement motive is apparently acquired early in life, is most often found in an environment characterized by mobility of classes, seems to be strongest in the middle class, and occurs in varying degree in all countries. Like all artists, those who are seized by the achievement motive seem more interested in what they are doing than in the social status or financial rewards deriving therefrom. They get more satisfaction from the sense of successful struggle and accomplishment than from pecuniary gain. The qualities needed are the ability to overcome obstacles, to exercise power without exceeding proper limits, to struggle, to persevere, to contrive, to be resourceful. Thus, as Elton Mayo, Chester Barnard, and others recognized long ago, the achievement motive involves character, temperament, and other qualitative factors as well as intelligence, ability, and rationality.

Professor Henry A. Murray, who devised the Murray Thematic Apperception Test, is considered the originator of this aspect of psychology. In an article entitled "Types of Human Needs,"[2] he notes that the achievement motive is an elementary ego need which may prompt any action or be fused with any other need, and hence the significance for this new departure in psychological research. "Actions which express what is commonly called ambition, will-to-power, desire for accomplishment and prestige," says Murray, include the desire "to overcome obstacles, to exercise power, to strive to do something difficult as well and as quickly as possible," which, incidentally, is not a bad definition of enterprise itself. There is also the demand for praise, commendation, and respect, factors that are increasingly emphasized in modern management. Then there are desires and actions in defense of status, which immediately suggest how a motive that stimulates enterprise may gradually shade off into a motive of bureaucracy.

Achievement motivation, says Professor David McClelland, is a highly individual matter and yet, like many other qualities, it is learned and not inborn. People are commonly judged according to what they can do rather than by who they are. In the developing West of the United States, for example, the initiative came from individuals and was little influenced by groups such as villages, national government, or business firms except as these offered encouragement. As McClelland notes, the town meeting served "as a means of coordinating the activities of a lot of energetic people," and the role of group activity, including government itself, was to control independent sources of initiative rather than to stimulate it in the first place.[3]

The achievement motive has nothing to do with caste, race, inherited wealth, or social position. In the United States, the strength of the achievement motive rests primarily in the middle class, the members of which are "upwardly mobile," whereas the inheritors of status, "having arrived," no longer need to strive, and the poor, being statusless, often lack the self-confidence needed for a start. This is one reason that in the United States the middle class has traditionally been the source of most business entrepreneurs.

The entrepreneur, says McClelland, is a person who acts on his own responsibility. He cannot know in advance how the venture is going to turn out; he gets the credit or takes the blame. He makes countless decisions on whether to expand or to contract: if he is too conservative there will be no growth; if he is too speculative it may ruin the business. McClelland also suggests that "group problem solving," apart from the enterprising individuals who may be included in the group, is likely to have only a limited success.

All cultures include at least some people with high achievement motivation, but the proportion must get above a certain significant level before a chain reaction of enterprising activity sets in throughout the economy. Nor can a lack of individual initiative be replaced simply by imposing goals on the economy and centralizing control and decision making at the top. About the most that groups or governments can do is to encourage a sense of personal responsibility, stimulate and reward imaginative risk taking, and offer guidance as to what is socially desirable.

The potentialities of achievement motivation are universal and, like bureaucracy or enterprise, need merely to be developed. The best method is through "character education of the very young" because this is when future patterns are determined. Most children require some "structuring" of performance patterns if they are to take their set early in life. The achievement motive is most likely to be outstanding, therefore, in cultures and in families that emphasize the self-discipline and the independence of the individual.[4]

THE ACHIEVEMENT MOTIVE IN ADMINISTRATION

Some of the researches in achievement motivation throw a good deal of light on the question of enterprise in administration and the manner in which it contrasts with bureaucracy. Thus, McClelland reports that, compared to individuals with low achievement motivation scores, those with high scores excel in various ways. For example, they:

> Work harder at laboratory tasks, learn faster, and do somewhat better work in high school even when their IQ's are no higher than the average

Work better under pressure and when no special incentives are introduced from the outside, such as money prizes and time off from work

Are more resistant to social pressure, choose experts over friends as work partners, and tend to be more active in college and community activities

Like risky occupations, perform better under longer odds, and choose moderate risks over either safe or speculative ones

Come from families that have stressed early self-reliance and self-discipline

Cannot tell accurately, when asked, whether they have a high achievement motivation score or not

These findings seem to mean that people with a high achievement motive are independent and nonconformist, want to do well anything they undertake, are predisposed toward innovation, and get a subjective satisfaction out of succeeding. Collectively, they constitute the group from which one would expect entrepreneurs to be drawn.[5]

To develop some of these points, the results of other research may be added and the whole divided according to topics in which we are interested.

Bureaucracy. In clinical tests it was found that, after a failure contrived by the tester in an achievement test, the children of parents who worked in bureaucratic groups showed a significant tendency to lower their needs for achievement, while children whose parents worked in small organizations with few levels of authority significantly raised their needs for achievement. Thus "social position, and presumably its concomitant, child-rearing techniques, is related to reaction to threat of failure."[6] People with nonbureaucratic backgrounds fight back harder than those whose backgrounds are bureaucratic.

Independence. Parents from the lower occupational levels do not encourage independence in their children to the same extent that middle-class families do. Possibly this is because they see less opportunity of independence being rewarded or less need of it in the type of work available, while the reverse is true of parents in occupations requiring initiative, self-reliance, and independence. This finding is a variation on the familiar psychological theme that people tend to respond to social expectations. The same study found that Protestant and Jewish parents expect independence earlier on the part of their children than do Irish or Italian Catholics.[7]

Achievement motivation probably has its origins in certain kinds of parent-child interactions that occur early in the child's life and that are emotional and unverbalized. The pattern appears as a rule around eight years of age and sometimes as early as five years. Achievement motivation is most likely to occur when the child is urged to obtain and is rewarded for achieving independence and mastery, accompanied by minimum restrictions after mastery has been acquired.[8]

Risky undertakings. Tests show that a high achievement motive predisposes people toward occupations associated with risk or with entrepreneurial activity, provided the type of risk and the popularity of the activity are taken into account. None of these tests supported the hypothesis that people with a high achievement motive prefer popular or prestigeful occupations.[9]

Environment. Starting with the assumption that achievement motivation rises and falls with periods of growth and decline in the culture, another study showed a coincidence between achievement motive and the three principal stages of Greek civilization. Thus, the highest level of achievement occurred during the growth period, the next highest in the climax period, and the lowest in the period of decline.[10] In addition, McClelland has found historical evidence that few cultures using slaves to rear children have been able to maintain high levels of achievement for very long, and he doubts whether the conditions of a bureaucracy can be relied on to call forth achievement motivation in any large measure.[11]

Perhaps enough has been said to show how psychology is contributing to enterprise theory and, indirectly, to bureaucratic theory as well. Apparently there are people who will do their best irrespective of special incentives and rewards. Such people are self-starters; they are independent; they set their own tasks and establish their own quotas; they are inventive and nonconformist;

they are not easily discouraged; they have unusual energy and drive; and most of them have developed this pattern during childhood. Achievement is a matter of both character and environment; it is both internalized in the individual and prompted from without; it is both self-nurtured and socially nurtured. Such being the case, the challenge to administrators is to discover and to adopt measures that will give people the chance to develop these characteristics.

EQUALITY OF EFFORT AND REWARD

Bureaucracy seems to thrive where a leveling influence is at work in the community. Levelers seldom distinguish between equality of opportunity for everyone and equal shares in the reward for everyone, including those who fail to produce. Society should, of course, provide for the unfortunate and the handicapped, but among able-bodied people it is neither Christian charity nor sound socialist theory to insist that all should share equally in the rewards of enterprise, however unequal their contributions may have been.

To deny the principle of equal reward for equal effort is partially to destroy the incentive to human improvement. Similarly, welfare legislation that disregards the relative efforts of people also weakens enterprise at its source: Why try harder when everyone comes out the same in the end? Machines are not yet so automatic as to bring plenty within the reach of all, irrespective of their effort. Even if automation ever should reach that point, again the effect would be to destroy the incentive on which enterprise rests. And even machines, of course, must be run by enterprising administration.

PROFIT AS A MOTIVE

Even if the administrators of large-scale industries were to recognize the force of the achievement motive and were to seek out and encourage gifted individuals, many problems of motivation peculiar to the field of management would remain.

One of these is how to make that great body of supervisors and employees down the line in an organization experience, even vicariously, the spur of competition and profit making that is felt at the top. Studies show this problem to be an increasingly difficult one, even in some of the most profitable undertakings. In both the United States and in Britain I have frequently heard the comment of middle-management officials: "Competition? Profit? We don't even know they exist. We have a job to do and a budget to do it with. I suppose the higher-ups think in terms of profit and I suppose they would be on our necks if we didn't produce, but competition and profit making seem very remote from our own daily routines."

Not even top officials are wholly immune from this reaction, especially in very large organizations where managers and submanagers usually acquire the employee attitude and identify themselves with other employees rather than with stockholding owners. From the very logic of his position, says Schumpeter, the modern top official acquires something of the psychology of the salaried employee working in a bureaucratic organization. Thus the modern corporation, although the product of the capitalist process, "socializes the bourgeois mind," relentlessly narrows the scope of capitalist motivation, and, if the process continues, will eventually kill the roots of capitalism.[12]

In a big organization, the motivation of the bureaucrat may stem from several sources. If he is one of those fortunate persons described by Murray and McClelland as having a high achievement motive, he will get his satisfaction out of mere struggle and achievement. So also do most people of the type that H. G. Wells called "learned-priestly," meaning people who are selflessly dedicated to an ideal. Or the bureaucrat may gain his satisfactions from what Hobson, Tawney, and others have called pride of craftsmanship, which is pride in work well done. Or again, he may like his employer, find his associates congenial and his work interesting, and so long as his salary equals that of others in comparable positions, he may be content. But effective as these motivations may be to most men, it seems reasonable to suppose that they could be considerably sharpened by the addition of the incentives of competition and profit making, if these could be made to operate with the force of which they have shown themselves to be capable in the economic history of the past.

The entrepreneur prizes his independence; but even the highest bureaucrat automatically gives up some of his independence when he signs his contract to work for a large organization. Accordingly, if we are to have the equivalent of independent entrepreneurs in modern business and government, it will be necessary deliberately to work at the problem. This issue is sometimes shrugged off with the statement that the scientist, the professional man, and the specialist always get an adequate satisfaction from their work and do not need the spur of competition and profit making, and that hence only the nonspecialist businessman and government official need these stimuli. But is this an accurate assumption? I wonder if Schumpeter is not right when he says that we should try to rediscover the meaning of the word "property," that curious phenomenon as he calls it, so full of meaning and yet so rapidly passing?[13]

THE IDEA IN ENTERPRISE

An organization that would remain vital needs ideas, because it is ideas that produce profits, economies, efficiency, and technological change. A so-called idea man is not necessarily an able executive, but a top official who is both is a world beater. A large part of Britain's effort since the end of World War II has been to try to exploit new ideas ahead of other nations by bringing the scientific discoverer and the trained executive together in the same person.

Moreover, in today's large undertakings, social ideas relating to human beings in institutional settings are as important as technological ideas, if not more so. One of Britain's leading scientists, who is also head of one of her largest corporations, has noted that vitality means change in some degree, for to be static is close to being moribund. And the price of vitality is constant vigilance and a fund of new ideas gained from a continual study ranging over the entire organization. This executive also notes that all inspiration and all new ideas come from some individual, and hence it might eventually become necessary for modern organizations to build themselves around certain independent and creative people rather than around groups of people stressing teamwork.[14]

If the discovery of new products and processes is requisite to industrial vitality, it may be asked whether the motivational and managerial considerations that apply in the area of ideas are the same as those in other areas of administration, and whether there is any transferability of these factors between the different areas. Fortunately this subject has been intensively studied by a team of British scholars headed by Professor John Jewkes, and their findings have been published in a book entitled *The Sources of Invention*.[15] This study raises issues that touch the heart of the innovative process.

The findings of Professor Jewkes and his colleagues do not seem to support Schumpeter's assumption that every creative aspect of the entrepreneurial process will eventually be reduced to routine. On the contrary, more than half of all significant technological invention during the nineteenth and twentieth centuries has resulted from the work of individuals. Most inventions have been the outcome of chance and not of goal-directed research. Where work is done in company laboratories, the small team seems more effective than the large one, and it is usually a particular individual who supplies the "big jump" in thinking, which is the heart of the inventing process. Indeed, the careful organization and close supervision of inventive effort seem to act as deterrents rather than the reverse.

To hold that the inventive process may become routine therefore seems to lack support, and even if such an outcome could be achieved it would be a distinct threat. Because bureaucracy invites ossification, the more effective system seems to be a reliance on eclecticism and trial and error. The essence of research and discovery is their focus on the unknown. The psychology of the inventor is complex and not wholly economic. Thus, "he is nearly always something of an artist or craftsman," says Jewkes, "prizing independence for its own sake." The innovator is "in the grip of inner compulsions" causing him to demand the right to decide how best in his own way to approach tasks, use talents, create procedures. Accordingly, when this privacy is invaded the creative worker is thrown out of balance. An effective way to defeat the scientific spirit, as a former director of Bell Laboratories once commented, is to try to direct investigations from above. Teamwork is always second best because there is no synthesis equal to that which takes place in the mind of one man.

Jewkes and his colleagues therefore reject the notions of writers who talk glibly about institutionalizing and even routinizing invention along with all other forms of initiative. Champions of collectivism, especially, present a "fuzzy" picture of invention as a social process, suggesting that if a particular man has not achieved what he had, another would have done so, and that every development in society is foreordained and culturally determined. These apologists, says Jewkes, are simply "seeing depth in darkness" because the record does not support their assumptions. On the contrary, if our main reliance were on full-time research by institutional staffs, there would be little invention; the larger the firm, the more does it become a center of resistance to change, and hence the more must it look for original thinking outside of itself.

It is disturbing, therefore, to have this study show that if present trends continue, the individual inventor even in an institutional setting will lose out and the group as innovator will become the dominant pattern. The reason for the current trend is partly that most money for research now comes from the largest firms. As of 1953, for example, half of the industrial research and development workers in the United States were employed in the seventy or eighty largest firms, where independence is largely lost.[16] In addition, degree-holding and other forms of bureaucratic status are increasingly emphasized. If these trends are not reversed, the future for individualism and inventiveness is not bright. It would be brighter if institutions would encourage the creative urge in their employees, leaving researchers free to work

Incentive and Idea 133

in their own way and confining company activity to devising better ways of putting new ideas into effect.

And here, incidentally, yet another difficulty may be noted, the difficulty of getting new discoveries converted into commercial application. In one of the nation's largest corporations, for example, the research department will come up with a new idea, and when they try to "sell" it to the various production units they encounter bureaucratic resistance. Typical reactions are, "That belongs to somebody else," or "We're busy, try such and such a unit." Although the reasons behind these reactions may be compounded of elements such as suspicion of the unknown, fear of failure, or preference for a sure thing, the main ingredient is this thing called administrative convenience. The nonreceptive production units are intent on their own work, their time is fully occupied, and they are loath to unsettle established habits and routines. They want most of all to be left alone.

Whyte's conclusions in *The Organization Man* are similar to those of the Jewkes study. The most productive laboratories, says Whyte, are those where independence is encouraged, individual differences are tolerated, temperament is respected, supervision is casual, immediate financial gain is of secondary importance, and there is no nonsense about "belongingness" and "teamwork." If the scientist is supposed to have misty eyes every time the company anthem is played, says Whyte, he cannot be expected to see quite so sharply when he returns to the laboratory.[17]

A final question is whether the temperamental and other conditions required for successful research and invention are equally needed in all other forms of innovation and enterprise. I think they are. Some of the greatest discoveries have been made by men who were trained in unrelated fields. In addition, when a researcher borrows a technique from another field and combines it with a fresh viewpoint, the result is apt to be more original than the work of a man who has been steeped in the lore of his own craft all his professional life and has never looked beyond it. In his book, *The Art of Scientific Investigation*, W. I. B. Beveridge drives this point home. Successful scientists, he remarks, have often been people with wide interests; discovery requires an open mind free from preconceived ideas; and when discoveries in one field are applied to another, the effect is often to set up a chain of discovery.[18] The new stimulates and refreshes the old. Stagnation in thought is as destructive as stagnation in institutional method. It is this fact that in recent years has caused some administrators to send men off on tours of duty, to executive development courses, to travel and observe in other places, all in an effort to revive their intellectual alertness.

The independent outsider is freer than the bureaucrat to challenge accepted ways of doing things. He propounds unorthodox ideas because he does not know they are taboo, looks for the new because he is not confined by the expectations of a group, and recognizes that every invention multiplies the possible combinations of existing ideas and widens the scope for originality.[19]

The more creative the work, the more is temperament a factor in the character of the person responsible for it. This is the lesson in Chester Barnard's essay on "Mind in Everyday Affairs"; this is why a two-fisted businessman often turns out on closer examination to be an artist. For the universal of all enterprise seems to be initiative coming from a compelling urge to do a certain thing, and this is temperament.

CONCLUSION

Of the four components of enterprise, the two dealt with in this chapter are psychological motivation, or incentives, and the innovation of ideas and discovery. The two remaining components, person and process, are discussed in the chapter that follows.

The initiative, innovation, and flexibility of enterprise are essential to efficiency and to high standards of production. When the factors of enterprise are missing, institutions become the victims of bureaucratic anemia. But like bureaucracy, enterprise also can be carried to extremes, resulting in dilettantism, false starts, disorder, lack of system, and similar disturbances. Here the best kind of bureaucracy must supply the correctives.

The highest expression of enterprise occurs in people who are self-starters and possessed of what the psychologists call the achievement motive. Such individuals seem to develop independence and high motivation early in life, especially under wise guidance and discipline from the family. A job of the administrator is to spot such people and to build his organization around them, to try to increase their number so as to set the multiplier of enterprise at work. But other incentives also are important, and over these management has a more direct control: profit and competition, for example, both of which need to be nursed back to full vigor if they are to play the role they once did in America and in Britain.

The traits of temperament that seem to accompany achievement motivation seem also to be the key to vitality in ideas. New discoveries, both technological and social, come from imaginative, independent, creative people. The conditions of bureaucracy are the worst possible ones in which to expect creativity to flourish. Even small-group methods have only a limited success unless the group includes at least one independent member able to carry the others along with him. But this is precisely the sort of thing that inventors are emotionally opposed to. Accordingly, the encouragement and administration of research, invention, and discovery of all kinds in a large organization is a difficult area of institutional management. But if it is not successfully tackled, the fountain of enterprise dries up at the source. Hence it is to these managerial considerations that we now turn.

Chapter **10** *Person and Process*

The managerial aspects of enterprise center on person and on process. The two principal problems here are, first, whether in the entrepreneurial function it is the individual or the group that is most effective; and secondly, what the role of management should be in adjusting to change and keeping the organization in balance.

Although for clarity the discussion of these subjects is topical, the challenge of enterprise, like the problems of bureaucracy it must deal with, occurs throughout the institution. This is borne out in testimony coming from the Administrative Staff College in England. In reply to the question, "How is vitality to be maintained?" a group of 240 junior executives drawn from private firms, public programs, and the nationalized industries made the following points:[1]

In the area of personnel there is need for new blood and early retirement, and the seniority system is a disadvantage. (Incidentally, the average age of the members of this group was around forty years.) Financial incentives are important and it was felt that the secrecy surrounding executive salaries should be relaxed. There was a strong desire to avoid dead-end jobs and to encourage a feeling of partnership in the program. Relative to organization, the main difficulty was said to be size, because most problems of vitality could be traced back one way or another to the effect of magnitude. Finally, in the matter of the directing function, most often mentioned were the need for unified and energetic direction, for tours of duty, for opportunities for wider observation and reflection, and especially for opportunities for overseas visits. Many of these problems fall within the purview of this chapter.

THE PERSON IN ENTERPRISE

Many kinds of people are involved in the process of innovation: scientists, personnel experts, work simplifiers, almost every variety of trained specialist. But the one most needed is the entrepreneur, the man who sponsors innovation and stimulates an institution to greater vigor. Such a man is a managerial innovator, and there is some danger that his species may be disappearing.

Until recently, entrepreneurship has been associated with the strong, independent, risk-taking individual who went out on his own, established a business, and made a fortune. This is the image that McClelland draws in his reference to the role of the pioneer in the western movement of the United States. But today the self-made business genius is increasingly rare. Men who formerly ran their own businesses now run big businesses. With time they are disappearing from the scene and candidates for their positions lack the hardening experience of their predecessors. Hence if invention, initiative, and enterprise are to continue to thrive, it seems to a growing number of people that most of it must come from groups of individuals instead of from independent individualists.

The Marxist insistence that the individual is less important than the historical situation, the process, the function, the innovative group, is an idea that is becoming accepted among capitalist businessmen who would legitimatize what they are doing. And insofar as these same businessmen are convinced by their own arguments, the type of leader in industry tends to change. Instead of being concentrated in the person of the pioneer, the enterprise function is now spread out over many people working in what is often a very large institutional setting. To call these groups "teams" or "task forces" or "components" does not alter their character. There are some people, however, who still think that to be worth the name, enterprise must be essentially, though not exclusively, an individual matter, and hence they look with misgiving on the tendency to accept the Marxist position by the back door.

Joseph A. Schumpeter has presented as clearly as anyone the new group view against which Whyte protests so strongly in *The Organization Man*. Schumpeter argues that the day of the individual entrepreneur is finished. In a world where nothing is left for entrepreneurs to do because system and process have become automatic, capitalism has taken on the characteristics of bureaucracy. Economic progress is mechanized and depersonalized; innovation is reduced to routine; personality and will power are no longer the useful characteristics they once were; monopoly in industry plays the same role as arteriosclerosis in the human body; and if economic progress continues it will be institutionalized, bureaucratized, and automatic.[2]

Although not everyone is prepared to go as far as this, many must agree that the entrepreneur type is in fact changing, and that function is becoming more highly regarded than person. It is only a step from these assumptions to the belief that if more were known about management by means of groups, there is probably little that the individual used to do that could not be done better by the team.

The intellectual ferment that has been at work on this subject in the last few years is mirrored in the definitions of entrepreneurship offered at the Harvard Conference on Change and the Entrepreneur, which took place in 1949. Three of these definitions stress the individual and one the process. Thus, the entrepreneur is

> One who contrives, discovers, and promotes innovations in a business enterprise

One who provides the dynamics of change; an economic opportunist who reaps rewards
The man who gets things done and not merely the one who invents
An activity or function, not a specific individual or an occupation[3]

The first two of these definitions might be called orthodox or traditional, the third stresses the role of the chief executive, and the last is as broad as all of management. Thus even a decade ago the new pattern of entrepreneurship was still not a settled one.

Schumpeter points the picture of the individual enterpriser as he used to be. Thus, during the nineteenth and the early twentieth centuries, America produced the most vigorous and successful group of individual enterprisers the world has ever seen; it is doubtful if they were ever equaled before or will be again. In them, the essence of enterprise was found in initiatives directed toward invention, bold and daring moves, and individual decision. In nineteenth-century America the traits of enterprise were individual traits and they included business talent, an aptitude for efficient administration, an ability to come to prompt decisions, and enough imagination to recognize opportunities that others overlooked.[4]

In this period also, emphasis was on what was new and there was a steady stream of invention. It was assumed that if progress were to continue, all methods of doing business must be in a state of perpetual change for the better. It was recognized that capitalist economies cannot afford to stand still because once they stop going forward, they slip backward. The dynamic factor in growth was seen to be invention, taking the form of new technologies, new markets, new kinds of organization, new methods of production and distribution, new types of consumers' goods. There seemed to be common agreement, says Schumpeter, that enterprise must be dynamic and vital or it would become stagnant and bureaucratic.

Thus the economic system was simply the sum of individual traits. People venture, risk, fail, lead, or succeed, all because of the spirit of optimism that adventure invariably creates. The system fed on this adventure and optimism and was constantly refreshed by it, despite concurrent internal revolutions in technology, the constant birth of firms, and the equally constant failure of firms that could not meet the challenges of the day. Enterprise in the America of this period, says Schumpeter, meant specific individuals—capitalists, risk-takers, managers—all of them purposeful men with strong drives and motivations.

The true entrepreneur, concludes Schumpeter, must have a world of persistence, drive, and contriving ability because his specialty is the overcoming of obstacles. Such a man is not deterred from his objective by a simple refusal to finance or to buy an undertaking, or by an attempt to thwart him, because he is a combination of drive and maneuverability. It is the flexibility of this latter quality that chiefly distinguishes enterprise from bureaucracy, because enterprise always lies outside the realm of routine, whereas bureaucracy depends on it.[5]

Is this picture overdrawn? If so, it is not by much. And, hopefully, it is less overdrawn than the picture of what Schumpeter predicts for the future. He argues that when bureaucratic methods, which he equates with scientific methods, were adopted by entrepreneurs at about the turn of the century, it was found that these methods paid off and the system became even more efficient than it was before. As scientific management showed what it could do, the individual became less necessary and was superseded by the group. But since progress itself has now been routinized and bureaucratized, capitalism will eventually break down, to be succeeded by socialism which will be passably efficient because under that system the methods of bureaucracy will be based on high worker morale.

What Schumpeter seems to have overlooked is, first, that the methods of scientific management were adopted by vigorous, individualistic entrepreneurs, and it is the combination of system and person that paid off; and secondly, that devoid of enterprise, bureaucracy is harmful even to socialism, as current attempts in Communist nations to counteract the effects of bureaucracy show well enough.

With bureaucracy now a fact in most large-scale undertakings, and the individualistic entrepreneur now nearly gone from the scene, must it now be assumed that individualism itself is no longer useful, and that enterprise may confidently be expected to result from process as once it resulted from the activities of vigorous, imaginative, versatile individuals?

Taking an approach to the subject quite different from Schumpeter's, another economist, Professor Robert Gordon of the University of California, has noted that until recently there was an idea that entrepreneurship was produced by the impersonal forces of the market and that the motive was an attempt to secure profits. Although the profit motive is still an incentive, says Gordon, today few economists think of enterprise as being wholly automatic, because in addition to the influence of the impersonal forces of the market there are also the unpredictable factors of management decision making, the activities of pressure groups, and the impact of external forces. And now that entrepreneurship is considered as something more than "mere price decision," economists will have to give increasing attention to managerial, institutional, and human considerations, all of which would be to the good.[6]

The British economist W. Arthur Lewis has studied enterprise on a world basis and reports on it in his book, *The Theory of Economic Growth*. The spirit of adventure, he finds, is a constant factor throughout history and has been responsible for most of the world's economic development. In every community there are always a few men whose natural bent is to experiment, and the rate of economic growth in a nation depends largely on the number of these innovators. But although individual initiative is the chief cause of growth, there must also be group initiative, especially on the part of government, whose guiding hand must be relied on to maintain equilibrium.[7]

If individualistic enterprise was efficient, if the system was even more efficient when the tenets of scientific management were added to the compound, and if economists are taking a second look at their traditional theories and beginning to understand the role of management in the growth of the economy, then surely Schumpeter was wrong in his prognostications. And if such is the case, then the role cf the individual in enterprise must be recognized again for what it is: a vital factor in institutional growth.

THE PROCESS IN ENTERPRISE

As the increasing scale of institutional management causes the individual to be superseded by the group, what is the rema:ning role of the individual and what is the role of the leader? How are the spark and the wisdom supplied that will tie the whole administrative process together and make it progressive? Within the general rubric called enterprise there are a number of distinguishable though related jobs that need to be done by individuals rather than groups, and they are all tied together by institutional management at the top.

Professor Arthur Cole of Harvard, editor of a study entitled *Change and the Entrepreneur*, has some interesting things to say on this subject.[8] At its best, says Cole, management is innovation, innovation involves both the individual and the process, and hence it would be unrealistic to stress either factor at the expense of the other. Cole notes that in the United States there are fewer solo performers than formerly and that this is probably a social loss. Although today most men are obliged to work as part of an apparatus, it is still their traits and skills that count for most in the work of the group. There is a world of difference between people who are energetic, resourceful, and effective and those who are lacking in these drives. Groups take on their coloration from the combined traits of their members.

If management is innovation, then the successful businessman must have certain kinds and combinations of skills which, however, are not invariably present. Most businessmen seem capable of handling only internal challenges, though they do that well. A second group is adept at handling external challenges also. And a third group excels at innovation in all areas—research, technology, organization and management, human relations, and the like. The ideal enterpriser would qualify in all three respects.

Quite a few succeed in the first two categories. But the number of superb innovators of the third type is always small in any society.

Although it is possible to distinguish these three general areas of institutional management, in practice the strength of enterprise is determined organically and not according to segments. It is the over-all quality of a particular institutional management that determines how readily a new idea or process is likely to be thought up in the first place, and how effectively it will be incorporated thereafter. Both developments depend on "the vigor and health of the whole unit."[9] This concept of a unified, organic institutional management therefore becomes the center of Cole's thinking about the whole question of entrepreneurship. In order to achieve this kind of unity, top management must encourage what might be called an enterprise-wide innovative mentality, built around key people and combining the order and system inherent in bureaucracy with the innovative qualities of leadership.

Entrepreneurship, continues Cole, is based on three main elements:

1. The *purposeful* activity, by means of which a program is initiated, maintained, and aggrandized for pecuniary or other advantage
2. The *external* situation, which includes the economic, political, and social factors that must be combined internally with the management process
3. A *time period*, to provide perspective, room for strategy, maneuverability, and some measure of freedom of decision

On the basis of this kind of analysis Cole concludes that the aggregate of managerial, external, and time factors justifies the differentiation of entrepreneurship as a useful concept and as a discrete category when laid alongside other "social uniformities."[10]

Not all men and not all institutions can be innovative all the time. A certain proportion of discoverers and leaders, on the one hand, and of imitators and followers, on the other, will produce an adequate national income. But any increase will be the result of the work of a larger proportion of enterprising people opening up new natural resources, adapting technology to new needs, and evolving new marketing methods and institutional contrivances. As a historian and hence impressed with the continuity of growth and decline, Cole sees differences in the personal qualities that are needed in the two main stages of institutional growth. Thus in the promotional stage, some men have a fleeting or collateral interest in the undertaking and merely serve at the outset as financiers, advisers, or promoters. Then in the maintenance stage something more is needed, a kind of staying power that was not formerly required to the same extent. Nevertheless, in the total enterprise complex, most managers must continue to promote the program while they are also responsible for day-to-day operations and long-term planning. In this process, it is not hard to see enterprise shading off into bureaucracy. In an institutional setting as elsewhere, the creative manager will have drive, zeal, rationality, and native ability, along with the more sober qualities of judgment and balance.

It will be seen that Cole's portrait of the modern enterpriser differs markedly from the nineteenth-century conception of the man of driving genius, at once impulsive and self-confident. Today the ideal administrator is a man able to deal with all aspects of management—the exciting ones and the routine ones— and at the same time able to inspire the whole organization to be inventive and highly motivated. Thus Cole avoids the jaws of the dilemma of the group *or* the individual by insisting that enterprise is both the group *and* the individual. And no doubt he is right. A high talent of management is to make the best possible use of the individual within the group setting. But even if this were invariably accomplished, I would feel more confident that enterprise would continue to be a consistently pursued goal of management if the accent were primarily on the individual, and only secondarily on the group.

ADJUSTMENT AS A PROCESS

Alert management must supply the spark and the wisdom that

tie the administrative process together, and a test of this function is the manner in which the program responds to change. Growth means not only internal expansion but also adjustment to external influences. Hence there must be flexibility, coordination, the ability to recognize opportunity, to see with a new eye, to alter set patterns quickly, to select individuals who will be helpful on one job and groups that will be more helpful on another.

A major innovation will cause a series of readjustments throughout the organization. If new technical processes are never introduced in a program, it falls behind in competition with its rivals. If such processes are introduced but they are not accompanied by the necessary administrative adjustments, then a rival who is more flexible will profit. If the social climate favors mobility, there will be a constant restlessness and expectation of change accompanied by an effort to adapt structures and methods to the requirements of new technologies. This is the lesson that successful administrators learn.

The economic implications of mobility in the social environment are these:

Capital must be mobile. When a business fails because it has not adapted to a new technology or for some other reason, funds once used in that undertaking should be channeled into a new one.

Industry locations must be mobile. When a firm finds that effective demand, or a better source of raw materials, or improved transportation are to be found elsewhere, it must migrate or lose ground to competitors.

Consumer choice must be mobile. If a line of goods is too rigid or becomes outmoded and consumers are not offered new or alternative choices, a competitor will fill the gap and the business will be lost.

Prices must be mobile. If lower prices resulting from efficient operations are not passed on to consumers, a rival will take advantage of the opportunity to reduce his price or to offer a desirable substitute. Continually rising prices handicap a nation in competition for world trade and constitute a brake on the nation's standard of living compared with other economies where flexible prices are the rule.

Labor must be mobile. If employment opportunities are better in a different place, a worker must either change his job or put up with less favorable conditions. To be able to move increases a worker's bargaining power and improves his condition.

Management must be mobile. If managers are offered better employment in another place, they must either move or lose the opportunity to improve salary and status, to broaden themselves, and to develop new skills having a higher market value. This kind of mobility may occur between organizations or within the same organization, and in either case it is a method of overcoming some of the objectionable aspects of bureaucracy.

The administrative implications of the principle of mobility are these:

There must be a continual search for new products, new technologies, new methods.

Enterprise objectives must be made clear, but top management should be prepared to modify them quickly so as to take advantage of new needs and opportunities.

Institutional policies must be adjusted to the requirements imposed by external influences, so long as this can be done without sacrificing vitality and self-determination.

Organization structure must be gradually reshaped when necessary to accord with newly defined objectives and policies, to keep pace with social change, and to allow the best use of human talent.

Top management should never hesitate to alter organization structure so as to make the best use of outstanding talent wherever it appears.

Operating procedures should be kept constantly under review so as progressively to simplify them rather than allowing them to multiply to the point where they are intelligible only to the myopic expert.

Outside influences must be welcomed in policy and operational matters so as to encourage freshness of viewpoint and constructive criticism, but must not be allowed to weaken direct channels of leadership and responsibility.

To illustrate some of these points, here is a story told by the head of British Overseas Airways. After World War II the corporation took a big chance, pioneered the De Havilland Comets, and became the first airline to operate pure-jet planes. But the experiment backfired. Structural faults were discovered in the new planes and at one stroke the company withdrew nearly one quarter of its passenger-carrying capacity.

It is at times like this that mobility and enterprise are put to the test. In this case, thanks to fresh thought, quick decisions, teamwork, and expedited results, the difficulty was largely surmounted. A "massive" reorganization of services took place with no great disruption of schedules. Additional piston-engine airliners were quickly acquired in the world market and flying staffs and ground crews were retrained to operate them. When the job was done, the top management of BOAC could claim with some pride that the corporation had generally maintained its position in the competitive field and had continued to operate at a profit throughout this difficult period despite the unexpected and substantial additional expense that was involved. The hope was expressed that the achievement might be regarded "as a practical demonstration of vitality in administration."[11]

In this area of growth and adjustment to change, the difficulties as well as the merits of enterprise clearly show themselves.[12] A few brief examples will serve to illustrate these difficulties.

1. The president of a middle-sized manufacturing company was suddenly confronted with an opportunity to secure a contract that would increase production by 22½ per cent. He agreed to take the contract and then told his colleagues about it. They were bewildered. Where do we get the trained personnel? What will happen to the smoothness of existing operations and to the quality of present production? How can we prepare our foremen and supervisors (not to mention labor unions) for this sudden increase? The president's defense was straightforward: if he failed to grab the business, a competitor would; opportunity was

knocking; in the past the company had always been able to adjust successfully; the challenge was good for it.

Was this opportunism or was it enterprise? Or is there any difference? The organization was annoyed at not being consulted beforehand and at first it failed to cooperate. Then the president called a meeting of management and labor, explained that he had probably been impulsive, asked for cooperation, and won it. Plans were made to assign responsibilities and although there were some early difficulties in smooth operation, they were soon overcome.

2. Following World War II, a shipbuilding firm found its business slack and saw no prospect of an immediate pickup. At the same time it had on hand a considerable accumulation of funds from wartime profits which it needed to invest. Since to expand the business was too risky, the firm decided to develop a sideline, and with its surplus it bought a stone-crushing business in another state. But the decision was made almost entirely by the president, and when his department heads and stockholders heard about it they made objections: if the firm tries a sideline it will not be able to concentrate on getting more business for the shipyard, which is its main interest. There is no obvious connection between shipbuilding and stone crushing, and hence the advantages of specialization are lost. And if the international situation should change, this capital would be urgently needed for expansion and would not be available.

The president's defense was much the same as in the preceding case: the opportunity seemed like a good one; capital should be put to work; if the new business were successful, it could always be sold at a profit later on; and the stockholders would gain from the new investment.

Again, was this opportunism, or was it enterprise? In the outcome, the stone-crushing plant was made a subsidiary and placed under a separate management. The president of the shipbuilding concern became president of the subsidiary and, as it turned out, was the only member of the parent business to take an interest in the child. But the new business proved disappointing and was soon sold, and even the president finally admitted that he should have concentrated on getting new business for the shipyard, as discouraging as that seemed at the time.

3. Some years ago the Immigration and Naturalization Service, with a budget of around $10 million a year, saw a chance to secure an additional $3 million a year for five years out of unallotted emergency funds held over from the depression. The Service therefore considered the development of an expanded educational program for immigrants seeking American citizenship, as well as for citizens who might benefit from such a course. Such a program would mean preparing textbooks and materials, giving instruction to half a million people a year, conducting nationwide radio broadcasts, working with many local communities, and so on.

The objections to the plan were these: so large a program needs careful advance planning; the trained personnel are not available; emphasis on this new activity will cause a neglect of established programs by top management; if the enforcement responsibilities of the Service suffer, Congress and the public would soon make their displeasure known.

The defense of the chief executive of the Service was that a program of citizenship education should have been expanded long ago; here is idle money that can be used profitably; once the program was started and if it were successful, Congress would continue to support it; a program of this kind would benefit, not injure, existing services; and it was a patriotic responsibility, no matter how much extra work was involved.

The program was decided on and was turned over to an administrator to develop. Except for oversight from the chief executive of the Immigration Service, the Service itself was not much involved. At the end of the five-year period the program was continued, but on a greatly reduced basis.

These three illustrations suggest that the line between opportunism and enterprise is often a hard one to draw. But they also suggest that the charge of opportunism is likely to be avoided when two conditions are met: first, if the organization has a record of being able to take growth and change in stride; and secondly, if it does enough advance planning. All that needs to be said about the first of these two conditions is that nothing counts like experience when it comes to absorbing growth and change. Organizations develop mental sets and skills for this sort of thing just as they develop institutional resistances in other cases.

The question of advance planning is a little different. If an organization has a definite grand strategy that includes such matters of policy as the kinds of activity it will or will not undertake, the extent to which it will go into sidelines or by-products, how big it wants to become, and at what point it will resist further growth, then it has the soundest possible foundation on which to make decisions relative to enterprise and will avoid the fits and starts that usually result from opportunism.

It should be noted, of course, that there is a difference between grand strategy on the one hand and on the other, the kind of planning and decision making that are fashionable today. Both of these latter functions are involved, to be sure, but they are merely the instruments of the grand strategy of growth and ambition that every enterprising organization must have. If the administrator has a clear image of the ideal scope of his organization and of the specializations it needs, then he will be able to play his cards with assurance. No chance opportunity is opportunist if it fits in with the over-all design.

But opportunity, chance or contrived, is never enough. To produce favorable long-range results, opportunity must be combined with the logical planning function associated with bureaucracy. No one has made this point better than Peter Drucker in *The Practice of Management*. Under modern conditions, he says, grand strategy is an indispensable function of top management. Corporations should plan at least ten years ahead and further if possible. The two entrepreneurial functions of a business are innovation and marketing, and the test of its effectiveness is the degree to which it attracts customers. To this end, long-range policies are far more useful than opportunist policies that are usually short-range.

Innovation is a slow process at best, continues Drucker. Adjustment is a constant need and in the last analysis, enterprise and innovative management always come back to the human equation: Can you get the right man? Managers are the most expensive resource of a business, the one that depreciates fastest, and hence the one that must be most often replenished. Here again, a proper decision will be based on the grand strategy of the business.[13]

Finally, if an institution is to take change easily in stride, it must avoid drastic reorganizations that unsettle its employees and disrupt the familiar flow of work. There has been a lot of fuzzy thinking on the subject of reorganization, notably in public administration. An organization is a living, continuing entity with established processes in the same way that the human body has established processes, and in either case the way to adjust to change is gradually, not by sudden upheavals and what is appropriately referred to as surgery. A drastic reorganization carries with it the same kind of shock that accompanies surgery on the human body, a point admirably made by the Fleck Committee in Britain that reported on the organization of the National Coal Board in 1955:

> Every large undertaking must look at its organization constantly. To do so is a routine function of management. We think that the Board have chosen a good moment to have the present large-scale review of their organisation, as eight years and more have passed since the Board was first set up and a re-examination at this point should be fruitful. But it has been put to us that, since it was created, the National Coal Board's organisation has been too often subjected on the one hand to special examination and on the other to ill-informed criticism without proper inquiry. Therefore, it has been suggested, *the present review should be the last of its kind for some time so that the organisation may have a chance to settle down and get on with its job.* We agree.[14]

In support of this doctrine, the committee pointed out that no organization can expect to operate properly without continuity in top management; there must be leadership at all levels but especially at the top; and that the positive direction and guidance which must emanate from the top in the coal industry must be greater than would normally be the case in a competitive industry whose pattern and traditions of management had been established for a long time.[15]

No more eloquent plea could be made, I believe, for recognizing the essential character of smooth bureaucratic operation combined with the responsiveness of leadership to growth and change.

CONCLUSION

To draw together the threads of the theory of enterprise, a brief summary makes the following points:

Enterprise is the initiative of individuals and of organizations that results in innovation, coordination, and flexibility in order that new opportunities may be seized and continuing adjustments made to change of every kind. To achieve these results, it is individuals who must supply the necessary imagination, originality, aggressiveness, and perseverance. Some people are more ambitious and innovative than others and should be given scope and freedom. Such people usually supply their own incentives, but in addition the positive incentives of competition and profit making must also be emphasized. In institutional management all kinds of discoveries and inventions are useful in some way, directly or by adaptation.

Since enterprise now commonly takes place within the framework of an institution, there must be group as well as individual initiative. Progress must be planned within the pattern of long-term strategies. Adjustment to change must be continual and orderly and not disruptive of efficiency and of institutional well-being.

In the case illustration that follows it is shown how the elements of enterprise combine with the basic elements of bureaucracy to produce a successful and imaginative business undertaking.

Chapter 11 *Marks and Spencer*

Here is a firm that does not advertise, but is nevertheless widely known throughout Great Britain and even in other countries, because its reputation for quality and enterprise travels by word of mouth. As the operator of a chain of cash-and-carry retail stores in Great Britain, Marks and Spencer occupies a distinctive position in merchandising.

Each store occupies a prominent site in its town and sells clothing, some dry goods, and a few food specialties, but not a full line in any department. They are not department stores or five-and-dime stores or even dollar stores, although until the onset of World War II their top price was five shillings. They cater to the middle-class trade and yet wealthy people also shop in them; they do a large-volume business but emphasize style and quality.

The firm's reputation among consumers is based on the fact that the merchandise is best value for the price, invariably of high quality, consistent from year to year and store to store, and in good taste and often original. In addition, the goods are well displayed, the stores are commodious and attractive, and the salesgirls are pleasant. Among other businessmen, bankers, and management experts, Marks and Spencer is known for its ability to adjust quickly to change. It welcomes new, even daring, ideas. The company has originality, open-minded executives, and efficient methods. The principles of scientific management are combined with shrewd sales methods. And the human relations approach is used in all dealings with employees and customers.

GROWTH OF THE FIRM

Michael Marks, the founder of Marks and Spencer, emigrated from Russia in the 1880's with no capital and established himself at Leeds, England, where he peddled a few articles in baskets for a precarious living. But he was resourceful and he prospered. In 1894 he took Thomas Spencer into partnership with a capital of £753. The partnership ended in 1903 and the firm operated as a private limited company until 1926, when it became a joint-stock company and soon thereafter began a vigorous growth.

The man most closely identified with the business in the public mind is Sir Simon Marks, son of the founder, who joined the business in 1907. Sir Simon has been chairman and managing director of the firm throughout the period under review; was knighted in 1944, the year of its golden jubilee; and is still its driving genius.

The corporate history of Marks and Spencer is divided into three main periods. The first was from the beginning in 1926 to Britain's entry into World War II in 1939, thirteen years during which policies that were to become the firm's hallmark were established; a phenomenal growth occurred in number of stores, size of staff, accumulation of capital, and payment of dividends; and the reputation of the firm was built up. The second period was during the war years and their aftermath when, due to short materials, rationing, and financial restrictions, activities had to be redirected and somewhat curtailed, although the firm still made money. The current period, which again has been one of expansion, began about 1950.

Marks and Spencer's annual report for 1958 shows the growth that has occurred. In that year there were 237 stores in the United Kingdom, properties were worth over £45 million, turnover amounted to almost £130 million, net profit was more than £6 million, taxes amounted to nearly £8 million, a 32½ per cent dividend was declared on ordinary share capital, more than £2 million was transferred to reserves, capital reserves amounted to almost £19½ million, and selling space had increased from 2 million to 3 million square feet in five years.

At different times in its history and due to various circumstances, the firm's chief emphasis has been on hardware, food, and clothing, in that historical sequence. Today, however, Marks and Spencer's reputation as a pioneer is in the field of wearing apparel for men, women, and children.

The firm has also had a food line during most of the modern period and it was in this area that the main readjustment took place during the war and postwar years. With 234 stores and 18,500 employees in 1939, four years later the firm found itself with only 3,000 of its employees still active in the business, and it had heavy capital investments and financial commitments. In addition, goods for retail were in short supply and clothing was rationed. Under these trying circumstances the firm expanded its food department, established cafeterias, and continued to make a profit. A comparison of its net dividends tells the story: £755,000 in 1947, £771,000 in 1950, and £3,441,000 in 1958, representing an increase of approximately 355 per cent in eleven years. Since 1939 the firm has wholly financed its own growth by turning its earnings back into the business.

In the first period of peacetime growth, 1926–39, the figures show what happened:

Year	Number of Stores	Turnover	Profit Before Tax
1927	126	£ 1,306,000	£ 75,000
1930	131	3,605,000	335,000
1933	150	8,356,000	817,000
1936	213	14,269,000	1,264,000
1939	234	23,448,000	1,782,000

During these years the firm converted its ordinary stores into superstores and added new facilities as rapidly as it safely could.

Its capital increased from £993,000 in 1927 to £10,100,000 in 1939 and earnings on total capital employed (before tax) increased from 8.2 per cent in 1927 to 19.3 per cent in 1939.

This is a remarkable achievement when it is remembered that it occurred during a time of severe economic depression when most firms were either curtailing their activities or going out of business altogether. It was not surprising, therefore, to hear the comment of a prominent economist in 1958 that "If there were a hundred firms like Marks and Spencer, it would be the best anti-depression insurance we could have."

During the second period of growth, following World War II, the figures are as follows:

Year	Number of Stores	Turnover	Profit Before Tax
1947	228	£ 26,339,000	£ 2,576,000
1950	231	51,104,000	4,651,000
1953	234	85,525,000	6,741,000
1956	234	118,874,000	10,130,000
1958	237	130,400,000	14,143,000

During these years, sixteen stores that had been destroyed by enemy action were rebuilt, conversion to superstores was accelerated, the location and attractiveness of stores were re-emphasized, synthetic fabrics and plastics were studied, testing and research were expanded, and employee welfare and training programs were stressed. During the same period, capital increased from £12,565,000 to £53,048,000 and the earnings on total capital employed (before tax) rose from 21.9 per cent to 26.2 per cent.

So much for the general outlines of the firm's growth and financial success. How has it been accomplished? The answer lies in the firm's policies and administrative methods. Policy is an ever-changing thing, maturing with experience, insight, and expanding confidence. In the case of Marks and Spencer, since 1926 this evolution of policy is clearly seen, if only in the speeches delivered at annual stockholders' meetings. But there has also been a remarkably consistent general orientation due, apparently, to the fact that even after the firm became a publicly held stock company, it has continued to be run largely as a family-type concern with a group of directors who are congenial, who serve full-time, and who are held together and inspired by the personality of Sir Simon Marks.

The record also shows the influence of its vice-chairman and joint managing director, I. M. Sieff, who has a keen interest in scientific management and problems of large-scale operation. The head of one of England's largest banks once said to me, "Many people think the reason Marks and Spencer has been so successful is that the two top men—a little like your theory of bureaucracy and enterprise—supplement each other so well." However this may be, both men seem to be not only theorists but also men of energy and action.

To be effective, the policies of an enterprise must be related so as to become as a single policy. But in a study of this kind it is impossible to deal with them in this integrated fashion, and hence I shall discuss them separately and then try to draw them together at the end.

CONSUMER ORIENTATION

Of the many distinctive aspects of Marks and Spencer policy, the starting point seems to be consumer orientation. At one of the earliest annual meetings of the corporation it was stated that "a consumer attitude of mind" on the part of both retailer and manufacturer is the key to economic growth. And at about the same time there was announced a thesis that has constituted the catalytic agent ever since: "In the last analysis, it is the consumer who provides the bread and butter for all."

An interesting discussion of this principle took place at the annual meeting of 1935. "As no business can escape change," said the chairman, "there is needed a quicker adaptation to changing demands at prices which the consumer can afford to pay. This, I suggest, is one of the main tasks of all engaged in industry."

Sir Simon then examined the usual objections to such a policy and showed how shallow they are. It is argued, for example, that growing cheapness is a menace and that restriction should be deliberately organized with a view to raising low prices. But, said the chairman, as a general policy, restrictionism is a cry of despair arising from a mood of pessimism. If restrictive prices are ever justified, it is only as an exceptional policy. The truth is that people's wants are far from satisfied. There has been something like a fourfold improvement in the British standard of living during the past century, and yet a look into most lines of activity shows that saturation has not been reached.

It is also sometimes argued that productive equipment is adequately occupied and that no additional productivity is needed. But, countered the chairman, one has merely to observe that factories are constantly falling behind in meeting orders for goods for which there is a growing demand, while productive equipment is standing still where the demand for goods is stationary or declining.

It is further argued that the advantages to the consumer of cost reduction have been gained at the expense of the producer. But here again the facts suggest a different answer: unemployment has decreased and gainful employment has increased side by side with the lowering of prices. More efficient employment has meant higher real wages for labor and higher profits for manufacturers. The purchasing power of the workman to obtain the things he needs spells the prosperity of both worker and producer.

Sir Simon ended his speech on this note: a low price does not necessarily mean low profits or low wages, nor should it imply inferior quality or bad design. If a product is made more widely available by the use of modern machinery, the application of science and research, and the better organization of processes, then a low price makes for a decent level of profits and wages and a sound quality of goods. By the use of up-to-date methods, capable organizers can supply the needs of the community. The key is high-quality materials and pleasing design at prices within the reach of the vast majority of consumers.

Such a policy, furthermore, is a deterrent to economic depression and a stimulus to steady growth. A false stabilization achieved through raised prices, restricted production, and similar expedients sometimes tried during the depression of the 1930's is self-defeating. Where progress has been made it has been the result of getting on with the job, industry by industry and trade by trade, by adjusting to new conditions, by reducing production costs through greater efficiency, and by closer cooperation all along the line. Such a policy would permit a growing number of industries, both old and new, to sell their products at prices which a few years ago would have been considered impossible, and at the same time to make a fair profit.[1]

DISTRIBUTION

If consumer orientation is the cardinal principle of enterprise at Marks and Spencer, then efficient distribution is the next one. "The main problem of modern merchandising," said Sir Simon in 1928, "is distribution. Ideal distribution eliminates as many intermediate profits as possible, and reduces selling costs and overhead charges to the lowest margin of profit consistent with good service."

How this was to be brought about was explained in the first annual meeting of stockholders in 1927. There must be superstores occupying the best location in each community. They must be handsome buildings because this is a constant advertisement, and they must offer comfortable shopping conditions. There must be sound quality of goods at inexpensive prices, and a range of choice. And finally, there must be a close cooperation between manufacturer and retailer, the manufacturer adapting to the needs of the distributor just as he in turn adapts to the demands of the consumer. This last policy eliminates unnecessary intermediaries and charges and permits a firm such as Marks and Spencer to Buy British, as it has to the extent of 90 to 99 per cent of sales volume ever since 1926, the higher figure being the one for 1958. Buying in the home market also facilitates large purchases, which in turn reduce prices to the consumer. But stocks must move in moderate, not overwhelming, quantity to retail outlets so as to increase the number of annual stock turnovers. Specifications are set and materials ordered in large volume and are then made up by the manufacturer as demand and styles change.

Since the location and attractiveness of its stores are so important a part of the Marks and Spencer philosophy, the policy since the beginning has been to purchase freeholds and buildings or to secure them under long-term lease, and then to renovate them as often as necessary. This procedure has required a vast amount of new capital and large liquid resources, of course; but, as the chairman remarked in 1928, a demand for capital is a sign of business progress. Thus capital budgets must be planned several years ahead in order that growth may be steady and well conceived. The firm's slogan has always been, "There is plenty of room for growth."[2]

Another reason that attractive surroundings are such a major part of the Marks and Spencer policy is a desire to avoid a hazard commonly experienced by most dry goods and department stores. They are so overcrowded and display so much merchandise that shoppers are confused. Hence it is better to restrict the number of items offered, limit the models in each line, and set the goods off distinctively so as to get the best possible presentation. Moreover, with fewer lines of stock, these can be followed more closely and improved more quickly. The retailer is in the lead, so to speak, instead of following along behind the manufacturer. But since this arrangement also restricts the shopper's choice, what is offered must be first-class for the price. With no advertising except word of mouth, the better the quality, the better the word becomes.

Finally, Marks and Spencer prides itself on never having a sale, as most department stores periodically must. Why should a store have a sale, it is argued, when prices are always below those of competitors for the same quality of goods? If an article or a color moves slowly, reduce its price quickly, not after it has been around a long time, and avoid a similar mistake in the future. Under such a policy, sales are not needed.[3]

RELATIONS WITH MANUFACTURERS

Another policy of Marks and Spencer that has continually paid off is its close, cooperative relationships with manufacturers so as to give the retailer the jump on competitors. Looking back in 1938 over twelve years of experience, Sir Simon remarked, "We have had to interest ourselves in every stage of production." This kind of integration, as the economists call it, can lead either to a production-to-consumer monopoly or it can produce great savings and exceptional efficiency in which the consumer shares. With Marks and Spencer, integration has meant savings and efficiency. As Sir Simon once explained it, "It is difficult for manufacturers who are not in direct contact with the public to be continuously responsive to the variations and fluctuations of the public demand. Our organisation fills that void for him, and being in active daily touch with the public we can act as the eyes of the manufacturer and transmit to him as promptly as possible the necessary information to guide his production activities."[4]

Any businessman will appreciate that if this collaboration is effectively accomplished, especially as to the innovative part, it becomes a most useful asset. Among other advantages it increases outlets for the producer's goods; makes possible the most efficient methods of production by substituting large volume in a few items for a limited volume in a variety of items; assures continuity of production; reduces seasonal fluctuations; creates economies in selling organization; gives the retailer a competitive edge over his rivals, especially if he sells identical items in large volume in many stores; encourages prompt payment and reduces bad debts; stimulates the planning of new lines that will sell; gives the manufacturer the advantage of the retailer's experience; and creates exceptional merchandise values which are then passed on to the public with a minimum of intermediate expense.[5]

The danger in such a system of collaboration, of course—and much experience in the United States shows it—is that the manufacturer will become so dependent on the big retailer that eventually the retailer can either squeeze the manufacturer's profit margin at will or he can take over the plant and operate it himself. Marks and Spencer have resisted both of these temptations, having always made it plain to their manufacturers that it has no such intentions, now or in the future. I asked one of the men who grew up with the firm if it had ever been lured in this direction. "No," he replied, "we believe in sticking to our last. We are retailers. That is a big enough job. Our observation is that the man who mixes his business can't do as good a job as one who sticks to one business. Besides," he added, "the public wouldn't like it if we became too large and too powerful."[6]

Sir Simon's reports at annual meetings are full of evidence that the 750 or so manufacturers and suppliers who work most closely with Marks and Spencer are not only prospering but also are improving their profit position as demand increases and economies are effected. Already by 1933, the chairman was able to report that suppliers and manufacturers had acquired "a consumer attitude of mind"; that none was ever satisfied with his achievement and hence there was no complacency; that Marks and Spencer had constantly helped manufacturers to reorganize on a more scientific basis of costing, thereby helping to improve their position in other markets. Our experience indicates, concluded Sir Simon, that most manufacturers who "have laid themselves out to develop business with us have shown increased profits."[7]

Throughout the firm's reports appear statements such as these: our manufacturers try to develop special values for us; we constantly study similar businesses here and abroad; even better values are possible if manufacturers will take the trouble to understand our requirements and our policies; we welcome all manufacturers who have something distinctive to offer; the scientific method of production and distribution is the path of advance, not only for firms but for the nation.

SCIENTIFIC MANAGEMENT

It will come as no surprise that a firm obviously so sensitive to consumer wants has also from the outset been a champion of scientific management. At the annual meeting of 1928, for example, the vice-chairman of the firm referred to "the scientific method of distribution" and the theme has persisted. In 1934 the same speaker remarked that "scientific management is applied right through the productive and distributive process" and is one of the secrets of the company's success. But he was not referring merely to machines and stop watches. Rather, the science of distribution and management, he said, is a certain outlook, a policy of constant readiness to adjust ideas and processes to meet changing conditions, an elasticity and an adaptability to satisfy new tastes and fashions.[8] This description of the scientific method in administration is also a first-rate definition of enterprise.

In its concern with quality and value, Marks and Spencer has also developed a technical research and testing service by which it judges the quality and durability of the goods of various manufacturers and develops improvements to be passed on to those with whom it works.[9] When radical innovations in cotton and wool substitutes, synthetic fabrics, and plastics occurred after World War II, for example, the firm decided to be in the forefront of this movement and hence expanded its fabrics laboratories. Food testing also was expanded.

Some idea of the importance of this research activity is gained from the firm's report for 1957, which noted a total annual expenditure on technical services of £500,000 and the employment of 230 people, of whom 60 were scientists, technologists, and technicians—all highly trained individuals. It will be realized that in a firm with an annual volume of business amounting to £130 million, this is a fine showing for research, especially since it is still exceptional for a wholly retail concern to pursue an activity that is more commonly the function of a manufacturer. The explanation is the cardinal conviction of Marks and Spencer that efficiency must be continuous from production through distribution.

EMPLOYEE ORIENTATION

A final major area of policy will complete this part of the

analysis. Marks and Spencer has long been employee-oriented as well as consumer-oriented, believing that one of these emphases is not likely to be realized without the other. Hence, the firm has stressed employee relations and welfare from the beginning. Even in 1935, in the depth of the depression, the annual expenditure on this item was £50,000, and by 1958 it was £850,000. But large as it is, this figure is judged by everyone, including stockholders, to represent one of the firm's most rewarding investments. Marks and Spencer has also pioneered in employee-training programs as the means of renewing and vitalizing leadership in all departments. The benefits of employee orientation are reflected in the reputation of the firm and the pride and loyalty of its employees, a feature that outside observers invariably notice.

In all stores, employee relations come under the unified direction of the manager, assisted by a staff manageress responsible for all matters relating to welfare, personnel relations, counseling, training, and the like. As early as 1937 the welfare department was offering its employees sports and social clubs, holiday camps, medical services, canteens providing meals at low cost, and rest rooms for relaxation periods during working hours.[10] The object of this policy is to maintain cordial contact with the staff, "to develop conditions which make for happiness in work, and to improve the general conditions of employment." The well-being of each employee, the lessening of strain, and the provision of personal help where possible are the concern of the welfare supervisors. Consequently employee morale is high and the atmosphere of the stores reflects this basic contentment.

It seems likely that at least part of the reason for the success of this policy is that Marks and Spencer has never lost its characteristics as a family firm. When the chairman or one of the directors hears of a case of personal hardship or bad luck, it is not unusual for the firm to go beyond what its rules call for because the human touch has never been lost. Militant unionists sometimes condemn this practice as paternalism, but there is no question that the employees appreciate and like it. It gives them a sincere, personal kind of attention that is an antidote to a bureaucratic ailment.

PATTERN OF POLICY

Can these several major aspects of policy be drawn together to show the over-all pattern that makes Marks and Spencer a distinctive enterprise? Although there is the danger of distortion through oversimplification, the attempt may be useful.

The objective of Marks and Spencer is to make a profit through a particular kind of merchandising. To this end, it offers a limited line of goods in stores that are centrally located, commodious, and attractive; where the merchandise is of better quality for the price than that offered by competitors, and is characterized by style, taste, and uniformity throughout the system; where markup is relatively small and volume produces a satisfactory reward; and where the business grows and finances itself out of its own profits. Hence, the policies of the firm are a blend which includes consumer orientation, the latest merchandising methods, cooperative relationships with manufacturers, the scientific method applied throughout, and a sincere emphasis on human relations.

In short, the best in scientific method and bureaucracy, combined with the best in human relations and motivation, together produce enterprise and vitality of such a high order that the firm of Marks and Spencer is frequently referred to as a model for all of British industry.

Marks and Spencer policy is not a formula, however, in the usual wooden sense of that term. It is more imaginative and flexible than that. It is a fusion of opposites, each factor important in its own right and even more so when tied to other factors to produce the firm's personality and its impact on the retail world. Nevertheless, there is more involved than policies. There are also individuals and administrative methods, and a brief look at these will complete the story.

ADMINISTRATIVE METHODS

The record of Marks and Spencer shows how administrative methods may be made to further policy objectives in a way that will produce both consistency and flexibility. Marks and Spencer administration is ancillary to policy objectives, not the reverse.

During the thirty-two-year period under review, the dominant fact about the administration of the firm has been the personality of Sir Simon Marks, its chief administrator and policy maker. Sir Simon has devoted his life to the enterprise; he has the instincts of the merchant but the flair of the financier and the ability to inspire men; he has spent much time in the stores and knows their personnel and the temper of the public; he has kept his finger on the pulse of every separate activity of the firm and yet at all times he has seen the business as an organic whole; he has known how to select able assistants and subordinates and he has worked harder than any of them. In short, during Sir Simon's career, the planning and coordinating functions of the firm have been successful largely because of the drive and human qualities of this man. Lacking such a person, the history of the firm might have been quite different.

Sir Simon and his closest associates have long realized that in management there is an optimum size that cannot safely be exceeded. The human mind can accomplish just so much with efficiency and energy, and no more. At Marks and Spencer this cutoff point is thought to be about 240 stores, a figure attained just prior to World War II and not greatly changed since then. If there are any additions to the number of units, they must be few, and a continuous multiplication of units is to be discouraged. Emphasis is on quality performance in the existing structure, not on uncontrolled expansion with all of its attendant life-sapping problems.[11]

The three main levels of operation in the business are top management, consisting of full-time directors; departments headed by salaried officials in charge of various types of merchandise; and store managers in the 237 local units. A fourth level on a regional basis is of limited importance. Relations between the central office in London and the stores center in, but are not confined to, the Store Operations Department, under the supervision of one of the directors.

In practice, problems of management at Marks and Spencer are not as great as the size of the business might suggest. The reason is that although 237 stores are a large administrative responsibility, there are certain advantages that most other firms do not enjoy to the same degree. For example, all Marks and Spencer stores offer substantially the same limited line of goods, even to sizes and styles, introducing an element of standardization that simplifies all aspects of central management. Sir Simon and his associates in the central office can visualize operations anywhere in the nation. They will know, for example, that what is displayed in the store at Oxford is duplicated in the store at Richmond or Manchester, and that the problems and techniques of management in all places are similar.

When new materials are developed, new styles introduced, or new quotas worked out for the stores, the functions of budgeting, purchasing, distribution, inventory, and so on are much easier than for a competing firm, such as a department store, where many more items are sold. At Marks and Spencer the central management suggests quotas, the local managers put in their orders, and these two forecasts are then reconciled, but since the lines are standardized the procedure is a simple one.

Moreover, in order to maintain flexibility and responsiveness to the consumer, the stores are stocked for only three months in advance and long-term contracts with suppliers are avoided. For their part, the suppliers are content with the arrangement because they appreciate that so long as they give satisfaction, the firm has every reason to retain the association. Furthermore, with only three months as the usual stocking period, any mistake by central or store management can be quickly corrected by adjustments in price. And finally, unlike department-store buyers, who must work on a revolving-fund basis and must turn their stock over before they make new purchases, Marks and Spencer achieves a greater resiliency by controlling financial outlays from the center.

The job of a store manager is to know what local consumers are buying, and the job of central management is to know what the country as a whole is buying. If these two jobs are well done in collaboration between the two levels, the scheduling of purchasing is about as accurate as it can be made. The relationship is a direct one between local store and central office, by-passing divisional superintendents whose responsibility is more for operations than for inventory and stocking.

A main tenet of Marks and Spencer's operating philosophy is that a closely defined jurisdiction tends toward stratification, discourages collaborative effort, and hence is to be avoided. On the other hand, too little definition creates the danger that some important matter may be overlooked. The solution is to allocate responsibilities generally and then to encourage teamwork and cross reference so as to bring all elements of decision making into focus.

This seemingly loose system is more likely to succeed, of course, when, as in the case of Marks and Spencer, the top echelon of director-managers has grown up with the business, the family tradition is still strong, the top people have adjoining offices, and competitions for personal power are not as pronounced as they may be in a business lacking family cohesiveness.

Although each director is in charge of a particular area of the business, this is not his only job, for he is expected also to think about the business as a whole and how it can be improved and coordinated. Consequently, although the board meets formally only twice a year, groups of directors, department heads, and store managers meet daily and even more often than that, as the occasion requires. Top-management procedure is characterized by informal collaboration that facilitates quick decisions and immediate action. In other words, what may be lost through loosely defined jurisdictions is more than made up by the advantages of constant and effective communication within the central office and between it and subordinate levels. As Chester Barnard has repeated, easy communication is a main safeguard against bureaucratic stratification and rigidity.

In spite of its general progressiveness and flexibility, however, and even in spite of the dynamic leadership provided from the top, Marks and Spencer is no more immune than other institutions from bureaucratic influences that threaten to cramp these flexibilities. The firm's experience proves again that size, organization, and careful attention to method are always accompanied by the dangers of overorganization and especially overregulation through internal forms and procedures.

In 1956 Marks and Spencer became rather acutely aware of this problem and instituted a thoroughgoing housecleaning of useless forms and procedures. There is a story that one day Sir Simon was looking through the stockroom of one of his stores when a clerk came in with a form to be presented before she could renew her stock. "Why do you have to have that?" asked the chairman. "Why don't you simply take what you need and save time?" When he was told that presenting the form was necessary, Sir Simon decided that the organization had better look into all of its forms and procedures to see how many were really needed. The project was taken so seriously by the board of directors that they examined each department themselves, asking, "Is this form necessary, can't it be combined with another, why not dispense with it altogether?" No outside consultants were employed; it was a face-to-face relationship between board members, department heads, and store managers, and the result was a considerable discarding of red tape and a speeding up of operations.

Thus, time clocks were eliminated because employees preferred an alternative system; the paper control of goods within stores was abolished; fortnightly reports on sales by categories were replaced by a simpler and more accurate method; detailed records of what was used and spent in staff canteens were abolished in favor of more emphasis on results; store ledgers showing detailed records gave way to consolidated reports to headquarters; the piece-by-piece stock count was replaced by a simple check list;

and centralized requisitioning and purchasing were modified in favor of the local purchase of items such as pencils and office supplies.

The effect of these measures was drastically to reduce the need for all kinds of forms and paper work, to give managers more freedom and discretion, to place more emphasis on face-to-face relationships as a substitute for formal ones, and to improve employee morale. A customer told me that as a result of the changes there was an economy in the overhead and an improvement in the efficiency of the firm that cut sixpence off the cost of a pair of nylons. Although I cannot verify this statement, it shows the interest with which the public follows the internal affairs of Marks and Spencer.

Another administrative objective of Marks and Spencer is to keep staff activities, including personnel, finance, building, and research, small and tied in with the stream of operations, never independent of or in competition with it. The firm realizes that if the center of initiative in administration is to remain in the executive group where it belongs, then specialist activities must be kept in a subordinate position. The result is a unified and responsive enterprise with extra supplies of energy at its command.

In this overview of Marks and Spencer organization, the departmental level has a special importance. It is here that an official in charge of a certain line of merchandise handles a unified function consisting of planning, specification, purchasing, pricing, distribution, control, and the like. So long as there are strong, competent, and imaginative people at this action level, the burden on top management and its staff assistants is reduced. Except for the dynamic leadership provided at the top by the chairman himself, it is the departments that are the center of gravity in the firm. As Sir Simon once commented, "Do this right and you can overcome any other weakness."

CONCLUSION

This brief account of policy and administration seems to show what makes a firm enterprising and progressive. It is policies in combination. It is not an administrative principle; it is administration as the servant of policy. It is not a single element of administration; it is the way all elements are combined. And in addition to skillful, vital policy and administration, it is also leadership and people. If these three ingredients—policy ideas, administrative vigor, and gifted individuals—can be brought together and harmoniously blended with the right elements of bureaucracy in their right place and proportion, then enterprise will be generated and vitality maintained.

Part *IV* *The Best of Both Worlds*

The best in bureaucracy is scientific management and technological progress; the worst is indifference to the consumer. The best in enterprise is innovation and energy; the worst is confusion. This concluding part of the book deals with the blending of these two opposites, how the best parts of each may be brought together in a combination that will produce energy in administration and vitality in institutions.

This blend is the result of administrative decisions deliberately made in matters of leadership, decentralization, responsiveness, and power, for these are the areas where the excesses of bureaucracy most often appear. It is for the administrator to decide whether his program will have the self-centered characteristics of bureaucracy or the consumer orientation of enterprise; whether it will have the irresponsibility of bureaucratic excesses or the responsiveness of enterprise; whether it will be bound up in the power manias of bureaucracy or balanced by the extrovert qualities of enterprise.

The first four chapters in this part deal with the four main areas of internal administration from which solutions to the excesses of bureaucracy are to be drawn. And the last chapter is a reminder of the reasons that administrative vitality is to be diligently sought, for the stakes are none other than the goals of the economy itself.

Chapter *12* *Integrative Leadership*

All large-scale organization needs strong, constructive, imaginative leadership to pull together all the elements of the program which otherwise tend to fly apart, and to focus the organization's attention on the consumer instead of on the bureaucracy's own inner tensions, moods, and petty concerns.

Unfortunately, the need for strong leadership is frequently either overlooked or denied. "There is no such thing as individual leadership," say some critics. "The responsibility of top management stops at the point where employees are given a congenial place in which to work," say others. Or, "group cooperation makes individual leadership unnecessary." None of these statements is true and, taken together, they hasten the decline of enterprise and the deep freeze of bureaucracy.

The larger the body, the greater the centrifugal force it develops and the greater is the likelihood that the parts will be separated from the whole; that segmentation will drain the program's energies and halt enterprise. It is integrative leadership that keeps the parts together, and hence leadership is more necessary in large bureaucratic institutions than it is in smaller, more informal, competitive ones. But irrespective of size, organization alone never solves any administrative problem. There must be some one person at the top to watch over the program so as to keep it together, to keep it responsible, to combat self-centeredness, to promote innovation and vitality. And there must also be extensions of leadership to subordinate levels so as to form a kind of network through which the influence of the top man is carried throughout the organization.

A position of leadership is not an easy one, which is why so many men are either abdicating or denying the need for the function. "If the right spirit is to permeate the organisation," said Britain's Fleck Committee, "teamwork rather than regimentation must prevail. But the men at the top must be sure that the undertaking is moving in the right direction. For the leaders to know when and how to step in and exercise the difficult role of decision, whether the purpose be to initiate new principles and methods or to end indecisive discussion or to reverse a trend in practice, calls for the highest qualities of industrial statesmanship."[1] Moreover, there can never be a "technical renaissance" or other new departure unless these conditions are met.

In the following discussion, integrative leadership is dealt with in these stages: first, the need in administration to make the best use of scientific management; secondly, the need to prepare for the special impact of technology; thirdly, the advantages of administration by objectives instead of by power and rote; and finally, the matter of education for leadership in an age of specialization and science. In other words, this chapter deals with the reconciliation of the enterprise factors of initiative and leadership with the bureaucracy factors of group introversion, and tries to show how scientific management and human relations are both basic to the blend that is administration by objectives.

If system, which is the nonhuman element in administration, can be joined with personality, which is the human element, the relationship will go far to reconcile bureaucracy and enterprise. A central manifestation of bureaucracy, it will be recalled, is self-centeredness and the building of walls both around and within a program. The effect may be both efficient and inefficient. The efficient effect is to promote attention to the details of organization, method, science, and technology. The inefficient effect is to neglect elements such as salesmanship, human relations, and response to change. To allow the matter to stand there is to fail in leadership. To develop the formal aspects of organization in an age of automation and isotopes but to neglect the human aspects of enterprise is to lose out in competition. The alert leader will correctly assess the situation and try to reconcile these two aspects of administration.

SCIENTIFIC MANAGEMENT

The scientific management movement was pioneered by Frederick W. Taylor at the turn of the present century. It deals with technology, organization, and method; it is essentially an engineering concept; and its distinguishing mark is the application in administration of rigorous scientific method.[2] Some of its more important assumptions are these:

First, a man cannot do a job until he knows what it is; the approach must be analytical. The odds are in favor of the best-informed individual, said Henry Kendall, and he added, "I regard the application on an organized commercial scale, of the scientific method as using and interpreting facts, as a vital element in the success of any business."[3]

Secondly, there must be a rational calculation of objectives. These vary with the nature of the undertaking, of course, but in a business undertaking the following statement may be taken as typical: Management, said Percival White, is "that activity whereby economic forces (land, labor, and capital) are utilized in combination, always with a view to profit, of one kind or another."[4]

Thirdly, there must be an understanding of the materials of production, an understanding acquired by laboratory testing by scientists, technicians, and engineers.

Closely related to testing is the need for costing and pricing, which is perhaps the most distinctive feature of the scientific method as developed by Taylor and his followers. The procedure is to start with the smallest measurable unit and then to study the way it is combined and recombined at successive stages of process and through the functional divisions of the organization until the basis is provided for determining unit costs and total efficiency. If, for example, the cost of producing a steel girder is known and this item is used in a dozen different places in the undertaking, the unit cost is a constant in determining the production cost at each later stage.

But since the material aspects cannot be separated from the processes of production, scientific management also seeks to standardize and to measure such factors as organization and flow of work so as to eliminate waste motion, inferior units, or any other unnecessary cost that weakens the firm's competitive position. Whether the object of study is material or procedural, however, the approach is the same: to go from the known to the unknown, from the establishment of norms to the combination of norms, from the creation of standards of performance to the control of standards throughout the undertaking.

Of the two main aspects of scientific management—the testing of materials and products, and the standardization of processes —the usefulness of the first is rarely questioned. It is the second category, which includes so large a human element, that encourages some of the excesses of bureaucracy. The difficulty comes about in this way. It is assumed that with enough care and skill it should be possible to determine the one best way of performing every function. And where inanimate things are concerned, this is so. But when the assumption is made to include organization and management, efficiency may indeed be encouraged up to a certain point, but thereafter the disconcerting fact of unpredictable human reactions creates a limitation.

People object to being compared to commodities, especially in large organizations where the objective is not made perfectly clear to everyone. People ask where the dividing line is to be drawn between standardization and routine, on the one hand, and the legitimate needs of human beings, on the other. It frequently takes a good deal of diplomacy and persuasion to gain their willing consent to the use of stop-watch and motion-study tech-

Integrative Leadership

niques. How are *they* to gain from allowing themselves to be regimented and speeded up? If individual employees fail to raise these issues, their unions make good the deficiency.

It comes down to the question of how to routinize and standardize the work of an institution and still make sure that individuals as well as programs will remain personable, spontaneous, and enterprising.

When the scientific-management movement became popular, the subject of organization in administration was added to the bailiwick of the engineer. Organization, said Urwick in 1935, is the subdivision of all activities necessary to any purpose and their arrangement in groups, which are allotted to individuals. The purpose of organization is "economy of effort obtained through specialization and co-ordination of work leading to unity of action." And, he added, there are certain proved principles of organization just as there are certain principles that govern the building of a bridge. These principles should be independent of and take priority over all traditional, personal, or political considerations because if they are ignored there will be a waste of effort due to lack of cooperation.[5]

Opposed to this largely mechanical view of organization is the modern view which, curiously enough, was stated as early as 1926 by John Lee: "It is a pretty fancy," he said, "that private industry is scientifically organized. As a rule it is nothing of the kind. Nor need this be said of necessity in disparagement, for it may happen that the personal head of a personally owned industry by force of his very personality is able to make up for considerable apparent deficiencies of organization. By his very freedom he is adaptable to circumstances. . . ."[6]

A single-minded passion for organization and system in the belief that one is observing the tenets of scientific management is a primary cause of bureaucracy; the absence of flexibility in such a viewpoint is also a primary cause of failure. Summarizing the results of a nationwide study, a group of Harvard professors noted that certain companies "which had employed an enormous amount of formal organization planning were running into trouble because of it." There is no such thing as the perfect organization that automatically runs itself, with exactly the right number of organizational compartments in exactly the right relationship one to another.[7]

The executive who makes organization a fetish, continue these experts, becomes a martinet and a perfectionist. He regards organization charts, procedure manuals, and internal operating rules as ends in themselves. If he recognizes the human aspects of organization it is merely "to keep it in its place," which, interpreted, means keeping it at a distance. He does not realize that an overemphasis on formality drains the life out of people and destroys their ability to initiate and to think for themselves. He does not understand it when his logical organization charts are made obsolete by the action of the informal organization that flourishes among people who work together. He fails to realize that no part of a program should ever be allowed to operate independently, as on a chart it appears to; much less should it be encouraged in that effort because the result is dispersed energy, and no attempt to bring the parts together again ever seems wholly successful.[8]

A controversial issue in organization theory is whether position analysis should be determined independently of the skills of the incumbents or whether skill and position should be combined. The bureaucratic position is that organization should be built around particular functions irrespective of the individuals who may be involved (i.e., organization should be an end in itself). The opposing position is the practical view of enterprising administrators that organization is primarily an arrangement of human beings, and human beings cannot be fitted into ideal slots in a predetermined structure. To follow this line too far, however, offers nothing but confusion. To take the best of both viewpoints, positions should be determined as a logical exercise in assigning responsibilities, but thereafter it is necessary to take account of the strengths and weaknesses of particular individuals, to modify the organization plan accordingly, and to keep on changing it when further developments make that desirable.

A justifiable complaint against scientific management in its original form was that it did not go far enough; that it should expand to include elements that would humanize it. Taylor knew this. He realized that cooperation is basic to efficiency, but he also recognized that too little was known in a systematic way about human relations to make possible a valid contribution to scientific management at that time. But since then, and especially since the end of World War II, human relations has become a main emphasis in administration and a remarkably good fusion with scientific management is already taking place in what is called administration by objectives, an approach that is discussed later in this chapter.

The modern view of the role of scientific management therefore is this: get the facts; develop managerial principles and relationships; establish standards of performance; plan procedures for maximum efficiency and economy; and determine a definite procedure for every step in a particular process.[9] If it can be assumed that scientific management must be combined with human relations to form a balance, that standardization must not be carried to the point of overlooking individual differences and discouraging initiative, and that the one best method is constantly subject to change and improvement, then scientific management is an indispensable tool of administration, not only in matters of technology and efficiency but also in the matter of human relations.

TECHNOLOGY AND MANAGEMENT

It is a little hard to believe that in the age of fission, fusion, and earth satellites, any matter relating to technology could be neglected, but such is in fact the case. It is not the fact or the benefits of technology that have been overlooked, of course, but the manner of its handling by management and its needs relative to other parts of the organization. This is a lesson that Great Britain learned after World War II. Invention alone is not enough. To make its full impact, invention must be accompanied by improved technical training programs for administrators and the appointment of more physical scientists to top posts in industry and in government to insure that the results of invention are put to use.

A broad five-year survey of industry and technical progress in Britain showed in 1957 the direct relationship between the growth of profits on the one hand and the rate of scientific and technological progressiveness on the other. Thus: ". . . most scientific progress is often in companies whose managements *are good in every other way;* in production, sales and costing, and, of course, in staff and labour policies—that is, they have all the normal attributes of a well-run and alert company, and so *have learnt how to spot and adopt the ideas and methods of science as part of their normal activity.*" And then this bow to scientific management: "Though all countries have some backward industries, there are parts of British industry which show a narrow and parochial approach to scientific methods for which there is no justification and . . . the worst cases reveal an ignorant complacency which is both alarming and inexcusable." Technological progress is part of the unified responsibility of management. Parochialism and inertia in technology will not yield merely to a "whiff" of the hope of financial gain; there must be "a radical change of mood and a clear sight of the necessary things to do."[10]

In an article entitled "How to Make a Captain of Industry," Bosworth Monck argues that "there should be more technical men as captains of industry, *because good technical men are often ambitious about ideas.*"[11] And yet he points out that as of 1957 in Britain, technical men were outnumbered in the board rooms of industry, including the engineering industry, by five to one; and that in one-third of these board rooms "no technically qualified voice is ever heard." Hence in Britain, at least, the gulf between technical and nontechnical men must be bridged; in the United States such a gulf is much less frequently encountered. But in both countries something more is needed beyond the mere generation of ideas and technical knowledge: "Ideas must be 'sold,' " says Monck, "not dumped; many men of ideas have not the necessary persistence or skill to 'sell' them."

Writing on "The Pressure of Technical Change," Sir Alexander Fleck argues that, more than anything else, leadership involves "creation," the creation of new concepts and methods, of new products and new techniques. The figures he offers underscore the challenge. Thus in the period 1880–1948, the average rate of industrial production in the United Kingdom was 1.5 per cent a year compound interest; in the United States the rate was twice as high. But in the period 1907–48, industrial output in the United Kingdom increased by about 2½ per cent a year compound interest and after 1948 it doubled, being almost 5 per cent a year.[12]

But as great as the pressure of technical change is, continues Sir Alexander, and as perplexing as are the management problems that are tossed up to the chief executive, the rate of technical innovation must be still further increased. In the United States and in some European nations, annual expenditures on investment in new capital average between 14 per cent and 22 per cent of gross national product. No nation that would assure its own progress can afford to do less. But this kind of expansion cannot take place without people, and the people must be qualified in technical subjects.

Hence there must be an effective demand for technical men in positions of leadership and the schools must offer a better training to that end. In the training of engineers and technicians an immediate improvement would be at least one good required course in management and social science. Similarly, for students in the social sciences and the humanities, there should be at least one good required course on technology and its social implications.

In addition, more could be done by management itself to help technicians and engineers to understand the needs of management, as well as to help professional administrators to understand the needs of technology. Thus, seminars on technology would bring together salesmen, auditors, and other nontechnical specialists for a practical course of instruction. Similarly, where engineers and technicians work together, they could be made familiar with significant developments in management, human relations, and economics. At such meetings, the most rewarding subjects are those that cut across two or more departments or types of work.

Further, some of government's economic services, such as departments of commerce, boards of trade, and the like, might increase the number of their publications that synthesize technical and managerial problems. Yet another possibility is to expand the training programs conducted by some labor unions aimed at increasing an understanding of administration, and correlating the technical, organizational, and human relations aspects of institutional management.

RATIONALE OF THE HUMAN APPROACH

The human relations approach to administration was pioneered in the period between the two world wars and since the end of World War II it has become a dominant feature of administrative management. The movement is based on the principle that people who are personally involved in a common undertaking come to feel that they are partners in it; that thereafter they work more willingly without special incentives, they accept more readily new ideas and ways of doing things, they even accept unpleasant situations—for a while, anyhow—whereas otherwise they would bolt and run.

In large institutions the psychological need of the individual is to acquire a feeling of separate identity and importance and a chance to develop his own life and personality, thus compensating for the deadening effects of the impersonality, conformity, and segmentation that inhere in bureaucratic organization. In a smaller, less bureaucratic situation, the psychological need of the individual is for a chance to follow the lead of his achievement motive as far as it will carry him. In both situations a common requirement is that individuals and programs should both have a feeling of success.

The point at which most bureaucratic theorists seem to have gone wrong in the past is in assuming that impersonality is a tolerable human condition. The fact is that in a large institution, the first effect of impersonality is to make people bitter and repressed, and to lead them into many forms of antisocial revolt. The second effect is to dry up the wellsprings of initiative, administrative effort, and institutional energy. Although the greatest psychological errors seem to have been committed in certain civil service systems, many large corporations have made the same mistakes.

In his book, *Civil Service or Bureaucracy?*, E. N. Gladden describes the debilitating dichotomy that has arisen between an anonymous civil service mentality, on the one hand, and on the other the need for a new outlook emphasizing initiative and personality. We must get away, he says, from the growth of a "slave mentality," from placing a "premium upon caution," from "routine procedures," from an overemphasis on conformity. Instead, we need "independence of mind," a "real freedom of spirit," and a recognition of accomplishment and of work well done.[13]

The "vices" of large-scale organization are cumulative, continues Gladden, and have proceeded far. Hence there is urgent need "to encourage and to reward genuine initiative." There must be a changed attitude toward anonymity. The promotion process must cease to create the impression that the individual is a passive actor who, having done his best on the job, must supinely await judgment from above. "To put the individual official back into the picture" would help to counteract the strong parochial tendencies[14] that constitute one of the greatest vices of a developed bureaucracy.

The real trouble with a large-scale bureaucracy, continues this expert on civil service, is that the individual "counts for nothing." Gladden describes the situation in these rather poignant terms:

The individual officer knows that he is not likely to receive full credit for what he does: sometimes those above him will not even be aware of the full implications of what he personally is doing. Some will do their utmost to take credit for his successes whilst leaving him to take the blame for any failure. And even when he receives due credit from his immediate superiors they still have the task of pressing his case further up the line. There are human reasons why they will sometimes fail in this. *The official himself cannot do very much about it since he cannot in fact know what is going on behind the scenes.*

The anonymous official, says Gladden, is given few opportunities to make his own representations to higher authority, "though of course he may obtain publicity as a member of the departmental drama society or by acting the goat at the annual Christmas party."[15]

In *White Collar,* C. Wright Mills has documented an analogous development in large corporations. Thus an impersonalized and anonymous system of control, where no one is sure who really has power, is frequently characterized by anxiety, fear, insecurity, and worry on the part of officials and employees. Consequently, "resentment, slowly produced by the routine of dull work, finds an outlet in strong anti-company and strong anti-union loyalties. . . ."[16]

Most people would probably agree with Gladden that "Bureaucracy in any of its guises is too expensive a luxury for any community to be willing to support it." But if the antidote of positive incentives is to be applied, it is not enough that higher management come to the defense of the anonymous ones. The challenge is also a social one in which the public, the press, political leaders, and the government-of-the-day must all take a firm and constructive stand.[17]

Both in industry and in government there is needed a well-thought-out program of weaving positive incentives into the daily routines of institutions. People resent it when they are ordered about to no apparent purpose, when nobody takes notice of their opinions, and when their skill and experience are ignored. Hence, without weakening the unified responsibility of leadership, ways must be found of consulting with subordinate officials and with employees before decisions affecting their interests are made. Policies must be open to full gaze. There must be no hindrances to the free flow of information. The key to cooperation is good faith and mutual respect between people who work together, and this requires honesty and fair dealing.[18] And finally, some means must be found to encourage property ownership on the part of employees by making it possible for them to acquire shares in the corporation or even to start a business of their own.

The trouble with most bureaucrats is that they are bored. And a bored worker is an indifferent one, never an inspired one. Thus, few people, especially in large institutions, work at anywhere near their real potential. They have no desire to improve. They tolerate their work so as to be able to enjoy their leisure. But being bored during most of their working hours, they somehow never learn to enjoy their leisure hours either. If people were happier in their jobs, a different cycle might be started. They might enjoy their leisure more; they might acquire wider cultural appreciations; they might become more intelligent and active citizens. All this is possible.

The question is, What will fire the ambition of a bureaucrat? People seem to want a combination of things that add up to dignity and self-respect. In addition to material luxuries, monetary emoluments also mean status, prestige, and the chance for one's children to rise on the social scale. As part of this success complex, people value certain personal relations: a liking for the boss, being treated fairly, being recognized for effort and for good work, being given responsibility and confidence. Some people will also try harder because of a sense of fear, but usually this is the fear of disappointing oneself and one's close associates, not fear of sanctions, because these are now little used in management.

Now the most enterprising people, as we have seen many times, are those who need no outside stimulus but whose drive comes from within themselves. They have achievement motivation. They are restless and impatient, ambitious and self-confident. They know what they want to become or what they want to do, and they pretty well **know** how to go about it. These are the people whom top management must look for. These are also the people who suffer agonies of death when sucked into the undertow of bureaucracy.

Achievement motivation is far more prevalent than is usually supposed. Most people want to be successful and often get more satisfaction from the struggle to improve than from anything else, including the usual tangible evidences of success. Achievement motivation is a combination of many things, including competition, drive, play, pride of craftsmanship, temperament, body chemistry, egocentric drives, and early training. Altruism and idealism are also part of the compound because many people still strive for unselfish reasons as they would not for themselves. Shakespeare had an insight into the passions of active, creative men, and, by extension, of businessmen who have been successful and still do not want to retire, when he noted that

> All things that are,
> Are with more spirit chased than enjoy'd.

It has also been said that "He begins to die that quits his desires."

Although the human relations approach in administration is now widely accepted both in business and in government programs, the test of it is the degree to which institutions can attract the kind of people who seek conscious self-development and associate this drive with their work. Where the number of such people is large it seems as though the institution must possess a formula that might in the long run be more important to mankind than the one that made atomic fission possible. No undertaking that understands this formula need worry too much about the pathologies of bureaucracy because with gifted and motivated employees there is less need for detailed rules and regulations and all the other props and gadgetry of bureaucracy. The stakes have probably never been better stated than by Louis Brandeis (later Associate Justice of the Supreme Court of the United States) in his testimony before the United States Commission on Indusrial Relations in 1914. Thus:

The grave objection to the large business is that, almost inevitably, the form of organization, the absentee stockholdings, and its remote directorship prevent participation, ordinarily, of the employees in such management. The executive officials become stewards in charge of the details of the operation of the business, they alone coming into direct relation with labor. Thus we lose that necessary co-operation which naturally flows from contact between employers and employees—and which the American aspirations for democracy demand. It is in the resultant absolutism that you will find the fundamental cause of prevailing unrest; no matter what is done with the superstructure, no matter how it may be improved in one way or the other, unless we eradicate that fundamental difficulty, unrest will not only continue, but, in my opinion, will grow worse.

The object of scientific management is to draw out the facts; the object of the human relations approach is to develop the human potential. Both are necessary, and when properly combined they are infinitely more potent than either approach taken alone. How is this combination to be effected?

ADMINISTRATION BY OBJECTIVES

A new approach in management, which includes elements of both scientific management and human relations, is what may be called administration by objectives, the effect of which is to develop the potential of the individual and to make him a willing partner in the undertaking.

If the objectives and policies of the enterprise can be made clear to the individual, he may find that his societal and personal ambitions, which together add up to his personal integrity, coincide with the institutional goals of his employment. At this point higher management assigns him an area of responsibility and allows him a good deal of latitude regarding method, the assumption being that if the goal of the program is jointly agreed on, the working out of method should be left as far as possible to the recipient of delegated authority. This authority should be increased as the individual's ability develops, and at the same time he should be cooperatively engaged in the further definition of larger, common objectives, so that eventually he will be qualified for responsibilities at a higher level.[19]

If this plan is carried out well, then officials and employees throughout the undertaking will develop loyalty and energy because to a considerable extent they are their own bosses. Top management will be free to coordinate, to plan ahead, to look for evidences of decay, and to stimulate enterprise, none of which is very feasible when administrators are burdened with the details of direction and control.

Administration by objectives gets away from the idea that an employee is like a key on a machine that moves when punched, and substitutes for that notion a philosophy that appeals to the selfhood of the employee and develops his potentialities. It means giving him a wider scope that will counteract the narrowing influence of bureaucracy. Such a philosophy is part of the success of Marks and Spencer in Britain; it is a revolutionary new policy of International Business Machines; in a practical way it may be most effective in keeping bureaucracy in check. This new approach, says Drucker, must become widely adopted as automation becomes more widespread, because only as technicians broaden their competence will they be able to plan and to operate complicated systems.[20]

The first implication of this new philosophy is that administration starts with policies and objectives that are widely and cooperately conceived. Vitality in administration stems from vitality in policy. Both must be cooperatively arrived at because involvement and participation are the source of motivation. Unfortunately, most large businesses seldom do carefully analyze their aims. It is enough, apparently, to say that the aim is profit; but profit is only one of many results of many policies in many areas of the business, and if any of these areas is weak profit will be less. A naïve conception of profit also discourages morale and efficiency. The sophisticated administrator will insist on the democratic planning of objectives and policies from which every individual in the undertaking receives his mandate. Such a mandate frees him from his bureaucratic prison cell and allows him latitude and opportunity for growth.

But not even a dynamic program runs itself, no matter how democratic a sense of participation may be. Idealists sometimes overlook the fact that efficiency is primarily the result of human drive and of human personality. The keenest exponent of the human factor in administration is Ordway Tead, author of *The Art of Leadership, The Art of Administration,* and many other books on management. There is a basic distinction, says Tead, between, on the one hand, administrative policy determined through representation and participation and, on the other, executive action carried out through delegated individual responsibility. Once agreed to, policy must be executed intelligently, promptly, and continuously. This implies effective oversight and requires unified responsible direction. There must be no lessening of clear responsibility, no confusion of authority, no ambiguity as to directive power.

The adoption of a policy profoundly concerns all who are to be affected by it. Consequently they should know in advance what is proposed and why. They should have a chance to offer facts and points of view, and should give their explicit consent as a condition of carrying out the new policy. There must then be responsibility for results. Insubordination and sabotage are intolerable, but criticism is proof of partnership. Hence, says Tead, the two principles that must constantly be synthesized in administration are representation or participation, and coordination.

The greater the area of delegation and cooperation, the more must coordination be emphasized. The principle of coordination assumes that an organization can function smoothly only as there is a definite, informed, advance agreement throughout as to aims, policies, and methods. Individual energy and scope for growth both depend on the manner in which the principles of representation and coordination are brought together. The neglect of either will cause a return to older methods of authoritarian rule.[21]

A main source of institutional energy, therefore, is the directing function, the unifying center that governs the conduct of the whole program. For it is here, in the chief executive, that policy planning and delegations, supervision and coordination, must be located. Here also is the center of decision, although the extensions of that function are to be pushed as far down the line as possible.

In a program of administration by objectives there is no substitute for frequent face-to-face relationships as an antidote to bureaucratic impersonality and loss of morale. A few minutes of conference between senior and junior officials are worth stacks of memoranda. The way to get rid of paperwork is to deal direct, and the way to coordinate is through the human touch: staff conferences, informal huddles, and a judicious use of committees that will allow full scope but will prevent the undermining of unified direction and control.

Administrators are often too remote from their organization, which is one reason that the excesses of bureaucracy are cumulative: top administrators never learn the extent to which pathologies have become lodged. The top men are insulated. Like the White House secretariat, they are cut off from the flow of work among the departments. This condition is most likely to occur where social position, prestige, rank, and attitudes of superiority are found. The problem is greater in Britain than it is in the United States, except where British businessmen are of the self-made variety like Lord Nuffield of the motorcar industry or Sir Simon Marks of Marks and Spencer. Like Henry Ford, these men get around to the shop floor and the assembly line. But in the military services, in the diplomatic services, at the headquarters of large corporations, and in the large departments in Whitehall and Washington—wherever protocol, dignity, and position are important—there the top men are remote from day-to-day affairs. There may be a tangle of red tape just below the chief executive's office, but he never learns the extent or the seriousness of it during his whole career in office.

The solution to this difficulty is to unbend and find out for oneself just what is going on. But this is often harder than it seems because social attitudes and traditions are stubborn things. It may be suggested that the top man should enlist the services of a personal assistant who would tell him these things, but once such a man is appointed he is assumed to be an "organization spy" and is treated accordingly. There is no substitute for the top man getting the worm's-eye view for himself.

It is only by personal relationships that an administrator can give all members of the organization the sense of the whole and of how the role of each is vital to the rest. And without this sense of relationship it is useless to suppose that people will develop a sense of belonging and of voluntary cooperation. If, as organizations grow in size, ways cannot be found to increase rather than to decrease direct personal relationships, nothing top management can do will overcome the impersonality that characterizes bureaucracy. For the plain truth is—and it has been proven over and over again in big business as in big government—that the overdevelopment of formal procedures in the absence of personal relationships drains the very life out of enterprise, no matter how energetic it was to begin with.

In this important matter, the twofold responsibility of the chief executive is to resist the temptation to do himself that which others can do with profit to themselves and to the institution; and secondly, he must build up the self-confidence of his juniors by frequent conferences in which he communicates enthusiasm as well as tactful advice. With this modest and sympathetic approach, the prevailing spirit of the enterprise becomes one of service, a spirit that customers never fail to be aware of, just as they never fail to be aware of artificiality and insincerity.

Chester Barnard has made many contributions to the solution of problems of large-scale management, not the least of which is his insistence that the higher an official rises, the less real power he enjoys; and that accordingly the task of the top executive is to create the conditions of enterprise, mirror the attitudes of his organization, set up easy channels of communication, delegate work, and motivate his subordinates. In other words, it is the chief executive who sets an example and creates an atmosphere in which people can do their best work.[22]

EDUCATION FOR LEADERSHIP

If our educational system continues to train men by precision methods for particular specialties, then it is doubtful whether the Bureaucratic State can be avoided. Men will be bred and trained for status, to fill a certain role in society or in the big corporation, and the gifted few who are innovators will never have a chance to develop their talents. To train some men this way and others as innovators overlooks the fact that the ability to innovate crops out in unexpected places and these cannot be predetermined. A proper educational system, therefore, should try to produce a balance in most people and to develop their potentialities as far as they will go. Such an approach would represent a fundamental attack on the problem of institutional vitality and the future health of the economy.

An educational policy that would emphasize balance and avoid the bureaucratic outlook would seek to train all men both in mental discipline and in cultural, humanizing subjects, relating the two so as to encourage a unified personality. At a certain point, those with aptitudes in particular fields, such as a science or an art, should have a chance to specialize. But by this time the individual's knowledge will be broader than if he had specialized from the start and any later training outside of his field—as when he is selected for a top administrative post, for example—will be that much more effective.

In between the two extremes of specialized scientists, on the one hand, and specialized artists, on the other, is a large group that includes all the rest of us, and it is from this group that most administrators will normally be drawn. Except that in the present atomic age an understanding of technology is indispensable to all administrators, the outlook of this type of person is different from that of the specialist, being a blend of mental discipline, cultural sophistication, an understanding of human relations, an ability to learn from experience and to synthesize the many complicated factors of institutional management into a workable scheme.

In administration, certain technical skills are needed, but even more needed are the social skills, plus the kind of personality and character that inspire confidence and make leadership a sort of second nature. Administrators cannot be trained merely as thinking machines, as automatons, and turned out in standardized units. Their job is planning, decision making, directing and inspiring others, exercising judgment, developing the qualities of the statesman. And little of this can be taught by formal means. Such skills will have their beginning in formal education, but thereafter they will be developed from experience and pursued for a lifetime.

To rely entirely on formal education would be to produce many able bureaucrats but few men of wisdom, drive, and understanding. If a man is narrowly trained he has the rest of his life to become human if he understands the need for it. If he is sloppily trained he has the rest of life to develop self-discipline, which is the basis of every creative effort. But here again, the need for self-discipline must be appreciated. In either case, the demands of institutional management offer the best possible challenge.

In some European and Middle Eastern countries the only access to bureaucratic posts in government and in industry is by means of the appropriate university or technical degree. There could hardly be a more direct contributing factor to bureaucratic pathology. Men not only have the same standardized professional presuppositions, which is bad enough, but they even wear the same school tie. And the effect is a smugness that discourages innovation and dissent and bars the outsider, the more certainly if he should be that dangerous fellow, the nonconformist.

The beginning of bureaucratic stagnation is an educational monopoly of this sort. The blend that is needed comes from diversity: of training, of geographical and school origin, of presuppositions, and even of prejudices. To mix all these elements in an educational situation creates a competition among old ideas and develops new ones. Only so can accepted doctrine and sanctified protocol be tested, criticized, and amended if need be.

In every field of endeavor the greatest innovators have been those who were most free and most independent. Professor Jewkes and his colleagues have shown that it is the "will and obstinacy of individuals spurred on by the desire for knowledge" that have most often produced innovation. Indeed, says Jewkes, an inventor is "nearly always something of an artist or craftsman" and hence he "prizes independence for its own sake."[23] The importance of independence has nowhere been more succinctly put than by the hero of Dudintsev's novel, *Not By Bread Alone:* "A discoverer," he says, "always thinks differently in any sphere of knowledge. Because he has found a new and shorter way, he rejects the old habitual one."[24]

A philosophy of education for leadership in a technological age must recognize that intellectual curiosity is a continuing quality and that discovery is just around the corner. The discipline of traditional education encourages the logic and order of bureaucracy, while the freedom of progressive education stimulates the venturesomeness of enterprise. If traditional education could allow for a greater degree of freedom and independence to enable gifted men and women to advance at their own pace, or if progressive education could pay more attention to self-discipline and reason, the result would be a blend of the best in both educational philosophies. Such an approach to education would make much easier the synthesis of qualities needed in enterprising administration.

CONCLUDING CAVEAT

The attempt here has been to show that system is essential to efficiency, but is useful only when combined with complementary human factors. Failure to make this blend has created many bureaucratic excesses that have warped the lives of countless people working in big institutions.

Certain aspects of administration are measurable and others are not, and to learn the point where this division occurs is part of the wisdom of the top executive. If an administrator tries to count things that cannot be counted, to measure things that should not be measured, he must expect that people will first chafe and then either give up or get out. This fact has been forcefully stated in the Harvard study entitled *Executive Action*, where, to illustrate one aspect of their thesis, the authors remark that "If staff departments must justify their existence by producing measurable results such as detailed progress reports, they may spend more time in performing measurable activities than in meeting nonmeasurable needs for serving line departments."[25] Thus, the executive must have a sense of fitness, recognizing that attitudes, beliefs, morale, ambition, human sensibilities, and a host of other things are far more basic to accomplishment than physical things that can be counted, measured, and stored.

The executive must also resist the feeling of loneliness that the top man is bound to experience at one time or another. There are two lines he can take. Either he can try to bolster his self-confidence by administrative gadgetry such as inflated staff activities, the use of outside consultants, and the adoption of the latest measuring devices in the naïve hope that these will prove to be substitutes for individual synthesis, teamwork, and decisiveness. Or he can assuage his loneliness by gregariousness, in which case he will deal personally with his subordinates and employees as often and as candidly as he is able. The latter course is easier on him, more acceptable to his employees, cheaper to his organization, and far more productive of results than the first one.

Much of the sympathy for a bureaucratic type of leadership amongst social scientists in the United States seems to stem from a mistaken view of the unity of supervision. Apparently it is assumed that unified leadership is necessarily authoritarian leadership, and that if the authoritarian personality is to be avoided, which everyone agrees is desirable, then leadership must be diffused and, in effect, broken down among groups throughout the institution.[26] This fuzzy thinking can do much harm to our institutions. No leadership is necessarily authoritarian. Unified leadership simply recognizes that for integration to take place the organization must be hierarchical, and that the man at the top has a *function* to see that all parts coalesce under proper supervision; that energies are stimulated from the top and released all the way down the line under conditions of fullest participation and with a maximum of planned initiative and delegated authority.

Organizational leadership is not an either/or proposition any more than any other aspect of institutional management is one thing or the other. The excesses of bureaucracy may be avoided by combining the best in technology and in human capacity, in the stop watch and the personal example, in organizational principles and individual exceptions, in precise planning and discretionary delegations of authority, in teamwork and in individual genius.

Chapter 13 Decentralization

During his active career as the head of General Motors, Alfred P. Sloan, Jr., came to the conclusion that decentralization is a primary means of combining the best elements in bureaucracy and enterprise. When managerial responsibility becomes concentrated among a few executives, the result is to limit initiative, create delay, increase expense, reduce efficiency, and retard development. A characteristic of bureaucracy is that most executives spend too much time worrying about the details of administration and meeting the critical situations that daily arise. The solution, said Sloan, is centralization of policy and decentralization of execution.

Bureaucracy is not caused by too *much*, he added, so much as by too little organization of the right kind, a kind that will transfer decision making and action as far from the center as possible and still achieve the objectives of the program. Within this framework, coordination assures adaptability to business fluctuations and allows for enough managerial freedom so that opportunities may be seized that an overly centralized program can never grasp to the same degree.[1]

This policy of what might be called administrative federalism has long been a cardinal principle of administration at General

Motors and even more so at American Telegraph and Telephone Company. This chapter examines decentralization policy for antidotes to bureaucratic excesses and uses the Bell System as principal example.[2]

THE A. T. & T. STORY

American Telegraph and Telephone Company is one of the few corporations in the United States that early developed a philosophy and a kind of personality of its own, a fact that has had much to do with its ability to resist bureaucratic excesses and retain an enterprising spirit. "The success of the Bell System policies," said Danielian, writing in 1939, "is explainable by the indirect, unostentatious, but nevertheless insistent, pursuit of their objectives through all available avenues of approach."[3] In so large an organization as A.T. & T., said Chester Barnard, a former official of that company, the essential problem is to develop cooperative action, on the one hand, and the individual, on the other, in such a way that they reinforce each other. What is needed is a "dynamic individualism which will express itself in initiative and resourcefulness together with control evidenced in patience and restraint."[4]

A.T. & T. is a holding company controlling twenty operating companies that span the United States. In 1958, the Bell System served more than 52 million of the nation's 64 million telephones and to this end employed about 800,000 men and women. There were 1,600,000 stockholders and the total physical facilities of the Bell System—local and long-distance lines, switchboards, dial apparatus, buildings, telephone instruments, and all other equipment—represented an investment of nearly $19 billion. Approximately 90 per cent of all toll (long distance) messages originating in the United States were routed in whole or in part over the system network. In addition, A.T. & T. itself owned 99.8 per cent of the stock of Western Electric Company, the dominant telephone manufacturing concern in the country, and Western Electric and A.T. & T. together owned the Bell Laboratories which conducts research for all the Bell companies. And finally,

A.T. & T. also provided networks of private communication lines for other businesses and for government agencies, plus long-distance pathways for interconnecting television and radio stations, but these and other special services amounted to only about 4 per cent of the total business of the company.[5]

All of the operating companies of the Bell System have their own separate corporate entities and officers, leaving to A.T. & T. itself, which operates out of 195 Broadway in New York, the following responsibilities:

Servicing the operating companies, for which fees are charged
Operating most of the long-distance business as a common facility for the regional companies
Conducting research through a pooled service, Bell Laboratories
Developing standard agreements with its manufacturing subsidiary, Western Electric

Our present interest is with the first category because it is here that decentralization is so prominent a feature.

Confronted with a task as formidable as that of the parent company in this enormous system, how can even the most expert management simply maintain order, much less keep the spirit of enterprise alive? And added to the problem of great size is the ever-present possibility that this industrial empire might be transferred to public ownership. A privately owned telephone monopoly on a continent-wide basis is the exception to the common rule, because almost everywhere outside of the United States telephones are a monopoly of the state. Leadership in the Bell System, therefore, has had to think not merely about efficiency and vitality but also about the very survival of the company as a private undertaking. Consequently policies have had to be based on the concepts of trusteeship and accountability.

The concept of trusteeship centers on problems such as these: How to keep a steady supply of top executives coming along, men who combine technical competence with an ability to lead. How to foster research and invention at the center and self-reliance and autonomy at the periphery. How to operate what many consider the best staff services in the country, and yet keep energy flowing down the line of operations where it belongs. How to do a proper job of public relations with state legislatures, economic interests, labor groups, and local consumers.

Our mandate, said the president of A.T. & T. in 1958, is this: "Give good service at reasonable prices. Deal considerately and fairly with people. Be progressive, not complacent." I know of no law, he added, to prevent reasonable freedom under regulation. A business such as A.T. & T. that does not encounter competition in the same degree as many others must be regulated. But this does not make it different from other kinds of enterprise. It reacts to incentives and to opportunity as others do. It also needs freedom, under regulation, to do its very best.

A.T. & T. has never ceased to emphasize decentralization as a basic policy. "Decentralizing not only provides opportunity, but helps people prepare themselves for more of it." The Bell System is an up-from-the-ranks business. No large interest dominates its management or says who the top managers shall be. These men come up step by step. Consequently responsibility and authority must be pushed out as far as they will go so that able people destined for the top will acquire the kind of training that comes from having to make decisions and then live by them. Decentralized authority helps people to increase their understanding as well as their skill.

A.T. & T. has no wish to grow bigger merely for the sake of aggrandizement, concluded the president. It does not want to step outside of the proper sphere of providing communications that serve the public interest. It simply wants to make service more freely and easily available to everyone.[6]

CENTRALIZED POLICY

Decentralized administration is hard to achieve safely unless responsibility for policy is securely located at the top, in the hands of the board of directors and the chief executive. If, in addition, a corporation is to operate as a public trust and remain enterprising, certain factors are of special significance.

Decentralization 203

In the case of A.T. & T. these special factors were once explained to me in this way. The success of a trusteeship corporation depends on the thoughtful establishment of objectives and policies. There must also be a kind of company philosophy which includes principles of management, attention to morale, and satisfactory relationships with personnel and with the public. The success of A.T. & T. is due in part to the vision of its early leaders, who created objectives that have not had to be changed much throughout the years, and established relations between 195 Broadway and the associated companies that also have not had to be much altered. Leadership is based on deliberate policy. In A.T. & T., the going concern is directed by its top executives, with the board acting as a reserve control. Clear-cut objectives and the company philosophy prevent the self-aggrandizement of individuals. There has been no trouble with this in the Bell companies, where it is a habit among executives to think of the company interest first. This is because most company men are taken directly from school, are made familiar with the philosophy of the company, and devote their entire career to the Bell System.[7] Thus the company combines policy and objectives and stresses the need for leaders of character and ability, men who might be called institutional philosophers.

Such a man was Arthur W. Page, who for years directed public relations for A.T. & T. and who had studied the role of the board of directors. In a small corporation, he said,[8] the members of the board are often partners in the business and hence few serious problems relating to policy and management are likely to arise. But in a big semipublic corporation the board generally consists entirely of officers. Hence a necessary double check that might be supplied by the owners of the business is lacking in the matter of policy formulation.[9]

The principal function of the board of a semipublic corporation, continued Page, is to pick good management and to get rid of it if it proves unsatisfactory. The typical duties of a board include meeting once a month, receiving financial reports and statements of condition, hearing reports on new policies or

P

changes, and presenting reports on business trends or political policies likely to affect the business. The board members' principal concern is with financial results, and they will not ordinarily inquire into management policies or methods so long as results are satisfactory. A.T. & T. has always been careful to choose board members who have not taken on too many other directorships and who cannot use their positions for their own or their company's benefit.

The most important contributions of board members, continued Page, seldom appear in the minutes of their meetings. Most problems are settled in informal consultations with management because it is better to handle difficulties in this way than to make an issue of them in formal surroundings. In case of any serious trouble, a group of directors can get together and lay plans to get rid of the management or to take other drastic action.

Stockholders have certain checks on company policy and operations, including capable men as board members; capable executives careful of their own reputations and that of the corporation; government regulation (telephones are regulated at both the federal and the state levels); and periodic investigations by Congress and by regulatory commissions. Nevertheless, when no single stockholder owns so much as 1 per cent of the outstanding stock, there is little that he personally can do in the matter of company policy. If things got bad enough, a number of stockholders might combine and try to correct the situation, but their chances of success are not great.

In the last analysis, concluded Page, the problem is not one of control or power so much as it is one of responsibility. A trustee corporation will succeed so long as it can attract men of character. So here again is the human factor in administration.

The officers and directors of A.T. & T., said an article in *Fortune*,[10] include a strong representation from the New England group by whom the company was founded. There are also men of financial ability and experience, and men whose interest is in the public service "coupled with a noticeable leaning toward what might be called an aristocratic liberalism." Hence, the three major traditions that have been merged are a New England tradition of family, a Wall Street tradition of finance, and a public service tradition compounded partly of wartime service in government and partly of Wilsonian democracy.

The tradition and philosophy of A.T. & T. were explained to me by Bancroft Gherardi, another outstanding figure in A.T. & T. history and noted as a developer of men. The source of the tradition, he said, is the fact that the founders of the company were gentlemen in the best sense, they sought congenial associates, and this practice has been continued. Realizing that the corporation's reputation for public service and sound public relations is the product of high moral and intellectual qualities, the company's nominating committees have deliberately selected men of this caliber.

Regarding the role of the chief executive, Gherardi commented that in general there are two types of person in such posts. There are those who are self-centered, domineering, and exploitative; and there are those who are socially sensitive, sympathetic, and dedicated. He believed that only the second type of executive can be lastingly successful because the self-centered individual cannot create a proper institutional spirit or guard against the inherent dangers of bureaucracy.[11]

Yet another element in the A.T. & T. tradition is a chief executive with the ability to lead, to explain objectives, and to get support for them, an executive possessing that uncommon sense of what to do and when. "Great administration is not primarily a matter of rules," remarked an officer of the company, "for they are incidental to policy; it is the product of inspiring leadership, creating confidence and satisfaction on the part of employees and the public." Unfortunately, there are not many chief executives of this type.[12]

In general, continued this officer, a man who has a narrow specialization will not be an effective chief executive. Walter Gifford, the then president of the company, had been trained as a statistician but he was primarily a policy maker and a philosopher, a contact man, one who liked people. Hence his personal relationships both within and outside of the company created its tone and made friends for it. A chief executive must also be able to see all parts of the organization simultaneously, broadly, and in relation to objectives. He must be sensitive to the effect of policies on employees and on the public. He must be able to transfer his skills from one situation to another, but this ability depends more on personal qualities than it does on training and most men lack the necessary temperament and predilection.

Finally, said this officer, if a corporation succeeds in getting the right man at the top, everything else will pretty much take care of itself because he will in turn pick the right men, he will emphasize objectives in a way that will constitute a kind of philosophy for the institution, he will recognize that many principles of management are merely common sense, and he will de-emphasize rules on the ground that informal cooperation is easier and more effective.

Many public utility and engineering concerns tend to neglect the human element in administration, but this difficulty has been avoided at A.T. & T. partly because in the early 1920's it was blessed with an outstanding personnel man whose policy was expressed in these terms: "Develop and encourage every policy, practice, custom, and tradition that will affirmatively tend to make each one feel that he is a part of the business, and therefore ready and anxious to assume all the responsibilities, both individual and joint, as well as to enjoy the privileges and compensations that go with that relationship."[13] This man anticipated the modern emphasis on administration by objectives, which is a condition precedent to effective decentralization.

DECENTRALIZED ADMINISTRATION

"If it didn't decentralize, A.T. & T. would fail," said an officer of the company to me on one occasion. "It couldn't be run from 195 Broadway even if all of its executives were supermen—as they are not." And a little later the president of one of the operating companies stated just as positively that "If the corporation didn't have definite lines of organization we could not respond to emergencies." Although there may be an apparent inconsistency between these two views, the fact is that decentralization is possible only as it is founded on definite lines of organization and responsibility that permit a quick response to emergencies. Here, then, is a large area of reconciliation in the theory of bureaucracy and enterprise.

It was Chester Barnard who stated the need for clear lines of organization. "In A.T. & T.," he said, "the lines of responsibility must be known and observed. Action sometimes cannot wait. To delay for conferences or research might be fatal." An example at the time was the investigations of the Federal Communications Commission, which sometimes required authoritative action by company officials without opportunity for consultation. When the light burns on the switchboard, said Barnard, the organization must respond at once. Speed is made possible by definite lines of organization, established practices, general understandings, and the capacity of people to respond in time of crisis.

In a large decentralized institution, continued Barnard, men who are left alone are apt to settle down into routine, habitual responses; their minds lose resiliency and drive, their outlook becomes dull, and they respond slowly to crisis or to opportunity. All of these difficulties can be avoided by alert management and clear lines of organization.[14]

The decentralization policy of A.T. & T. was successful because the corporation picked good men, gave local companies independence, created an atmosphere of cooperation, and issued no peremptory orders. It tries to give helpful staff advice to the operating companies but without obligation on their part. It moves men around all over the country to make them familiar with the whole system. It keeps able staff men at 195 Broadway, promotes men for merit, and has succeeded in avoiding favoritism to a surprising degree.[15]

An objective of top-level policy is to encourage freedom and initiative at the local level where, as Barnard contends, the real power in any organization rests and where, in this case, the customers are served. As a local company official once observed,

Administrative Vitality 208

"In every community the commercial manager is the recognized head of the system. In fact, the public doesn't know that other department heads exist. We therefore have the advantages of specialization by function and of integration, too. The local manager handles all public relations; he is the symbol of the corporation; he tries to gain public recognition; and all other departments defer to him." And then this comment on how conflicts between the rival claims of order and flexibility are met: "The rule is to have your lines of authority clear, but if common sense tells you to be flexible, don't let petty pride interfere. Good will and understanding alone make organizational structure work effectively."[16]

In other words, administration must seek the best of two worlds, the blend of order and enterprise. The Bell System lays the structural foundation for such a blend by creating a specialized functional organization that runs throughout the corporation, with each man having only one boss. There are simple lines of authority and superficially the arrangement looks like a military type of organization. But where the military pattern tends to concentrate authority upward, at A.T. & T. the fact of its combining with a policy of decentralization reverses the flow of authority downward and spreads it out at the lower levels of the organization.

It is interesting to note how the same decentralization policy is regarded differently at headquarters and among the operating companies. According to Gherardi, "A.T. & T. never issues orders. This makes for morale and progressiveness. A one-man show is a 'hen-and-chickens' type of organization. A.T. & T. tries to create independence and at the same time an institutional mind. The fundamental problem is that of encouraging individual initiative and responsibility within a corporate philosophy."[17] As illustration, a poll was once conducted by which the parent company sought to determine whether the operating companies wished to introduce special long-distance rates on Sundays. Most of the companies did, and when the dissenters were then asked if they wanted to go along with the majority, all except the Pacific company agreed. There were special considerations in that area and the company said it would consider joining later. Thus a successful general policy was adopted and nothing was lost by the fact that it was not made uniform among the operating companies.

The field viewpoint on decentralization policy, as it came out in a group interview in the Chicago area, was that 195 Broadway acted primarily as a clearinghouse, not as an innovator.[18] Thus, the popular conception that A.T. & T. does most of the thinking and planning is wrong. More ideas originate in the field than at headquarters, and this includes ideas that field men take with them when they move to New York. The usual procedure is for the operating companies to communicate new ideas to A.T. & T. and to ask for an opinion. The companies also tell A.T. & T. how they are meeting particular problems that may arise. A.T. & T. develops ideas that are suggested to it, tests them in the field, and appraises the results before making a general recommendation.

When problems arise among the operating companies for which no adequate solution is at hand, the company calls on A.T. & T. for ideas on how to handle them. If the problem is a new one, A.T. & T. may say that it has nothing on it and to let it know how the matter has been solved, when it is. If several different companies call headquarters on the same problem, A.T. & T. may question others on how they are handling the difficulty and then it will try to develop a suggested practice. If A.T. & T. knows how a particular problem is being handled successfully by some companies, the information is widely circulated.

As practiced by A.T. & T., administrative federalism is a little like Justice Holmes' description of political federalism as "the insulated laboratories of the forty-eight states." New ideas may be tried out in one place, those that work may be widely adopted, but no unit need conform unless it wants to. When the Illinois company wanted to insert advertisements in the main columns of city telephone directories and it was known in advance that headquarters did not approve on the ground that the practice might be carried too far, the functional official in Illinois got permission from his president to take the matter up at 195 Broadway. It was agreed between them in advance that if the reply was, "No, we don't think it would be a good idea," then they would go ahead with the plan anyway; but if the reply was "Hell, no!" then they would look into the proposition a little further. The first of these replies was made, so the Illinois company went ahead, and soon other companies did the same. At this stage A.T. & T. simply sent out a letter cautioning them to go slow and to try out the idea fully before giving it wide effect.[19]

THE ROLE OF STANDARDS IN DECENTRALIZATION

The discussion so far may have given the impression that even a large corporation can become so flexible as to tolerate a considerable degree of deviation and experimentation—and so it can. Nevertheless, there are certain technical areas where standardization is indispensable. In A.T. & T. this need is met, first, when the parent company establishes standards and makes inspections; and secondly, when it tests results on a comparative basis.

In the Bell System, everything that can be standardized for purposes of comparison is standardized. The system determines, for example, the average length of time required to install a telephone, to complete a call, to change an installation, and what a fair rate of wrong numbers may be. Everything and every process that is measurable is measured in the interests of efficiency and uniformity. Another objective of the same policy is to stimulate competition and improvement among the operating companies.

According to experienced field men, the method works something like this: the quality of the work of plant and traffic men is checked by supervisors, using the sampling process, and control is by means of comparisons. Indeed, it is this comparison of similar data from different operating companies that is one of the most interesting features of administrative federalism as practiced by A.T. & T. because it supplies an element of competition in an industry that is in fact a monopoly and hence has no competition from the outside.

As for investigations, "The only time the higher-ups investigate you," said an A.T. & T. field man, "is when the performance is above or below the average." If performance is above the average, then there is the possibility of poor quality, irritation of the public, or short cuts at the corporation's expense. And if performance is below average, then higher management tries to discover a better system. In one case, for example, unpaid accounts in a certain district were reduced by a substantial margin. Immediately the head man in Chicago sent for the district man and asked him how he did it. The new procedure was a sound one and there was an attempt to get other functional men to adopt it.[20]

At the same time, however, A.T. & T. tries to take the curse off standardization by the use of discrimination and common sense. In the Chicago Central Observing Office of Illinois Bell, for example, daily tests include all phases of the work from the time a subscriber signals until all parties have been disconnected. Observations are made from the viewpoint of the subscriber. Quality of voice is noted, slow answers are recorded, and results are checked against statistical averages.[21] The records of these observations are then published for each central office, the dual purpose being to show quality of service and to furnish objective material for executive control purposes. If certain records are low, the district manager is questioned and, if he asks for it, special supplementary tests are made. But since district managers differ in personality and temperament, some welcome this form of staff activity and others resent it. Hence, "As the managers are personally known, allowance is made for these characteristics and the staff proffers this information only to those who would welcome it."[22]

As already noted, the standards developed by A.T. & T. and their comparison and interpretation are the basis for a kind of internal competition that helps to overcome one of the greatest hazards of large, monopolistic enterprises. In fact, telephone men will sometimes argue that standards set in this way result in more competition in technical matters—but not necessarily in price—than if the separate companies were fully independent. The several areas of comparison and competition are within districts, within state or regional limits, and among different companies.

Comparisons are more detailed in some kinds of work than in others because of the nature of the activity. In a continent-wide system, moreover, there is always someone who is out in front, and this also creates competition. Men with good records are usually willing to share their information with officials of competing companies, if only because they know it will eventually become the possession of 195 Broadway anyway.

For a number of reasons, knowledge and know-how are disseminated more quickly in the Bell System than in most other companies. For one thing, telephone officials travel a great deal to observe at first hand. Wide use also is made of national, regional, functional, and local conferences where men learn by a direct exchange of information. Frequent tours of duty help to spread information between levels and among companies. And finally, the corporation has always tried to locate its vice-presidents and coordinating officials on the same floor of the same building in order that they may confer as often as they need to.

Competition extends even to engineering in the Bell System, a crucial area where new technologies and commercial innovations are made. The four centers where engineering functions are located are the associated companies, Western Electric, Bell Laboratories, and 195 Broadway, and among these "there is a good deal of rivalry."[23]

THE STAFF FUNCTION

It seems unlikely that the decentralization policy of A.T. & T. would work so well were it not accompanied by a skilled staff activity and its careful coordination with line operations as carried out by the associated companies. Indeed, its staff work, its decentralization policy, and its careful selection of executives constitute what most outside observers consider the three most prominent features of the corporation's management.

There are two ways of operating a big business, said a management expert in U.S. Steel. One is the outright holding-company device where men are hired and fired according to their success in operating the business. The second is the A.T. & T. method of building up a staff at headquarters, integrating it with the field units, and then maintaining a reciprocal flow of personnel. This, thought my informant, is the better method, but it requires staff men with certain human traits, and the main question is temperament. Such men are born with an ability to get their satisfactions in seeing results achieved by others. Skilled staff men should be paid as much as skilled line officials—and in A.T. & T. they are. The company also studies promotions to both line and staff positions "for years in advance," which is another clue to the success of its decentralization policy.[24]

It is in connection with its staff activities that A.T. & T. stresses its policy of tours of duty. During their formative period, men who show promise are sent to 195 Broadway and then after three or four years they go back to a line position in the field. At a certain point it may be discovered that a particular individual has an outstanding talent as a central-office staff man; he has the necessary characteristics of temperament plus a certain wisdom and levelheadedness, a philosophical cast of mind and a native diplomacy, that "go down well" with the field. Such a man may be kept in a top staff position for the rest of his official career. But if a staff man shows any inclination to become stale or to act remote, these being signs of boredom and bureaucracy, he is quickly transferred back to the field because action at that level keeps a man alert and discourages complacency and inertia.

An effective method of maintaining vitality is to provide powerful inducements for gifted people. A.T. & T. does this for its staff men by offering salaries comparable to those of operating officials. A man receiving $200,000 a year, for example—a figure attained to only by the president in the past—will receive a pension of $90,000 a year after forty-five years of service, and $40,000 after twenty years of service. A man whose salary at retirement is $50,000 will draw $22,500 a year if he has worked for forty-five years, and $10,000 a year if he has worked for twenty years. In 1958 a man who had been retired for several years was receiving $25,000 a year as a consultant to the company, and $11,600 as a director and member of the executive committee, in addition to his pension. The immediate past president was receiving a pension of $70,234 a year. All of which shows that A.T. & T. places a proper value on the services of its central staff men.[25]

EVALUATION

Considering the size, the variety, and the nature of its business, A.T. & T. has made a success of its decentralization policy. The relationship between headquarters and the operating companies is an unusually cordial one. In most corporations there is a constant struggle between the need of a division in the field to conform to general policies enforced from the center, and the universal human tendency of such units is to seek independence. There follows a pulling and hauling between headquarters and the periphery, between the poles of centralization and decentralization. A local manager will resent what he regards as interference from the main office and will try to get as far away from it as possible. And when in the view of headquarters this has gone intolerably far, he will be pulled back into the fold and "reorganized," only to renew his determination to escape. A top executive who recognizes this phenomenon will know how to drive with a light rein, for nothing destroys cooperation more quickly than a rigid and uncompromising attitude. It is this light rein that A.T. & T. seems to have achieved. To illustrate, a former president of Ohio Bell once told how he was considering some important organizational changes and consulted several vice-presidents at 195 Broadway. Some of these officers were opposed to his scheme, so he asked Walter Gifford, the then president, what he should do. "You think it's a good idea, don't you?" asked Gifford. "Then why don't you do it?"[26] It is significant, of course, that the Ohio man consulted at all; but this will not surprise experienced executives who know that a wise man will always consult and that there is a difference between consulting and a feeling that someone else is making up your mind for you.

In order to check the findings presented here, at the time we made this study my assistants and I consulted the regulatory authorities in Washington and in Illinois to learn their impressions of A.T. & T. management. The head of the company's legal department had already explained that legal matters were highly centralized at 195 Broadway because it had to take a unified position before the courts; the companies would suffer if they took inconsistent positions; and a precedent is sometimes more important than the amount of money involved in a particular case.

The result is that 195 Broadway is the intelligence center for all legislation introduced in the several state legislatures and in Congress that is likely to affect the Bell System. In addition, the parent company keeps informed concerning local cases, all briefs are submitted in advance, and in important cases A.T. & T. either provides high-paid legal talent or local attorneys go to 195 Broadway for consultation.[27] Also, some local and regional attorneys are kept on retainers, which is good politics, especially if the man happens to be a former judge. However, I have never heard any suggestion of unethical practices on the part of A.T. & T., such as trying to influence legislators by undue means, because as Arthur Page once said, "If you set out to bribe a legislator you wind up in most cases by being blackmailed."

The only strongly adverse statement we heard from a regulatory official was that the Bell System was so big that it cannot be effectively regulated either by the FCC or by the state regulatory commissions; that it is virtually impossible to determine what the service to a subscriber is worth; and that under the guise of decentralizing, the system confuses state regulatory bodies to the point where it is impossible to discover which costs are joint and which are separable. With its vast power, furthermore, A.T. & T. adopts a policy of prolonged litigation which drains the finances of the state commissions. In one case (the Lindheimer case in Illinois, which went to the United States

Supreme Court), litigation dragged out for over a decade.[28] It is only fair to point out, however, that this criticism applies primarily to the *power* of the corporation and only incidentally to the efficiency with which it decentralizes for administrative purposes.

From the member of the Federal Communications Commission who conducted the telephone investigation of the 1930's came this comment on A.T. & T.'s administrative federalism:[29]

> The choice of presidents of the operating companies seems to be under the complete control of the president of the parent company. Correspondence examined by the FCC showed that an outgoing local president seemed to have little to do with the selection of his successor.
>
> The legal department at 195 Broadway exercises a close control over the field in all matters of legislation and adjudication (as already noted). But wherever possible, the local telephone representative always fronts for the company.
>
> A vital interest of A.T. & T. is that only Western Electric Company equipment may be connected with a local Bell System, and even a minor court case that threatened this subsidiary would result in intervention by A.T. & T. The fact that Western Electric is free from government regulation is considered another vital interest.
>
> A.T. & T. exerts control "whenever a vital Bell interest is threatened." As already noted, a precedent may be more important than the amount of money involved. Since an idea detrimental to Bell interests may spread rapidly, it must be headed off at the start.
>
> Control is exercised from 195 Broadway, not in a directly disciplinary fashion, but by indirection. Acquiescence to Bell's wishes "is just drilled into employees until it becomes a part of their subconscious." Whenever a question arises that might jeopardize a "vital interest," a Bell System executive automatically considers only one side: "He doesn't think of crossing Bell policy." The hope for continued service and advancement "lies in conformity." It is possible that executives in the Southwestern Bell company demand and receive more independence than those in other companies because that unit was the last to be formed and therefore has many holdovers from the former independent regime.
>
> Finally—and in many ways this was the most important revelation—the nature of the dominance by 195 Broadway is such that if a regula-

tory commission could control that office, it would control the Bell System.

Here again, of course, testimony is more on the adequacy of administrative regulation than on the extent to which the company policy of decentralization has succeeded. Nevertheless, these remarks offered interesting offsets to any one-sidedness that might have been acquired as a result of talking with so many engaging telephone company officials.

On balance, it seems likely that an evaluation by a vice-president of Illinois Bell is sufficiently accurate. "Each company," he said, "is permitted to run largely as an independent business and to make its own decisions. The suggestions from headquarters greatly influence those decisions. If, however, a company decides to shift its organization around, to create a new department, or to merge others, it is at liberty to do so. It does not need to follow the suggestions of A.T. & T. unless it wants to. But for reasons of system cooperation, it usually winds up doing so."[30]

The cohesive factor in the whole Bell System appears to be more a matter of common targets and principles of management than a fear of exerting one's independence. And this seems to come about as close as possible to combining the desirable elements of bureaucracy with factors of enterprise in large corporations.[31] A.T. & T. tries to guard against centralization and abuse of power by having clear objectives, clear policies, and a clear philosophy of administration; by assuring a constant supply of leadership at the top through promotions from within; and by decentralizing almost every aspect of operations, maintaining an effective central staff activity, and then articulating the two in a unified operation. "Why does Bell organization look so similar everywhere I go?" I asked on one occasion. "Because," came the reply, "men are transferred around so widely that we tend toward common ideas as we broaden our experience."

Chapter 14 Responsibility and Response

Few relationships in large-scale administration cause more uncertainty than the seeming polarity between responsibility and response, and yet the fact is that they have more in common than they have of difference. Both are an attempt to satisfy some interest outside of the agent; both are a principal-agent relationship, and in a democracy the principal is always the public.

A bureaucrat is cautious on the subject of responsibility. He will not act without proper authority, and in this sense he is responsible. But by the same token he is reluctant to step outside of his terms of reference and assume additional responsibility because it disturbs his routine, or it may be something new and he distrusts the consequences of innovation.

These limitations on the initiative of the bureaucrat limit his ability to respond when response is necessary. And in administration, the ability to respond is needed all the time: consumer preferences, the social environment, the impact of public policy, internal crises, the occasional need to reorganize, all demand an alert eye and a ready response. The problem, therefore, is how to maintain a sense of responsibility and at the same time encourage responsiveness, on which the resiliency of the program depends.

In administration, responsibility may be narrow in its stress on strict accountability, in which case it reinforces the bureaucratic excesses of impersonality and red tape. Or responsibility may be broadly considered and emphasize social accomplishment, in which case it contributes to the enterprise factors of discretion, initiative, and the like. Dictionary definitions tend to support this interpretation: responsibility may be defined as either strict accountability involving guidance, or as self-reliance and "doing it on one's own." In other words, the term responsibility has the connotations of both bureaucracy and enterprise, and the administrator who understands this may guide the concept in either direction at will.

Indeed, if the possible connotations of responsibility are traced out far enough, they will be found to include many factors associated with progressive, vital administration: the use of incentives and delegations and the encouragement of self-responsibility and self-growth. The real question therefore, as Toynbee and others keep insisting, is whether responsibility becomes a personal trait voluntarily exercised or is an impersonal duty enforced from the outside. In the first case, enterprise thrives, but if responsibility must be enforced from the outside, then bureaucratic pathologies are generated.

The concept of response likewise may be regarded from different angles. If it is narrowly defined, response will turn inward to center on the we-group, in which case it encourages bureaucratic self-centeredness. Or it may turn outward and stress consumer orientation, in which event it will center on those who are the patrons of the program and it will encourage enterprise and vitality.

And again, like responsibility, the connotations of response also may be personal or impersonal. A response that is personal will show sensitivity and sympathy, but response that is impersonal will be merely an answer, as in a lawyer's brief, and there will be no attempt to exceed the terms of reference. A third connotation, however, is response that is "an accord," which is a combination of answer plus sensitivity, which in administration encourages the vitality factor of consumer orientation.

These dictionary definitions confirm what administrators usually learn the hard way: responsibility and response may be either legalistic and burdensome or personalized and energizing. In the world of practical affairs a combination of both is invariably required and the test of management is the extent to which it is able to effect a blend compounded of accountability and discretion, fixed standards and individual initiative, elements of trusteeship and elements of managerial freedom. If either set of opposites is allowed to dominate, the extremes of bureaucracy or the extremes of enterprise will throw the program off balance.

RESPONSIBILITY AND PUBLIC POLICY

"The Big Cannot Be Free," said David Cushman Coyle, and so they cannot, because size means power and power must be controlled against the possibility of abuse.[1] External controls on the power of management are funneled through government by interest groups expressing the wishes of various segments of the public. In a situation in which size and power are increasing, there are three main alternatives of public policy, depending on which interest groups win out before the legislature and before the executive branch.

The first alternative is a hands-off policy on the assumption that the problem will correct itself when human nature has "matured." But meanwhile the abuses of power mature along with human nature—if it does—and in the end the sanctions that must be applied are usually more drastic and more limiting on the freedom of endeavor than would have been the case had action been taken earlier.

The second alternative is for government to set up a regulatory body—such as the Federal Communications Commission or a state labor relations board—to force management to live up to its trusteeship obligations. But although this is sometimes a necessary device, the effect is to bring the impact of two parallel groups of managers, one private and one public, to bear on the conduct of a single institution, thus weakening unified administration and checking enterprise.

The third alternative is to nationalize a large undertaking and try to protect its necessary managerial freedoms under a unified administration responsible to government. Leaving aside the important question of what happens to private enterprise generally under this policy and concentrating on the managerial aspect of it, the fact is that under nationalization, managerial freedoms are often more theoretical than real because of constitutional obstacles that seemingly cannot be avoided.

At this point it may be objected that if the government does not own it cannot effectively control, and that if it does not control it cannot maintain the necessary equilibriums in economic affairs. But this conclusion does not necessarily follow. If private management is responsible, self-disciplined, and statesmanlike, then government has no reason to interfere with its administration and public officials are free to give more attention to economic planning and policy than would be possible if they were also burdened with administrative responsibilities for major business functions. This position on public policy is the liberal one and seems most likely to achieve the objective of power widely distributed, plus energy and self-determination throughout the economic fabric.

There are two major conditions, however. Such a division of responsibility depends, first, on a sufficient number of administrators who cherish their freedom and are prepared to assume the statesmanlike role that freedom requires. Second, it depends on a sufficient number of energetic leaders in government who recognize the pitfalls of bureaucracy and eschew the temptation to extend their own power at the expense of a devitalized economy. Thus institutional managers and government officials alike must subscribe to the philosophy of freedom and trusteeship upon which the success of the free managerial system depends.

A basic principle of public policy, therefore, should be to prevent concentrations of power in the first place. If administrators lack the statesmanlike qualities that are needed in the control of size and power, then government must take some kind of action. Unfortunately, almost any action that government takes to restrict the abuse of power also restricts the freedom of management to experiment and to apply the principle of self-determination. In the last analysis, therefore, the extent to which controls are necessary depends on the number of what may be called public persons resulting from all the cultural and social influences of a given time and place. The qualities needed include public spirit, operational morality, and intelligent self-discipline.

The main obstacle to this solution is the fact that many big semipublic corporations are directed by men who labor under the mistaken impression that they can claim the best of the two worlds of capitalism and socialism and not pay the price in a large measure of public control. Businessmen who shortsightedly subscribe to the philosophy of "I will get mine while the getting is good" will have no fair complaint if socialism and bureaucracy become everywhere prevalent, for it is the businessman's initial lead in the card game that determines future moves in public policy.

From the standpoint of the citizen, accountability is apt to be measured by the number and severity of external controls imposed on management, and politicians also fall into this habit of thought. But the administrator, who must, by the very nature of his position, exercise power, is inclined to think that he never has enough of it, so difficult are his responsibilities. He knows from experience that every increase in external controls feeds the bureaucratic excesses of rigidity in his institution, limits its ability to respond to the consumer and to change, impairs its efficiency, and weakens unified management, which is probably the most serious fault of all.

The voter and the politician say, "Pass a law"; but the administrator says, "Don't pass it if it can be avoided because every law sets up scores of new rules and regulations that drain the vitality out of administration." Indeed, the seeming conservatism of many businessmen is more often due less to a reluctance to accept something new than to a realization of how injurious external controls can be to unified and enterprising administration.

The outstanding characteristic of administration is the interrelatedness of its parts and the need to coordinate and to unify them in order to achieve objectives as efficiently as possible. So whenever a second group of men is set up to do a part of the job, unity becomes impossible or at least exceedingly difficult. A commission, for example, is created to regulate public utilities and is empowered to issue orders on managerial questions such as accounting, depreciation, and auditing systems; allowable profits and rates of return on investment; salary limitations for top officials; allowable charges for holding companies and service groups; standards of service to the consumer; standards to be followed in labor relations; the establishment of safety regulations; and many other matters depending on the type of utility that is involved. How can the administrators of the utility thereafter take a personal interest in enforcement? For the most part, they are concerned with ways of neutralizing the effect of outside control, if not, in fact, circumventing it.

It is not suggested that public control can be dispensed with if the public interest is to be protected, but there is a way of mitigating the effects of dual management that has been explored in England and to some extent in the United States, with some favorable results. It is sometimes called the public-policy as contrasted with the administrative-regulation approach to the control of power. The principle is that wherever possible, a law chartering a corporation, a trade union, or some other governing group should contain socially desirable standards and restrictions so that control is internalized in the body of the law instead of being externalized through a separate regulatory commission. The result is self-regulation as a partial substitute, at least, for public regulation.[2]

There are many kinds of standards that might be defined in this way. If the projected undertaking is a monopoly, for example, its profits should be limited. If it is to have a sense of public duty, directors should be chosen for their demonstrated attachment to the public interest as well as for their skill in practical matters. If a government enterprise is to operate as a business, it should bear all costs customarily borne by competitive enterprises in the same field. If it is to have financial freedom as well as internal operating freedom (and it is not likely to have the one without the other), it must be allowed to raise its own funds in the capital market. If it is to enjoy the needed managerial freedoms, it must be empowered to pay executive salaries comparable with the best in private industry, to determine differentials in salary scales, to hire and fire without reference to a civil service system, to promote promising men quickly so as to catch them in their prime, to adopt incentives that have proved useful in the private economy. It must also be free to purchase in the open market and to expand or to contract its operations in harmony with the usual economic barometers. In short, in its internal operations, a public enterprise should be modeled as closely as possible after the most progressive and unified private enterprise and merely have its monopoly powers limited by statute.[3]

If this part of the analysis seems to have stressed regulated and nationalized industries more than private ones, it is only because the problem of drawing a realistic line between public accountability and needed internal operating freedoms has become more acute there than anywhere else. But in a different order of magnitude the same problem also confronts major institutions in the private sector of the economy, and hence it is useful to think in terms of first principles which at the appropriate time and place may be applied to both categories of enterprise.

If past experience is any guide, it may be expected that as power and economic concentration increase in the private area, the demand for administrative regulation also will grow. Top management, especially in the United States, appears to discount this fact, for it continues to regard with complacency the uninterrupted trend toward oligopoly and restricted competition that characterizes our industrial empires. If either socialization, with its attending insistence on centralized responsibility, or administrative regulation, with its pattern of dual responsibility, is to be avoided, the remedy would seem to consist in one of two courses: either the trend toward monopoly must be deliberately and voluntarily reversed or public policy should include more effective preventive measures such as limitations on the size of corporations and guarantees to protect the public interest written into charters in the manner outlined above.

A vote for external controls is a vote for bureaucracy and a vote for internal controls is a vote for enterprising administration. How the public casts its ballot is largely determined by how well management reacts to its public responsibilities. If administrators neglect the public or try to deceive it, they will have their hands tied by regulation; but if they are as thoughtful of the public interest as the most trusted statesman, they may retain their managerial freedoms. What has so often been called creeping bureaucracy is less the familiar stereotype of officials conspiring against the public than it is the public tying the hands of officials to the point where they are no longer free to respond to the needs of the public.

The larger the administrator's program, and irrespective of whether it is labeled private or public, the greater is his role as broker serving many interests. One of these is the bureaucracy itself. Others are particular individuals, the informal social group, professional groups, pressure groups, stockholders, labor unions, his own industry, and government at all levels. But most of all the administrator is broker to the consumer, the men and women who buy his goods and services, for on their good will depend the program's vitality and survival. The administrator who would respond to that interest must also be responsible or he will wind up unable to do either. In other words, it is only by combining responsibility and responsiveness that he can count on the full benefits of both. Without responsibility he will be stripped of his freedom, and without freedom he cannot respond. It is as simple as that.

EXCESSIVE LEGALISM

A sense of responsibility may sometimes be carried too far. Thus, an excessive respect for authority ties the organization up in a straitjacket that confines response within very narrow limits. An administrator with a rigid respect for authority never takes any action unless everything in the way of instructions and legislation is spelled out to the last detail, so that even punctuation becomes important. An enterprising administrator, on the other hand, stresses action and looks to rules and regulations as little as he can.

More than this, however, legalism may become a national trait, a distinctive habit of mind, so that its influence covers all kinds of undertakings. Tied up in red tape, the administrator dare not venture without the full support of authority on every point. He would not think of acting on an informal delegation of authority or on his own initiative because conventional rules forbid it; hence all initiative must come from the apex of the hierarchy. Consequently, top officials wind up doing most of the work and their subordinates are underemployed. In time, this limit on their freedom corrodes men's souls and makes them unresponsive even in emergencies.

This problem of legalism is an acute one, unfortunately, in many underdeveloped nations, and since something like two-thirds of mankind now live in such nations, the matter has a wide practical importance. But legalism is also a prominent characteristic of developed bureaucracies such as Max Weber recommended, stemming as it often does from an overemphasis on system by work planners with a passion for detail. Nations in which legalism is emphasized are apt to be the most bureaucratic, and those in which more discretion is allowed are the ones most able to respond quickly and to energize their people in time of economic or political emergency.

The French bureaucracy is traditionally legalistic and stresses *paperasserie*, but, as already noted, its business and public leaders have been able to escape many of the debilitating consequences of legalism by the use of a considerable degree of shrewdness and flexibility outside of but parallel to the theoretical legal system.

The German bureaucracy stresses pronounced hierarchy and neatness of organization more than it does legalism, but the effect is much the same. The Prussian tradition is bureaucratic, as Max Weber well appreciated. It is efficient in the sense that a machine is efficient. It is weak in its failure to recognize the necessity for delegation, discretion, and initiative. The German bureaucracy is superb at planning, but finds it hard to improvise and to respond quickly to change.

The British bureaucracy is different from both the French and the German variety. The British have a congenital suspicion of logical precision, perfection of organization, blind adherence to principle, and regimentation at all levels of work. The British administrator prefers to trust to mutual agreements and a sense of what is proper and in keeping with commonly held values. Both in government and in private enterprise, managers are encouraged to think for themselves and to develop initiative. To the outsider, and especially to French and German bureaucrats, this attitude looks suspiciously like anti-intellectualism because it seems to lack tidiness and logic. But in this the critics are wrong. The British system is intellectual in that it requires people to think for themselves about problems and their solution and not to depend exclusively on what the rule book says on every small point.

The American bureaucracy lies somewhere between the German and the British. The United States is the home of scientific management, but equally the home of the human relations approach and of rugged individualism, and hence its bureaucracy is both legalistic and individualistic. The differences are based more on history and culture than they are on nationality. There is an inclination to trust informal traditions and the individual, and emphasis is often on individual thinking, which is the enterprise approach. Nevertheless, the mental cast called legalism is not absent, nor are the characteristics of bureaucracy that accompany it.

The solution to the problem of legalism is a philosophy of administration that recognizes the importance of decentralization, delegation, and administration by objectives and the solving of individual problems.

Legalistic administration is not the same thing as respect for law, which is a wholly legitimate attitude. The approach recommended here does not minimize the importance of law as a protection of civil liberties and human rights. Indeed, the record of both Britain and America in this respect underscores the importance of this kind of law in administration, for Britain is the home of "the rule of law" and the United States is the home of its equivalent, "due process of law." It is only the operational phases of law in administration and the stifling of initiative and response among administrators at all levels that must be combated. As a general thing, lawyers *qua* lawyers are rarely able administrators, while administrators show no disrespect for law when they use methods that are more respectful of the intent of the law than of its letter. The plain truth seems to be that an excess of legalistic caution makes enterprising administration almost impossible. Hence, while the best in law and in administration must be protected, the requirements of both must be reconciled one to the other in the interests of vital administration.

LEGALISM AND "MANUALITIS"

One of the worst aspects of legalism is a "disease" that exasperated administrators call manualitis. All large organizations must have a body of rules and regulations which are often codified and filed in loose-leaf volumes, and few aspects of bureaucracy offer more difficulties to the enterprising administrator.

I once asked the head of a division of a large organization whether they had an administrative manual and he replied, "Yes, a steel cabinet full." And this was literally true; there were no less than forty-five series of manuals on different subjects, circulated to various levels of organization, all loose-leaf, all with neatly coded numbers, all locked away in the files seemingly so that no one could see how bureaucratic the organization had become. I asked if these were operating manuals. "No," was the reply, "we are a specialist staff agency; the operating divisions have their own manuals." When I asked how the two series were coordinated, he said that the only way people learned what was in each other's manuals was when they met in conference; there was no central clearance or attempt to integrate the work of the two parts of the same organization.

Generally speaking, a manual includes three kinds of material: instructions (sometimes called directives), descriptions of procedure, and information and background material. The usual arrangement is by function or topic and some subjects are gone into in great detail. A specialized manual on office management, for example, will tell the employee what to do after opening a letter, how to keep cupboards tidy, and other procedures that any proper course in home economics would teach.

As a rule also, each division of the organization is authorized to issue its own instructions, subject to review by the head of the division, which is one reason the number of publications and their size become so great. A division may have a special official in charge of this work, a man as eager as the next fellow to keep his job and expand his work, so that the appetite for written rules and regulations becomes insatiable.

Abundance is the real source of the trouble. It becomes impossible to tell where the writing of letters to oneself should stop. Anyone who can think of something that has not been written on in the past becomes a local hero for his discovery. Eventually nothing is overlooked.

Moreover, since different manuals go to different people, again the demand is increased and so is the intriguing variety of the job. In one organization I put the question, "If one manual deals with the specialist activity and the other with operations, and both relate to the same product, what is the local manager supposed to do?" I got a look which made me realize that I was being naïve. I thought the reply was going to be, "Why he reads both, of course," But no, it was, "He reads neither. His assistants read them and when he wants to know anything he asks them."

So then I asked, "If your organization has several linear feet of manuals in a single cabinet, how do you keep employees from throwing the book at customers and how do you encourage employees to think for themselves?" Again I caught a disapproving look. I thought the reply would be, "Oh, in time, the operating man gets so he can carry around in his head anything he really needs to know." But it was this: "The way we keep overdetailed rules from having harmful effects is to balance them through our personnel policies. We choose men who don't pay any attention to rules but who go ahead and get things done."

This seemed like a good idea, so I asked, innocently, "Then why have the manuals at all?" To which the answer was that, first, we have always had them; secondly, it makes the field consult the headquarters more often than it otherwise would ("which it would not do at all if it could get away with it"); thirdly, people at headquarters like the feeling of security that comes from knowing what the rule is on every possible subject; and finally, "I guess we ought to review them and simplify them more than we do, and we talk about it periodically, but somehow we never seem to get around to it." Besides, "Since the system is loose-leaf, we can always change the rules and procedures if we want to." And when I asked why they didn't coordinate instructions with those of related divisions as a means of simplifying them, the reply was that "Everyone is jealous of his own jurisdiction. No one objects to talking about cooperation, but when it comes to giving someone else control over your own instructions and procedures, that's a different matter."

In one organization they not only have a separate division to operate the expensive punchcard machines that process and code instructions, but they even have a separate editorial section to see that when communications go out to the field they make use of the King's English.

When I express surprise that written instructions have become so profuse, a number of defenses are suggested:

We have lots of coordinating conferences, and these counteract the red tape. Our functional people meet every two months, our interdivisional heads four times a year; we are constantly having conferences.

As long as operating people don't take instructions too seriously, where is the harm in a manual? But a few minutes later one will be given a picture of a field employee on a lonely road in the dead of winter with his manual open at page 217 and reading it word for word. We appoint independent people and if they pay any attention to the manual at all, it is by getting someone else to read it for them.

These may be the means of mitigating the effects of manualitis, but they do not offer a cure. Here are some suggestions. First, most top managers today are too far removed from operations to know for sure how much red tape there is locked up in the filing cabinets of their organization. *Such men delegate but they do not supervise.* Too few of them are able, like Sir Simon Marks of Marks and Spencer,[4] to discover excessive red tape by prowling around the sales floors where such excesses show up. Hence, a greater degree of deliberate supervision by the top executive would help to keep red tape under control.

Secondly, if instruction books are to be maintained there must be a conscious attempt to keep them short. The temptation to write "diaries" should be resisted and the maintenance of the manual should be located in one place where different aspects of different subjects can be brought together and coordinated with the flow of operations.

And finally, top management should make it a sworn obligation to review administrative manuals and red tape at least every five years. If the organization and methods unit is the culprit, abolish the unit; or if such a unit is lacking but might be useful in bringing about work simplification, then create one. Rather than undertake a review of this kind, some executives prefer to believe that no amount of red tape can do any real harm unless it is taken seriously. But the fact is that people who play such games with themselves are candidates for the institutional psychiatrist.

PSYCHOLOGICAL OBSTACLES TO RESPONSE

Some of the greatest obstacles to responsiveness in internal administration are psychological in origin and seemingly are to be expected when many people work together in a large organization. Under such conditions, people have understandable reasons for wanting to be cloistered. They do not like to be poked at and the way to avoid this reaction is to substitute administration by objectives for regimentation by detailed order. Secondly, employees often feel lost in the huge sea of institutional impersonality and look for a cove where they can enjoy privacy; this desire is taken care of by encouraging the social and informal groupings that exist alongside the formal structure in all large organizations. And finally, as already noted, people positively like a maze of rules and regulations that are unintelligible to the outsider because it gives them a special feeling of superiority and importance. This last propensity is a most difficult one to handle and the most successful attack is probably to offer positive incentives and satisfactions that make achievement visible and rewarding. People respond and act responsibly when their surroundings are healthy and normal; they act neurotically in both of these respects when their surroundings are dull and frustrating.

Another psychological factor in the behavior of the in-group in administration is the cynicism with which the objectives of the program come to be regarded. An experienced bureaucrat becomes a past master at saying one thing and doing another. He knows when he is pulling the wool over the eyes of a colleague or a superior, but he does not think of his behavior as being morally wrong because to him it is all a game and he plays to win. And the more bored he is, the more play-acting he does, the emphasis invariably being on how to get the better of someone, especially the boss or the policy group (the legislature or the board of directors). When this happens, the administrator must look for the sources of boredom and then try to substitute a positive game for a negative one.

This cynical role playing which is the cause of so much wasted energy is reflected in the definitions that a newspaperman found circulating in the bureaucracy in Washington.[5] Bureaucrats develop dynamic vocabularies to cover up their cynical behaviors, and the following are examples:

Implement—v. (bureaucratese), what you do to carry out a decision, policy, or program when you are doing nothing.

Finalize—v. (bureaucratese), signifying formal adoption of decision, policy, or program with tacit agreement that it will be given a quiet burial, or "implemented."

Team—n., a mutual protection society formed to guarantee that no one person can be held to blame for a botched committee job that one man could have performed satisfactorily.

But anyone who has worked in Washington or in any other large bureaucracy knows that cynicism alone is too harsh a judgment. These coinages are also the working of a bureaucratic sense of humor, which is frequently delicious and without which people would take themselves more seriously than they are normally inclined to do, even in a bureaucracy.

In the last analysis, there does not seem to be any substitute for compelling goals if people are to be motivated to respond and to act responsibly. But since many of the larger goals of mankind, such as the good life, respect for the truth, and the possibilities of social and individual improvement, are often vague and poorly expressed and appreciated, we waste our affections on lesser goals: the idea of the "impersonal" civil service, for example, which insulates bureaucracy instead of inspiring it;[6] the idea that there is something called administration *per se* instead of what administration sets out to accomplish; and the belief that bureaucrats are so professionalized that theirs is neither to reason why nor to question the end of policy, but only to obey orders. Only when bureaucrats are encouraged and allowed to think for themselves about policy and its implications will they stop playing stultifying games and act responsibly and responsively.

COMBATING SELF-CENTEREDNESS

If outside controls and excessive legalism are limitations on the responsiveness of institutions, so also is the self-centeredness that flourishes among the in-groups in large-scale organization. To combat this tendency the administrator must divert the attention of the group from itself to the larger objectives of his program; he must try to make the group increasingly self-critical, and so self-assured that instead of avoiding responsibility there will be an attitude that invites it. If the administrator succeeds in these efforts, he may be able to substitute self-discipline for the mass of detailed regulations that add to red tape, delay, and rigidity in the face of new situations.

In his attack on bureaucratic self-centeredness, the administrator must first answer the tacit question of every employee: "What do opportunity and responsibility mean to me, in my job?" because this query is the center of the employee's world. The administrator must then supply the answers to a number of other relationship questions: How de we serve the consumer, the long-term interests of the program and its personnel, the efficiency and motivation of the organization, and the individual's sense of competition and self-development? But whatever the answers may be, they must be oriented around the individual employee and his own concern with, "What does this mean to me?"

Self-centeredness cannot be denied, but its horizons can be extended and the responsiveness of employees stimulated. This is done by defining and redefining objectives, by establishing policies to take the place of rules, by developing initiative through delegations of responsibility, by a philosophy of administration by objectives.

Next, the administrator must provide definite aims for his employees by setting up clear standards of performance. As shown in the study of A.T. & T.,[7] such standards are not only the instruments for measuring the success of particular units and operations in the program; they also supply the immediate incentive that wipes out the blights of bureaucracy, boredom, and indifference. In setting standards of performance, the bogey must be determined not by the yardstick of past performance but by an estimate of what each unit *should* be able to achieve. Account must be taken of physical conditions, which are sometimes hard to alter; and where there are any organizational or administrative weaknesses that hold back performance, these must be put right.

To supply incentives is not the only advantage of standards

of performance, of course. Another is to give employees a sense of costs, because such standards are directly or indirectly based on cost-analysis data. When everyone concerned with production is provided with a set of standards to guide him in his work and to help him in judging performance, he will take a personal interest in costs and may be motivated to keep them to a minimum. Hence cost-analysis factors must be made as clear-cut as possible and widely published within the organization. In addition, standards of performance are also the means by which top management keeps control of the situation, checking progress according to a predetermined schedule and spotting lags where they occur. The work is better done if the units are organized alike and use similar administrative techniques.[8]

In applying standards of performance, however, it must not be forgotten that uniformity is never an end in itself, but only a tool for determining what causes and justifies variations from the highest standard that can be set at any time. When uniformity becomes a fetish it reinforces the excesses of bureaucracy instead of mitigating them.

The horizon of the in-group can also be broadened by an intelligent public relations program aimed at making employees well informed and motivated; by appointing outsiders to the board of directors for the fresh viewpoints they offer; by a judicious use of advisory committees for the same purpose; by occasionally bringing new blood into executive positions; by tours of duty from headquarters to the field and back again; and by selecting and promoting people on the basis of their ability to adjust and to handle other social skills.

In the administrator's attack on the self-centeredness of bureaucracy, he will find that the more clearly goals, policies, individual responsibilities, standards of performance, and cost analyses are established in advance and widely understood, the less is the need for detailed instructions and peremptory orders. But he will also find that where an undue stress on order is a limitation on freedom, a certain amount of order is essential to freedom, to the exercise of discretion and initiative, and to the over-all consumer orientation that a vital institution must have. Most administration can stand the application of a good deal of system without becoming objectionably rigid, so long as organizational and financial tidiness are handled with energy and changed when need be.

In the attempt to turn the in-group from self-centeredness to responsiveness, the stakes are higher than might be supposed. If the condition of the group is allowed to follow its normal path, then stratification and segmentation will prove a severe hazard to the vitality of the program. A unified institution is responsive and responsible, but a stratified institution, being atomized, is neither. When people refer to "the huge, sprawling bureaucracy," they seldom realize that what they are thinking of is not its numbers and cost so much as the diffused and segmented aspects of its nature.

RESPONSE TO CHANGE

An attitude of responsibility to the public and response to the consumer must be accompanied by an ability to respond to change in the environment and to the need for change in the institution itself. More or less severe alterations in the organizational structure of the program may be indicated. But the more the excesses of bureaucracy become established, the harder it is to effect significant change and hence the more useful it is to understand what methods are likely to succeed.

A first step is to recognize the limits of what has been called the principle of functionalization. The orthodox view of this principle, as stated by Webster Robinson, is that all the proper functions of a business must be recognized, granted existence, combined where similar or complementary, and placed under the direction, supervision, and control of properly qualified executives who have only one, or at most only a few, similar functions under their command.[9] This principle is a sacred canon of bureaucracy and especially of a civil service system.

The opposing view, modified by a respect for the human element in administration, denies the possibility of arranging the lines of organization so that functions and divisions exactly coincide.[10] The reason is that every function is related to every other one, and hence efficiency and morale depend on the degree to which teamwork is facilitated and segmentation avoided, on a knowledge of what everyone else is doing, and avoiding work in blind isolation.

To change the patterns of organization is usually much easier, however, than to try to change long-established habits of behavior, which is the aspect of change that is most vital to responsiveness. The chief obstacles are the inertia that characterizes institutions even more than it does individuals and which increases with every addition to the size of the program. Some of the factors that operate here are, first, every organization has its own distinctive characteristics growing out of its history and its traditions; secondly, the imposition of a change that is premature or that is not really necessary will cause confusion and bitterness; and thirdly, change or the threat of change arouses in most people feelings of resentment and anxiety that cause them to indulge in excessive conformity, on the one hand, or heel-dragging, undeclared warfare, and lack of cooperation in many forms and guises, on the other.

Indeed, in many ways this type of institutional (bureaucratic) resistance to a proposed change is the hardest problem the administrator has to cope with simply because it is so elusive and takes so many forms. Bureaucrats rarely defy superior authority openly, nor will they often show their personal dislikes directly. But covert, indirect, subtle defiance is something else again. It appears, for example, as procrastination. Action is promised but it keeps being postponed and no one person is to blame. Or if the group is widely opposed to some top-management policy, all parts of the connected program save one will perform on time, but the missing one is out of step. Since most administrative programs require the harmonious synchronization of several different units, the failure of one may be fatal and hence this form of resistance is a most effective one. In other cases there is delay but eventual compliance, followed by a general slowing down of work and an atmosphere of icy indifference which the experienced supervisor learns to associate with the preceding "crisis."

These are but samples of the many forms of institutional resistance to change, and most administrators can add almost endlessly to them from their own experience. What is the solution? There is no single answer, but a few rules do indicate the general approach. Thus, when people pout or drag their heels, the administrator must not merely guess about the cause; he must meet the issue head-on by direct questioning. If the response seems unreasonable he should say so, but first he must try to understand it by putting himself in the group's position. If little disturbances tend to accumulate, the administrator must look for deeper and usually unexpressed causes of discontent. If it is clear that he has been at fault, he must not hesitate to admit it, thus insisting on the right of each side to its integrity and to respect from the other. And once the atmosphere is cleared of tension, he must seek positive goals on which both sides can agree and combine, rather than a prolongation of strife that makes mountains out of molehills. But perhaps above all, the administrator must realize that friction is a natural and healthy condition. In a vital organization, argument is a sign that its members are free and uninhibited, instead of pent-up and frustrated, as is so often the fate of the neurotic bureaucrat.

The administrator who would bring about change in his organization must first pick the right time, which is after the need for change has appeared and the reasons for it have been studied. Then he must see that his officials and employees are intellectually and emotionally prepared for the change he contemplates, and he must get those who are later to be affected by it to plan it themselves. No employee can be expected to respond to what he does not understand and his tacit question, "What does this mean to me in my job?" must be satisfactorily answered.

These three basic considerations involving tradition, timing, and people are the framework within which most proposals and strategies will be threshed out one against the other. It will be necessary to avoid stereotypes, to emphasize instead the distinctiveness of the program and to build what is new on its traditions and a respect for its pride. To change the behaviors of people, furthermore, it is necessary to change also their thinking and their attitudes, to anticipate and to seek out anxieties, to talk difficulties out in a kind of mental therapy. It is helpful to analyze new jobs and new responsibilities as clearly as possible so that people will be reassured and not left in the dark. The administrator must give his own time to training employees in the *how* as well as in the *why* of the change. If new skills are needed in the new setup, they must be developed. And finally, there must be a close scrutiny of the whole process to see that there is no missing link in the new arrangement and that all parts of it move together synchronously and in balance.[11]

I once listened for several hours to ten junior executives, drawn from ten different employments, discuss methods of adapting to change and of maintaining vitality. These are the points they apparently thought most significant:

Excessive secrecy has a devitalizing effect on effort and especially on that of senior executives.

A way to break down resistance to change is to show how to do a new thing yourself.

In recruiting for new positions, look for independent men and then set reasonable tasks, gradually increasing the complexity of the job as ability is shown.

Those who react strongest against change at the outset are often the most loyal after it has been made.

The effect of technical change is to question whether the individual's skill is worth as much as it was before.

Change is not the same as vitality; vitality requires a fresh mind, but change is a constant challenge.

Pinpricking lowers morale; sensitivity is highest at the lowest and the highest levels; it is least in the middle ranges.

The way to keep alert is constantly to ask the question, "Where are the trouble spots likely to be?" and then concentrate on these first.

Everyone has a blind spot. Policies are likely to change when a new man is brought in because he sees things that his predecessor had become used to.

But, asked this same group, "Is there any executive mind so fresh that it is not exhausted after nine months on the same problem in the same locale?"

CONCLUDING OBSERVATION

Pathological bureaucracy thrives on diffused authority and lack of self-determination, causing people to become indifferent and cynical. If institutions are to be both responsible and responsive, therefore, certain conditions must be present. The mandate should be clear, limitations on power incorporated into the mandate so far as possible and not enforced separately by a public authority, the organization put under the direction of one man, jobs and responsibilities clearly assigned throughout the institution, standards of performance established as incentives and as the means of internal control, and the main orientation of the program focused on the consumer. Finally, the top management should help to build a series of loyalties that are internally consistent and that center around the employee's insistent question, "What does it mean to me, in my job?"

There is no inherent conflict between the rival claims of responsibility and responsiveness, for each may be used positively or negatively to supplement or to weaken the effect of the other. The key to the reconciliation of the two is to stimulate the response of the program to all parties of interest through unified and motivated administration based on internal controls and self-discipline. And finally, unified administration depends in part on the presence of unified personalities, men and women who can resist the paranoias, the cynicisms, and the play-acting of large-scale organization for the sake of adventure and self-development.

Chapter **15** *Power and Security*

Some bureaucratic institutions are aggressive and seek power for its own sake, but most of them seek power for the sake of the security they believe it assures them. The difficulty is that security lies not in power but in enterprise, the ability of the institution to stay vital and to move forward with self-confidence. This chapter deals with the third of the major characteristics of bureaucracy, the introverted search for power, and suggests the means of releasing and redirecting these wasted energies.

Power is simply the energy to accomplish something. It must therefore be properly released and directed, not too narrowly confined, on the one hand, nor dissipated, on the other. To release energy is to develop the potential of the individual, the firm, even of the economy. But in a bureaucratic organization power is often dammed up or misdirected. Dammed-up power is frustrated energy that ends in indifference or revolt. Misdirected power is energy introverted, wasted on some minor objective and accomplishing less than it should. The result is a kind of narcissism, a pathological form of self-love and self-absorption which puts responsiveness, initiative, adaptation, and enterprise outside the range of possibility.

In institutions as in individuals a certain amount of introspection promotes self-criticism and hence self-improvement.[1] But an institution that is excessively introverted is not likely to be able to adjust to outside circumstances. A state of anxiety, frustration, and failure causes it to build up defense mechanisms against external threat. Psychological tone is weakened, administrative efficiency is lost, energy is wasted in petty aggressions, infighting, evasiveness, oversensitivity, and similar useless activities. All of which is the antithesis of the freely flowing, healthy energy and efficiency that characterize an institution in which the group directs its energies toward goals it has helped to define in the first place and is highly motivated to carry out.[2]

The purpose of releasing power rather than allowing it to become introverted is to develop a kinetic situation in which the relation between the institution and the forces that act on it from the outside is a favorable one, and adjustment is dynamic toward human ends. A condition of happiness is the freedom of the individual to develop his potential ability. The role of leadership is "to help others to do," to assist them to overcome egocentric drives, to work in an "open atmosphere, which is one based upon informal relationships centered in mutual confidence."[3]

OPENING UP CLOISTERED AREAS

Wherever cliques are found, there also will be found cloistering and self-containment. Cliques are useful insofar as they satisfy some of the deepest needs of the individual, such as gregariousness, status, prestige, and security. But carried too far, cliques tend to become exclusive, noncooperative, resistant to change, and unwilling to merge their interests with the larger interests of the organization. The statesmanlike approach to the problem is to recognize the need for cliques and then try to combine them with other elements in administration so as to turn the energy of the group outward, from bureaucracy to enterprise.

It is security or the lack of it that determines the pathological limits to which group introversion is sometimes carried. There are many causes for these organizational tensions and no one has analyzed them better than Alexander Leighton in his book, *The Governing of Men*. Some of the more prominent reasons are the failure of administrators to anticipate new sources of tension in advance; social disorganization within the group; inadequate channels of communication; divided or inadequate leadership; imbalances that result when a belief system is being changed by pressures from the outside; and the conflict between generations, for the new characteristically challenges the old.[4]

Insecurity is often caused by a social lag between challenge and response, says Leighton, and when this imbalance occurs we must expect "exaggerated compliance, apathy, *poorly directed aggression*, suspicions, attacks on scapegoats, and pathological rumors," all being evidences of emotional states and conflicting systems of belief.[5] It is the phrase "poorly directed aggression" that supplies the clue to the cause of irrational behavior in bureaucratic situations: what appears to be a quest for power is in reality an attempt to re-establish a sense of security.

For many people, affiliation with a group is a kind of compensation for the personal ownership of property which was formerly so much more widespread than it is today. Both in Britain and in the United States, for example, a chief anxiety of business leadership is the degree to which workers seem to draw closer to their labor unions and away from managerial leadership. This could be because workmen no longer own the means of their own livelihood, they have only their time to sell, and they dislike being wholly dependent on the power of others. If so, then an appreciation of the difficulty is the starting point of progressive management intent on winning back the loyalty and confidence of its employees. The means must be found of giving people a greater sense of property ownership, skill ownership, personality ownership—in short, their status as free moral agents must somehow be reinforced. Enough has already been done along this line to show that the approach is a useful one; the experience of Marks and Spencer, for example, is instructive.[6]

Three main areas seem to have a special bearing on the problem of bureaucratic cloistering and a compensatory quest for power. These are the insularity of specialized and professionalized skills, the vested interests of labor unions, and the question of institutional size.

SKILL AND PROFESSIONAL EXCLUSIVENESS

Professionalization is a large category under the general rubric of specialization and applies particularly to fields such as law, accounting, engineering, medicine, teaching, and the like. Professionalization is distinguished by its special educational requirements and degrees and its development of codes of ethics and professional conduct. But in addition to the professions, in industry there are also many kinds of specialists concerned in the development of machine technology. At the top, these specializations center in the engineering profession and at the lower levels they fade off to the ability to handle a single small operation as part of a more complicated one.

Every advance in technology increases specialization in industry and administration. And if not accompanied by a corresponding emphasis on synthesis and coordination, specialization tends to make institutions objectionably bureaucratic, self-centered, and resistant to change. A kind of informal stratification sets in until, as James Burnham and Harold Lasswell among others have noted, skill and professional differentiations in a country such as the United States are more influential than class structure.

Even in England the influence of class structure is steadily declining as ancient privileges are weakened and industrial wealth displaces landed wealth, with a consequent broadening of the base of national leadership. The cleavages between skill groups create formidable problems of administrative leadership. Sir Oliver Franks, in his Reith lectures in 1955, sounded this warning: "If we saw clearly how directly the greatness of Britain depends on our productive efficiency we should find that extra bit of drive. For making our industries adaptable and flexible is not just the problem of employers and workers. We are all involved, for in the end success or failure flows from the climate of opinion, the scale of values of us all."[7]

Specialization has been assumed to offer a superior advantage to large-scale organization, but this belief, says W. Arthur Lewis, is an error because the problems created by specialization are serious. The activities of specialists must be coordinated, for example, in order to assure balance in administration, in the human mind, in the ability to cooperate.[8] A specialty may be anything from a particular area in chemistry to the knowledge of how to set a certain nut onto a certain bolt with a certain washer in its right place. As industry requires ever more and wider areas of knowledge, specialists tend to know more and more about less and less. As they become narrow they begin to feel insecure, and then to compensate by joining with their fellows and placing an undue value on what they do know. There follows a chain of consequences: segmentation, stratification, parochialism, cliques —in a word, the cloister. Each skill group begins to think of itself as superior to and independent of every other. To coordinate many specialists within a single organization becomes harder all the time.

But suppose the idea of specialization is examined with a new eye. It is true that some industries are more technical than others, and the more technical the process, the greater is the tendency toward routine specialization. But is it equally true that in technical fields, most of the work at the lower levels is *necessarily* routine and allows little room for interest or variation? Is it true that in nontechnical fields, such as education or hospital administration, emphasis is more on people than on things? Is there any basic dichotomy in the structure of industry and its institutions that requires some people, depending on where they work, to become as routine as the machines they operate, while others are free to act like human beings? Or do people always act like human beings no matter where they work? They do, of course, and when the environment is inimical, human behavior becomes bureaucratic.

It seems like a step backward, therefore, to assume that certain kinds of work should be based on the machine involved rather than on its operator, and that the operation of a machine may be so simplified and repetitive that workers are relatively interchangeable.[9] Rather, the more technical the process, the more must the human factors be emphasized, especially where routine operations are concerned. Where this course is followed it helps to counteract the hazards of specialization, especially at the technical level.

Overlooked by reason of its very simplicity, it took an enterprising mind with a fresh eye to apply the human principle in a practical situation where its advantages were immediately apparent. The remedy for overspecialized routine consists merely in an arrangement whereby specialists do several parts of a particular job instead of one small part only. Peter Drucker tells how International Business Machines increased the interest, the morale, and the efficiency of its workmen by getting away from the assembly-line technique and returning to an emphasis on craftsmanship. This revolutionary reversal of form has paid off and will doubtless be copied by other industries including those that are highly technical, as IBM is. It is only intelligent self-interest, says Drucker, to realize that it pays to employ the whole man instead of the splintered man, and that to enlarge the job increases a man's capacity. The more you tap people's potential, the more do you tap the source of energy and efficiency.[10]

The studies of William H. Whyte, Jr., which led to his book, *The Organization Man*, point to the same conclusion and to a corresponding remedy. For the better part of a century, says Whyte, management has been busily dividing functions into the smallest possible components and subcomponents of operation. The method of the assembly line was accepted as the epitome of efficiency. But assembly-line operations created an assembly-line mentality and an assembly-line morale. Compartmentalization bred the boredom of monotony, loss of incentive, neurotic behavior, and emotional negativism toward the company and its policies.

The remedy, says Whyte, is to give as many people as possible the chance to do the whole job—to wire the whole set, for example, instead of a single relay, or to plan several aspects of a large job instead of only one phase of it. A broader role would give men that wonderful thing which is challenge; would make them want to respond with enthusiasm; and would help them to regain their self-respect,[11] or what Ordway Tead calls their integrity or selfhood.

But the administrative remedy, adds Whyte, is not enough. We have reared a whole generation to be psychologically attuned to assembly-line techniques and educationally equipped to fit into the pattern of large-scale organization. We must now revolutionize our assumptions and our methods. Our schools and universities must emphasize content and not merely technique, relationships and not merely detail, thinking and not merely rote, values and not merely fitting the individual into a preexisting organization box with a neat label over it.[12]

Among bureaucrats, professional people are outstanding for their attitude of superiority and exclusiveness which, from an administrative standpoint, constitutes a pathological aspect of bureaucracy. The difficulty seems to be the basic problem already mentioned, a feeling of insecurity and a compensatory desire for power and prestige. But in addition, the professional person often seems to think that his integrity is somehow jeopardized if he collaborates too closely with a professional from some other field. If institutions could operate in watertight compartments, there would be little trouble with professional prima donnas, who would be content merely to give each other a cold shoulder when they met at the coffee break. But most programs require close collaboration and give-and-take in a common effort, and the cold shoulder is not enough.

Professional exclusiveness is also partly a matter of personality and of upbringing. Some professionals stand out in terms of cooperation as much on the plus side as many of their confreres do on the negative side. Generally speaking, the less able the individual, the greater is his tendency toward exclusiveness; and since there are never more than a few really top people in any field, the consequences are often enough to try the patience of the most patient administrator.

As Whyte suggests, the solution of bureaucratic exclusiveness lies partly in a different system of education. If the *relationships* among technical fields as well as their differences could be made clear at the outset, the neophyte professional might come to realize that other functions in society may be at least as important as his own. The current broadening of programs in engineering, law, and even in some medical schools is a laudable step. To break down artificial barriers between departments in schools and universities and to employ teachers who are broadly trained is another advance. Unfortunately, there is a vast amount of knowledge and variety of techniques that must be mastered, and broadly trained teachers are scarce.

Nevertheless, there is evidence of progress, at least in the United States, where the problem is more serious than in Britain. Thus, as organization consultant I once worked with a group of government accountants who were trying to broaden their sights and to apprehend the administrative considerations that combine with fiduciary spending to produce efficiency; they succeeded admirably. During another period in the Department of Justice I found a number of lawyers applying themselves to becoming better executives. And as consultant to a group of physicians I have been impressed with their ability to discuss the common principles found in both mental health and large-scale administration. This line of advance will eventually break down the parochial barriers that rob administration of its vitality and dissipate professional energies on not-too-elegant infighting amongst men who are old and experienced enough, seemingly, to know better.

The top executive in his role as leader can do a good deal to encourage cooperation, creating the right atmosphere and breaking down emotional barriers amongst prima donnas (at one point I even acted as "psychiatrist" to a psychiatrist), but something more than that is needed. It takes a deliberate effort on the part of the top executive, working with the factors of education, early environment, the psychological needs of the individual, and the trappings of bureaucracy, to turn the trend from a negative one to a positive one that will promote the vitality of his program.

THE VESTED INTERESTS OF LABOR UNIONS

Yet another group with which administrators must contend, and whose behavior is similar to that of all specialists and professionals, is labor unions. They also sometimes misdirect their energies in a search for security and status, and in this case the result is restrictive practices and interunion bickering at the expense of the employer. The problem is a growing one in all industrialized nations, but recent studies in Britain will show the general lines of the difficulty.

In a brilliant discussion of "The British Economy and Its Problems," Drew Middleton, an American newspaperman long stationed in London, noted the promising strides Britain has made in postwar recovery, but ended on the sobering note that further advance is jeopardized from several quarters. One of the most serious of these is the failure of trade union leaders to take a more progressive viewpoint. It was Middleton's opinion that the strongest resistance to change is located in the middle ranks of labor's officer class; that the Trades Union Congress, labor's governing body in Britain, has great responsibilities but little formal power; that each union is self-governing; that the unions are "quick and brutal" in punishing those who break their rules; and that, because of their shortsightedness, the unions frequently oppose the progressive measures that are necessary to modernize plant and equipment and increase productivity.[13] His English commentators are convinced of Middleton's fair-mindedness and the main lines of his analysis seem to be confirmed by the studies of others in the same field.

The first problem is that of restrictive practices, and here Middleton finds that management must share some of the blame. Together or separately, union leaders and businessmen prevent the most effective use of labor, of technical ability, and of materials; or, what amounts to the same thing, they obstruct the use of incentives that would stimulate the productivity on which Britain's future position in world competition depends. This peril is greater, says Middleton, than the threat of prolonged strikes, although these are always serious enough.

Restrictive practices also take the form of price fixing. In a notable case in 1955, for example, Britain lost a hydroelectric contract in Australia because eight British firms out of twenty submitted identical bids. In another case, twenty-six companies bidding on an electric cable contract for New Zealand did the same thing.[14] Such practices are no less familiar to the American businessman than they are to the Englishman.

Middleton also noted another threat: the gradual disappearance, under the dual influence of mechanization and labor union policy, of differentials in wages, thus creating a damper on effort and ambition. On the assumption that equality is more important than incentive, the unions will insist, for example, that London bus drivers be granted wage increases only if provincial bus drivers receive corresponding increases, irrespective of differences in arduousness of work or in cost of living. This attitude of the unions seems to be due partly to ideological assumptions and partly to union politics, for the leadership apparently feels more secure when everyone shares equally and differentials are avoided. Employers, it might be noted, are under similar pressures, and if they were to give in to them to any wide degree, a main incentive to individual effort would be lost.

But perhaps the most serious problem created by the British labor unions centers on what is called demarcation, a main area of interunion conflict and one with which this discussion is especially concerned. Middleton's conclusions are confirmed by David Nicolson, who describes, for example, how it is necessary to employ men from six or seven different trades to fit a window in the side of a ship, and how even the specified materials may have to be altered to avoid disputes between different trade unions in the shipbuilding industry. Again, in a ship's galley, a plumber supplies and fits all water and drainage pipes and a mechanic lines off the steam and exhaust pipes to boilers and ovens. But in the latter case a coopersmith must measure and make the pipes if they are large-bore, and a brass finisher must do it if they are small-bore. And in the end both workmen will turn the product over to a mechanic to do the actual fitting.[15]

Under these conditions, jurisdictional strikes are seemingly inevitable and some are very costly indeed. Middleton mentions one notable case where work was delayed six months, 400 workers were dismissed as redundant, 200 strikers found work elsewhere, the earning of valuable dollars was jeopardized, and foreign competitors gained as the result of the work stoppage. Because of the demarcation principle, wage costs in basic industries such as shipbuilding may be as much as 6 per cent higher than they would otherwise be.[16]

What is the reason for these irrational and costly stratifications when their harm is so apparent and their seeming benefits so meager? Middleton's answer is that the innate conservatism of the leaders and the rank and file of the unions makes it impossible to persuade them that new machines and new methods mean higher wages because more is produced at lower costs and with greater efficiency. The unions are apparently unmoved by the evidence of experience in the United States, where labor is more responsive to the introduction of new methods that have greatly increased production, wage levels, and standards of living.[17]

Part of the difficulty may be that tradition is so much stronger in Britain than it is in the United States, and in this case the tradition is the result of a long hard fight by the unions to achieve their present gains. But a more significant factor seems to be a fear of losing status and position and all the other rights and privileges that are protected in the wage contract. In short, it is a feeling of insecurity based on irrational fears and resulting in a wasteful dissipation of energy. By and large, there are no better workmen in the world than the members of the British trade unions. Their countrymen know it and so do they. But they fight for power and security, even when they thwart efficiency and productivity and in the long run will reduce their own market

S

baskets, because, so they think, to give in to the demand for new methods of production is a threat to their security.

A realization of this fact is the point of departure for a solution of the problem. If management and labor can establish a relationship of confidence in which give and take is voluntary and both are working for mutually beneficial ends, then there is hope of redirecting energies from petty ends to creative ones. If a change in attitude can be accomplished by changes in the system of technical education and apprenticeship by which men enter the craft unions, the process will be speeded. And if, finally, union leaders will inform themselves in matters of national production and efficiency, they will be more receptive to changes in industrial organization and process. It is a promising omen, therefore, that in recent years Britain's unions have devoted a good deal of attention to administration and economics in their own training centers.[18]

Dealing with the problem of the influence of labor unions on management in the United States, Clark Kerr finds that the unions sometimes hamper efficiency and stifle progress here also. In too many cases the American worker is still subject to a web of rules that becomes more thickly woven as a result of the presence of the union. The problem is not as severe as in Britain, however, because although ". . . undoubtedly many union rules do retard production . . . there is no evidence that the over-all effect has been anything but relatively minor, and some new methods have been better received *because of union consultation* than they otherwise would have been in the light of the inherent conservatism of the work-place."[19] Basically, however, says Kerr, union leaders need to become attentive to "the invisible empire of bureaucracy" and managers equally attentive to the psychological troubles of unions if there is to be a full use of power by the millions of men and women who are the members of organized labor unions.

THE EFFECT OF LARGE SIZE

All of the sticky problems of bureaucracy that have been dealt with in this book are increased—in some cases many times over —when they occur within the framework of large-scale organization, and hence large size is a central problem of power structures. In any healthy organization there will generally be a steady growth of the whole institution, and this is natural and desirable so long as it is the result of deliberate planning and the proper use of energy and does not exceed the optimum for that particular program. But growth that is bureaucratically produced and becomes merely giantism is vulnerable to attack. Is there any way to determine the optimum size for a given undertaking, size beyond which efficiency falls off with every increase in scale?

Of the many forces that influence institutional growth, what is the role of the need to feel secure? The question relates both to institutions and to their employees and administrators. On the latter score, "Large organizations in particular," says Robert M. McMurry, "have a very specific attraction for those with an unusual need for security, and so come to have a disproportionate share, a super-saturation, of the passive, dependent, and submissive. This condition would not be such a threat to the morale and organizational integrity of an enterprise if it were recognized for what it is and its implications understood. But," he adds, "this is rarely the case."[20]

This opinion might be the key to the solution. When bureaucrats reach the stage of lethargy, two things happen: they begin to fear for the survival of their institution, and they develop a feeling of guilt. This combination of fears causes behavior similar to that of a man who is slipping: he grabs at whatever will sustain him without being too particular about what it is. Similarly, bureaucratic organizations also may grab for power, the possession of which cannot be justified by any rational view of public policy or administrative procedure. Such institutions realize they are slipping; they are afraid; they feel guilty; and they are no longer as particular about their methods as an institution that is still in its prime.

Assuming this psychological explanation to be correct, the remedy is to attack the problem at its source; eliminate fear by making the program energetic and enterprising; give it a sense of direction and its members a worth-while challenge.

Paradoxically, there seems to be more security anxiety in large organizations than in small ones, a fact that appeared from interviews that I conducted during the 1930's with the heads of extremely large corporations. Such a fear might be partly explained by the almost superhuman proportions of their administrative problems, but in addition it seemed as though many of the executives of these giants realized that their programs had exceeded optimum size and might be vulnerable to all sorts of dreadful threats that were little understood: "labor troubles," for example, or nationalization, or even expropriation.

Yet despite the growing doubts about the benefits of limitless size, in both Britain and the United States there seems to be an acceleration in that direction, especially toward conglomerate, diversified undertakings. It is fashionable to take on side lines, even many side lines. A firm in Texas, for example, has no less than fifty varieties of business enterprise under one control. Millers in the Middle West are making highly technical experimental balloons. A manufacturer of soap sells fish at retail. A shipbuilder buys a stone-crushing business. What a bizarre list could be made!

The serious side of this development is its shameful violation of a fundamental principle of capitalism: that the individual who starts a specialized business operates more efficiently than a government which must be all things to all people. "Stick to your last," is a simple but wise dictum. Conglomerate undertakings are the specialty of socialists, and capitalist businessmen seem in a fair way to doing the groundwork for their ideological opponents. Moreover, as noted above, another aspect of this noonday madness is that size in itself is a cause of bureaucratic excesses. Hence a failure to observe the cutoff point in growth, the point beyond which size is a hazard to enterprise, is again to undermine capitalist institutions and to pave the way for socialism.

There is no quarrel with size that is technologically induced because if the technological aspects of the undertaking are efficiently handled there are always the means of overcoming the human problems that arise. Nor is there any fundamental difficulty about firms that stick to one line but cover a large geographical area; with enough decentralization the attendant administrative problems can be largely overcome. The real trouble is with the holding-company type of operation that builds echelons of coordination on top of each other to the point where they can no longer be efficiently managed. Whether these pyramids are of the banker type or the management type, both are immediately classifiable as bureaucracies, substituting remote control for face-to-face relationships and power for influence, confining men within narrow limits, robbing them of a feeling of security, neutralizing their incentives, and impeding their self-development.

OPTIMUM SIZE

The search for optimum size is a search for "manageable and comprehensible" units. But how are these to be measured and what are their limits? Peter Drucker, whose previous writings have in no sense been inimical to big business, says in *The Practice of Management* that big is too big when the chief executive can no longer work directly with the chief-executive team; when the bureaucracy has so many levels that even an able man cannot normally rise from the bottom to the top and spend enough time on each level to be thoroughly tested in performance; and when the undertaking spreads to so many different lines that it can no longer establish a "common citizenship" for its managers, be administered as an entity, and establish common over-all objectives.[21] This seems like a practical yardstick. If the mind of one man cannot integrate all aspects of a single business, then there is not likely to be any integration worth the name; the effect is increasingly to lose enterprise and to rely on bureaucratic methods instead.

Additional guidelines come from Harry A. Hopf, a management engineer who studied optimum size in life insurance companies.[22] The optimum, said Hopf, is that state of development which, when reached and maintained, creates an equilibrium among the factors of size, cost, and human capacity. In business and in government, he continued, "the evil results of a well-nigh reckless disregard" of these inherent limitations are widely evident. The difficulty will be intensified, moreover, because of the increasing age at which executives reach the rank of president or chairman of the board and hence find themselves physically and intellectually less able than under former conditions of comparative simplicity to cope with questions of size, progress, and growth. Hopf could find no point at which the span of control in executives is automatically reached, however. Some men who reserve their attention for important matters and train assistants to take care of details are able to maintain regular organized relationships with a dozen or even more subordinates without unduly taxing their capacity. Span of control is also increased as an understanding of operating policies is acquired by the members of the organization. And here again is the question of administration by objectives, as dealt with in a previous chapter.

Another management engineer who has studied the question of institutional size is John H. Williams. Although there is no optimum size for organization in general, said Williams, there is an optimum size for each particular organization, depending in each case on:

1. The extent to which the personal equation as distinguished from a repetitive function enters into the service or product of the corporation. A concern that renders a service must be smaller, to be effective, than one whose product is turned out through repetitive or continuous-process methods.

2. The extent to which authority is decentralized under conditions of cooperation between the managers and those receiving the delegated authority. Beyond a certain point in size, if authority is confined to top management, decisions are so far removed from the point of action as to create delay and confusion.

3. The extent to which accounting procedure is standardized to permit effective comparisons between units in terms that will be stimulating to their managers.[23]

Although Williams does not deal specifically with the human factor, he at least shows that he is aware of it.

The human factor has been dealt with very well in two studies by the Acton Society Trust in Great Britain. In *Size and Morale* there is shown a positive relationship between increasing size and accompanying problems of morale. Some difficulties, such as a higher incidence of sickness among employees, are apparently inherent and there is "little or nothing" that management can do about them. Further, all morale problems are normally intensified by size and hence the greater the size, the harder must management work to overcome them. Lowered morale is the result of work situations in which men feel lost in the crowd and hence lack the same sense of responsibility and loyalty to individuals and to ideas that they have in smaller working groups.[24]

Furthermore, says the Acton Society Trust, being an administrator in a large organization is an entirely different thing from being an administrator in a small, independent one. In a study of British hospital administration it was found that the tradition of the former private-hospital board members was one of independence. They were masters in their own house, conducting administration with that flexibility which independence allows. Once they became part of a great national system, however, "they found it irksome, and indeed sometimes incomprehensible that they should have to confine their recommendations within the framework of higher policy decisions and limit their function to that of an advisory and subordinate body."[25] The plain truth is that in a large-scale organization, for most people the opportunities for initiative are limited to the formalities of an impersonal hierarchy, and for enterprising men the condition may become well-nigh intolerable. All of which tends to confirm the belief of Louis Brandeis, expressed to me shortly before his death, that when Western man eventually decides that excessive size is harmful, it will be because of its effect on people more than its effect on efficiency, which derives, of course, from the human element.

One of the best treatments of institutional size is by a British writer, H. P. Barker, in an article entitled "Have Large Firms an

Advantage in Industry?"[26] He distinguishes the industrial from the nonindustrial incentive to growth, the first being normal and the latter seeking after diversification and power. No firm, says Barker, can be enterprising where there is a hotchpotch of objectives, because a prerequisite of efficiency in any undertaking is that its employees shall understand and respect its purposes in order to build their lifework around them. But in a giant corporation, simply because of its size, the objectives are likely to be of this hotchpotch nature, and hence size is a disadvantage.

Large firms undoubtedly do have an advantage, however, in the matter of stability, because they are more powerful, they have greater resources, and they are able to cater to mass markets. But often they lack adaptability, which is the special advantage of optimum-sized and smaller firms. In the latter case there is less inertia and internal vested interest than in big firms. The small ones can seize opportunities more quickly and can provide the working environment for genius more easily. Small firms also increase mobility in the economy because if they fail they go out of business, whereas if a department of a large firm fails it is often perpetuated simply because of internal, vested interests or considerations of prestige, and the result is to weaken the more prosperous departments in the corporation. Already, Barker finds, there is far more subsidization in large firms than is generally realized.

And finally, says this writer, "If it be true that large undertakings are sometimes lacking in entrepreneurial drive, it is because men in whose stomachs the fires burn sometimes find themselves contained in a spongy cocoon of benevolent negativism of the kind that makes it hard to close a factory which has ceased to be useful, to change the job of a man who could be better employed elsewhere, or alter the pattern of activity which has been overridden by changing events."

All of these tests of large size are useful, but perhaps the ultimate one is what allows human talent to be most effectively used. Expansion should be cut off at the point where the top executive can no longer synthesize the work of his program and deal with his subordinates personally. There is no substitute for face-to-face relationships. The multiplication of hierarchical levels reduces inspiration from the top to people down the line from a steady flow to a thin trickle.

If the family concern could overcome the problems of administrative succession and the recruitment of leadership from outside the family circle, this form of undertaking might be the most desirable that could be found. It has the advantage that its leaders are inescapably interested in the success and reputation of the firm. When this is true, two of the main defects of the impersonal, bureaucratic corporation are largely overcome: the family business has more concern for its employees because they are the family's "own" people; and secondly, decisions are likely to be long-range and survival-oriented rather than short-range and self-destructive, which is the fatal weakness of the grab-while-you-can policy.

The basic weakness of the family concern, and the Achilles' heel of aristocracy in any form, is nepotism, automatic succession, failure to infuse more vigorous blood into the concern when the Mendelian law works unfavorably to the succession, or when wealth and ease have drained off the ability of the heirs to face challenges with energy and resourcefulness. Many firms have shown statesmanship in solving this problem, a notable instance being the Du Pont Company. In Britian there are many examples of family firms that have invigorated themselves over several generations, either by breeding and training men in the family tradition who are as competent as their ancestors or, when this fails, by absorbing similar men into the family group.

In the long run it may be that a combination of family pride, plus high standards of performance justifying recruitment from the outside, is the most effective formula that can be developed if what is wanted is high morale and durability and not merely quick production in large quantities by impersonal methods. At its best, the family firm is a strong offset to the pathologies of bureaucracy and a stimulus to enterprise.

CONCLUSION

In institutional growth, say the authors of *Executive Action*, the path of least resistance is to add to the levels of supervision. But inevitably this means distortion of communication between the top and the bottom. The better method, therefore, is to "improve the capacity of existing executives and supervisors to carry out the coordinating function."[27]

"To improve the capacity" of people, who are the mainspring of administration, suggests how power relationships and the quest for power and security may be redirected toward more fruitful ends than is often the case in large-scale organization. To combat excessive bureaucracy and inertia, there must be a greater reliance on the role of the individual in enterprise. Men must be bred and trained as synthesizers, there must be more attention paid to the values and standards by which men are bound together in voluntary association, there must be more confidence in the designs of businessmen when they deal with labor union leaders, there must be more modesty in the attitude of professional men and specialists toward their colleagues, and a little more humility everywhere in the search for truth and the public interest.

Chapter 16 A Vital Economy

A vital economy is one in which physical and human resources are combined by management to produce steady growth under conditions of equilibrium among the factors of natural resources, capital resources, technical development, and the availability of technical and professional skills, including those of the administrator. Moreover, once dynamism in the economy has been engendered, it must be maintained or it will slip back to frustration and despair, which are the breeding ground of violence.

The basic question is what institutional methods and policies will enable whole peoples to organize and grow toward self-determination and optimum conditions of freedom, with managerial skills so widely distributed that the economy and its political system can afford to be democratic in practice as in theory. There is a growing awareness that skilled management is the catalytic agent in economic development. Nations with ample natural resources cannot put them to economic use, for example, until trained leadership and managerial skills are available, and nations that lack natural resources may still achieve economic greatness under the right kind of administration.

Managerial skills may be progressively lost, however, as well as gained, and a main concern of this book has been to discover the reasons for that loss and how gains may be assured. It has been assumed that the answers are more likely to be found, not by an examination of the usual formal categories and limited processes, but rather through a look at the economy and its institutions from the standpoint of organic growth.

Such an approach underscores the cultural factors that help to create the environment in which institutions operate. It also shows how management, being a synthesis of many elements, can be analyzed realistically only in terms of blends, not discrete categories. A dynamic economy stresses relationships and the manner in which they blend. Like a corporation, the economy also works toward objectives that are consumer-oriented, and hence the role of human values and preferences must be acknowledged. Dynamic growth depends on a close look at these values and preferences, an understanding of the potentials of the situation, and a constant sensitivity to change.

Again like a corporation, whole economies also are in competition with each other. The difference in their competitive power is often a small one—a matter of a few percentage points—and usually depends on the skill of management. But cultural conditioning also enters into the situation, and the organic-evolutionary approach takes this illusive factor into account. In many so-called underdeveloped nations, for example, a chief cause of backwardness is a traditional view of all kinds of economic activity, including farming, as inferior and lacking in social prestige. Hence people with managerial ability are not attracted to them and the economy lags compared with a nation where business has always enjoyed a higher prestige.

What is most needed in some of these underdeveloped nations, therefore, is an appreciation of the fact that vigorous economic activity is basic to an improved standard of living, and that hence the most gifted of its people should seek opportunities in industry and in agriculture. Indeed, not much progress of any kind, unless it is with foreign capital and foreign management, is possible unless economic activity can be accorded its proper value. Again, the organic approach to the study of institutional vitality takes these factors into account.

Bureaucracy is inherent in all social organization. The so-called underdeveloped countries are held back not only by their negative attitude toward business but also by strong elements of bureaucracy in administrative systems that have not altered in a long time. Administrative skills are a highly perishable capital and sometimes decline more rapidly than they increase. According to Arnold Toynbee, Turkey once had the best administrative system and the best administrative training schools of any nation in the preindustrial era, and yet today, although she is trying hard to overcome them, she still suffers from the twin handicaps of the low prestige of business occupations and a tradition of administrative centralization that makes delegation almost impossible. The same judgment might be made concerning two thirds of the nations sitting in the General Assembly of the United Nations today.

Even in advanced industrialized countries such as Great Britain and the United States, there is a problem of how to secure an administrative blend of rational and traditional elements. In such nations, many generations of industrialization have left a distinctive mark. Science and technology stimulate big business; size aggravates bureaucratic excesses the solution of which depends on finding a better balance between the human and the nonhuman factors in management. Thus where bureaucracy is a problem in all nations, it is an infinitely greater one in nations whose institutions are big. Great bodies move slowly and progressively lose their vitality and their responsiveness. "Mobility," said *The Economist* in 1956, "is Britain's most important problem."[1] So, whether a nation is industrially underdeveloped or advanced, a common need is how to secure responsiveness to change. The solution is a proper relationship between bureaucracy and enterprise. The success with which the relationship is achieved is the key to a vital and expanding economy.

BUREAUCRACY

If a business would prosper and thereafter hold its prosperity, what must it do? Its product must be of the highest quality and attractiveness that science and technology can offer. Its methods of production must be the most efficient that can be devised. Its administrators must be able not only to assure these two essentials but also to tie all parts of the program together, to make decisions quickly and wisely, to inspire employees to superior effort, and to develop new and better ideas instead of relying on set formulas that discourage innovation.

If this is what an individual firm must do in order to prosper, this is equally what a national economy must do—on a more complicated plane—if it, too, is to prosper. In either case, both machine efficiency and keen human motivation are essential; the orderliness of bureaucracy must be combined with the human qualities of enterprise, and creative routine joined with creative experimentation.

The implications are clear. Max Weber was right in his analysis of the ingredients of bureaucracy but wrong in his conclusions. Equating order with efficiency in the operation of machines, he applied the same formula to people. But machines need not of their own will adapt, and people must. Machines do not have psychological needs, and people do. Machines do not invent, and people must. Thus where machines must have order, people need order plus something else.

Weber thought of bureaucracy as a kind of legal machine constituting the most efficient form of organization that could be devised. He was right in his analysis of bureaucracy as a form of organization which prominently exhibits the characteristics of hierarchy and authority, specialization and professionalization, rules and fixed procedures, and a resulting impersonality. But he was wrong in assuming that each of these characteristics is always beneficial. Most of them are beneficial in some degree and harmful in excess. This is especially true of formal rules and regulations, and a test of dynamic administration is the extent to which these can be replaced by voluntary cooperation and informal relationships. Weber was wholly wrong in thinking that impersonality is indispensable to efficiency, because in fact just the opposite is the case. Weber overlooked the human element in administration and hence made no provision for flexibility and responsiveness. The more his theories are applied without modification, the more do they become a major obstacle to administrative vitality.

What are the advantages of bureaucracy? The best thing about it is orderly analysis leading to orderly procedure. Science and technology depend on both. So also does scientific management which is based on costing, accountancy, the elimination of waste, and the simplification of processes. Although human elements also are involved, the main emphasis is on a degree of logic, uniformity, and symmetry that will create a balance in the program. Order is based on rational arrangement, priorities, logical distribution of functions, and clear categories. But a blind reliance on these factors causes an accumulation of excessively complicated and formal procedures that destroys efficiency and morale, whereas a proper handling of them is the basis for work simplification, which is an aspect of vitality.

ENTERPRISE

Enterprise is a constantly renewed supply of incentives and ideas, of creative individuals and responsive institutions. Enterprise is social as well as physical innovation. Enterprise breaks with the past when necessary; analyzes consumer needs and finds ways to satisfy them; produces new goods and services and the means of improving them. But enterprise is impossible unless the methods are rational and systematic as well as intuitive and inventive.

Enterprise is largely an individual matter. It is based on what the psychologists call achievement motivation, a quality that develops early in life if the conditions are right. Enterprise also is shrewdness, or what is sometimes called business acumen. It is the ability to move quickly, to take calculated chances, to make the best of what one has, and to take advantage of opportunity.

Like bureaucracy, enterprise also is a condition or an atmosphere. It stresses responsiveness by unorthodox means if need be, while bureaucracy emphasizes order. Enterprise relies on the individual to take the lead in new ideas, as bureaucracy relies on habit to protect the old ones. Enterprise denies that there is a permanent one best way of doing anything, because there is always a better one if it can be found, and the prevailing atmosphere assumes that it will be. Enterprise has no political or institutional coloration. It can be developed in a monopolistic undertaking as in a competitive one; in government departments as in family concerns; in conglomerate corporations as in the corner drugstore; under socialism as under capitalism.

Nevertheless, certain conditions are more conducive to enterprise than others: an expectation that innovation will occur; self-confident and resourceful people; incentives to experimentation and discovery; the encouragement of freedom, competition, and new ideas; minimal vested interests; congenial work surroundings; and adequate research facilities. And all of these conditions are more likely to flourish under capitalism than under socialism, under competition than under monopoly, and in a society where individualism is appreciated than in one where it is disregarded.

But although the greater freedoms and flexibilities of capitalism and democracy offer a more congenial setting for enterprise than socialism and minority rule, even in a democracy the influence of government on the economy is strong. If the government is enterprising and progressive, the economy will have the same characteristics. The British understand this relationship and deliberately try to improve the quality of their government and its administration, but in the United States we still prefer to believe that private enterprise thrives on a government that is never allowed to become too efficient. But the fact is that as policy maker, stabilizer, and tone setter for the economy, government largely creates the climate of private enterprise. If more government leaders were better grounded in the principles of

A Vital Economy

economic growth, it would help to produce the fractional advantage on which the success of a national economy depends in world competition. It is not suggested that to this end government leaders should be transplanted businessmen; merely that at some point in the training of such leaders, they should be made familiar with the facts of enterprise and bureaucracy.

Enterprise is primarily, though not exclusively, an individual matter, and hence individual initiative must be relied on for innovation in big institutions. There has recently appeared a strong assertion of the opposing thesis, that if it is based on *group* activity, enterprise and innovation may be made virtually automatic.[2] If this dogma, which originated partly in Marxism and partly in an oversimplified behavioral-science approach, should ever be widely accepted, it would surely drain the vitality from administration. Indeed, the group theory seems already to be doing so in the U.S.S.R. Students of Soviet administration report, for example, that the state managers of business trusts who make the greatest reputations and run the most successful undertakings do so by using their wits, even to the point of taking chances and being insubordinate, in order to circumvent the centralization and rigid procedures they are supposed to follow.[3] There is a saying in the West that every effective management "has a little spice in it," and this seems to be a need also of Communist administration.

The truth is that in administration both the individual *and* the group are needed. Invention cannot be automatic because it is never a sure thing. It is individual ingenuity and resourcefulness that count. But the individual does his best work with the help of a favorable environment and with the cooperation of others in carrying out his idea, and hence he needs the group. If the individual is the spark, the group is the engine. The sooner we are clear about this, the sooner will the group device discharge a useful rather than a harmful role.

A PROPER BLEND

Both bureaucracy and enterprise contribute to institutional

vitality. To rely exclusively on one or on the other, or to carry either to extreme, is to create a harmful imbalance in administration and hence in the economy. The test of administrative effectiveness, therefore, is the skill with which the best characteristics of bureaucracy and of enterprise are brought together in a creative blend to produce a new synthesis.

Enterprise is carried to extremes when administration is disorderly, where people and programs are lost in a confusion of duplicating and overlapping jurisdictions, objectives are obscured by passing enthusiasms, and administrators are merely promoters with little ability to follow through. Promoters have a certain social value, but not as administrative leaders.

Bureaucracy is carried to extremes when emphasis is on rules, regulations, and impersonality. When bureaucracy becomes pathological, the attention of the group is turned inward on itself instead of outward toward the consumer. Bureaucrats avoid personal responsibility if they can, whereas enterprising people are self-starters in this as in other respects. A bureaucratic group gives the impression of being power-hungry, emphasizing vested interests and encroaching on the freedoms of others, whereas enterprise is service-oriented and hence does not have to seek compensation in a grasp for power.

The root cause of bureaucratic excesses is management's failure to take account of healthy human drives seeking self-expression and social recognition. Thus, instead of impersonality being the right environment for effective human effort, it is just the reverse; the right environment is one in which people are offered scope for selfhood and a chance for individual success. To promote these human needs in extremely large, technical undertakings is not easy; but since the requirement is there, management has no choice but to accept the challenge.

The administrative strategy by which bureaucracy and enterprise may best be brought together in a proper blend is called administration by objectives. According to this approach, institutional objectives are democratically defined and redefined so as to give each unit in the program a clear idea of its role in the total scheme. Insofar as this procedure succeeds, detailed rules and regulations and volumes of manuals may be de-emphasized in favor of short directives of immediate application. The result is to free officials and employees to exercise as much scope as their abilities allow, to encourage their initiative and ingenuity, and to increase their satisfaction in their work. Some people are apparently born with achievement motivation and the ability to assume responsibility. Others have little of either quality and must be content to work as specialists or in nonadministrative posts. But most people can assume more responsibility than they now have if they are wisely and sympathetically dealt with by their superiors. When potential abilities are thus developed, the supply of resourceful leaders is replenished and the program becomes vitalized and consumer-oriented.

Administration by objectives also involves broad delegations of decision-making and empirical problem-solving authority, plus decentralization of administration to the field, where field units are used. But so long as the objectives of the program are clear and loyalty is assured (which is more likely under a democratic arrangement of this kind than where all direction comes down from the top), then the time and energy of top management are released for the coordinative, planning, and public relations activities that are the primary responsibility at that level.

Delegation and decentralization must be accompanied, however, by an assured responsibility on the part of individuals and institutions in such matters as honesty, compliance with public policy, and meeting standards of efficiency. To this end, appropriate policies and standards may be defined in basic charters and mandates, thus providing for accountability, avoiding interference by regulatory bodies, protecting managerial freedom, and creating an environment in which people are stimulated to seek out wider responsibilities instead of trying to evade them.

A final implication of administration by objectives is that with this approach people and institutions achieve power and status not by grimly holding on to whatever power they may possess and covertly plotting to gain more, irrational as the effort may be, but rather by energetically competing for quality of product and the preferences of the consumer, goals that are sufficiently compelling to call forth a free flow of administrative skill.

THE ENVIRONMENT

The attempt to blend the orderliness of bureaucracy with the resourcefulness of enterprise is more likely to succeed if the social climate is favorable, both in the undertaking itself and in the community. Administrators are not without certain weapons as they face up to the accumulated traditions and prejudices of the environment. In underdeveloped nations there are many examples of administrators who have set a new tone in their sphere of influence simply because they saw what was needed and were quietly persuasive. In the tradition-encrusted institutions in modern industrialized nations, some administrators have brought about effective revolutions due to their courage, persuasiveness, and intellectual vigor. Indeed, much is possible under the leadership of the right kind of person, acting both as administrator and as a citizen of position and influence.

Such a man can support gifted people in his own program and in those of others with which he is in contact. He can work for an educational system that combines training in self-discipline with individual freedom, science with the humanities, and logic with values. He can combat intellectual stratification and insist that the specialists in his program shall understand the relationships among the professions as they do the details of their own profession. The administrator himself will study what psychological research offers in the matter of incentives and will apply the principles of psychological motivation, not to manipulate, to exploit, or to brainwash people, but to help them to grow toward selfhood and happiness in a dynamic economy.

The administrator will also help to increase a respect for law and civil liberties, insisting that law is based on justice and the promotion of human values. But realizing that legalism creates an excessive regulation, he will promote the philosophy of administration by objectives, with its large ranges of managerial

A Vital Economy

freedom and discretion, accompanied by legal sanctions held in reserve if power is abused.

In the development of public policy the administrator will support the political economy approach, which combines institutions and men to produce plenty with an effective blend of order and initiative in administration. Consequently he will try to keep power widely dispersed; to encourage property ownership; to protect competition as a basis of efficiency and progressiveness; and to resist the temptation to regiment and regulate people to the point where they are no longer free to be efficient.

The capstone of this edifice is a dynamic economy, one that is constantly expanding and changing, setting challenges for itself and successfully and wholeheartedly responding to those challenges. Such an economy places a high value on mobility; for, as the biologists have discovered, life is motion, and although activity is not necessarily creative, mobility is invariably requisite to vigor. Mobility takes many forms: industrial and social invention; replacing obsolete machines and methods with better ones; allowing some businesses to fail and others to start with the capital that is salvaged; encouraging workers to choose their employment in a competitive market; increasing the alternatives for executive employment; and widening the range of consumer choice. The last of these is the most important of all because if both industry and government are consumer-oriented, in all other areas there will be flexibility and responsiveness.

The capitalist thinks that bureaucracy is a bad word, but the socialist likes it. The socialist thinks that enterprise is a dangerous word, but the capitalist supports it. And both are wrong. It is the best in bureaucracy combined with the best in enterprise that equals institutional vitality and a dynamic economy.

Notes

CHAPTER 1. VITALITY IN ADMINISTRATION

1. See, for example, W. Arthur Lewis, *The Theory of Economic Growth* (London: George Allen & Unwin, 1955), pp. 51–95.
2. Eli Ginzberg and Ewing W. Reilly, *Effecting Change in Large Organizations* (New York: Columbia University Press, 1957), pp. 1–39; and Chris Argyris, *Personality and Organization* (New York: Harper & Brothers, 1958).
3. Sir Alexander Fleck, "The Pressure of Technical Change," in *Vitality in Administration* (London: George Allen & Unwin, 1957), Chapter III.

CHAPTER 2. PIONEERING IN BIG BUSINESS

1. Two of the best of these biographies tell the story of Standard Oil: Ralph W. Hidy and Muriel E. Hidy, *Pioneering in Big Business* (New York: Harper & Brothers, 1955), which takes the story from 1882 to 1911; and George S. Gibb and Evelyn H. Knowlton, *The Resurgent Years, 1911–1927* (New York: Harper & Brothers, 1956). I have also read with great interest James Gray, *Business Without Boundaries: The Story of General Mills* (Minneapolis: University of Minnesota Press, 1954), and Robert G. McClelland has written *A History of Phelps Dodge* (New York: Alfred A. Knopf, 1952).

The principal concentration of interest in the biographies of businesses is at the Research Center in Entrepreneurial History at Harvard University, which publishes a journal, *Explorations in Entrepreneurial History*. The Center has also published a number of case studies, including *Men in Business* (1952), *Railroad Leaders, 1845–1890* (1953), *The Welland Canal Company* (1954), *The New England Merchants of the Seventeenth Century* (1955), and *Henry Varnum Poor, Business Editor, Analyst and Reformer* (1956), all by the Harvard University Press. The same press has also put out Thomas C. Cochran's *The American Business System, 1900–1955*.

A number of administrative histories have also appeared in Great Britain. Two of the best short accounts, sponsored by the Royal Institute of Public Administration, are G. E. Milward (ed.), *Large-Scale Organization* (London: Macdonald and Evans, 1950), and D. N. Chester and F. M. G. Willson, *The Organization of British Central Government, 1914–1956* (London: Allen & Unwin, 1957), the latter showing the adjustment of British government to new conditions.

There are many more histories of businesses that might be cited, of course, many of them written by popular writers rather than by historians; I have mentioned here only those on which I am chiefly relying in this chapter.

2. For reference, see note 1.
3. Hidy and Hidy, *op. cit.*, p. 38.
4. *Ibid.*, pp. 34–35.
5. *Ibid.*, pp. 56–58.
6. *Ibid.*, p. 337.
7. *Ibid.*, pp. 65–66.
8. *Ibid.*, p. 332.
9. *Ibid.*, pp. 172, 173 (italics added).
10. *Ibid.*, p. 211.
11. *Ibid.*, pp. 306–307.
12. *Ibid.*, p. 471.
13. *Ibid.*, p. 468.
14. For reference, see note 1.
15. Gibb and Knowlton, *op. cit.*, pp. 36, 42.
16. Hidy and Hidy, *op. cit.*, pp. 71, 72, 74.
17. Gibb and Knowlton, *op. cit.*, p. 607.
18. *Ibid.*, p. 580.
19. *Ibid.*, p. 608.

Notes   275

20. *Ibid.*, p. 610.
21. *Ibid.*, p. 525.
22. *Ibid.*, p. 627.
23. Interview with Mr. Northrup Clarey, Standard Oil Company (New Jersey), in New York, March 5, 1937. At this time Clarey, who was in charge of public relations, said that there were approximately 150 separate foreign and domestic corporations in the Jersey structure. The administrative arrangements of Standard Oil were confirmed in interviews with company officials in 1955 and 1956. On the broader implications, see A. A. Berle, Jr., *The 20th Century Capitalist Revolution* (New York: Harcourt, Brace and Company, 1954).
24. Gray, *op. cit.*, p. vii.
25. *Ibid.*, pp. 5, 12.
26. *Ibid.*, p. 71.
27. *Ibid.*, p. 134.
28. *Ibid.*, p. 200.
29. *Ibid.*, pp. 152–153.
30. *Ibid.*, pp. 224–225.
31. *Ibid.*, pp. 242, 286, 293, 306, 311.
32. Sir Geoffrey Hayworth, "Lever Brothers and Unilever Limited," in G. E. Milward (ed.), *op. cit.*, p. 168.
33. *Ibid.*, p. 168.
34. *Ibid.*, p. 172.
35. *Ibid.*, p. 171.
36. *Ibid.*, p. 177.
37. *Ibid.*, pp. 177–178.
38. *Ibid.*, p. 176.
39. A. D. Bonham-Carter, Director, Unilever Limited, "The Motive Power of Higher Management," in the symposium, *Vitality in Administration* (London: George Allen & Unwin, 1957), p. 63.
40. Hayworth, *op. cit.*, p. 178 (italics added).
41. *Ibid.*, p. 179.
42. R. A. Lynex, "Imperial Chemical Industries Limited," in Milward (ed.), *op. cit.*, pp. 144–165.
43. "ICI in a New Age," *The Economist* (London), May 22, 1954.
44. Sir Alexander Fleck, "The Pressure of Technical Change," in *Vitality in Administration*, pp. 36–37.

Notes 276

CHAPTER 3. SOME THEORIES OF GROWTH

1. I was first given this lead by my biologist colleague at New York University, Professor M. J. Kopac.
2. C. Brooks Worth and Robert K. Enders, *The Nature of Living Things* (New York: Signet Key Books, 1955), pp. 79, 146.
3. *Ibid.*, pp. 4, 129, 143, 161, 223, 224–225.
4. J. T. Bonner, *Cells and Societies* (Princeton: Princeton University Press, 1955), pp. 13, 21–22.
5. Worth and Enders, *op. cit.*, pp. 21, 169.
6. W. Arthur Lewis, *The Theory of Economic Growth* (London: George Allen & Unwin, 1955), and *The Principles of Economic Planning* (London: George Allen & Unwin, 1949).
7. Lewis, *Theory of Economic Growth*, pp. 143, 148.
8. Lewis, *Principles of Economic Planning*, pp. 17–19, 93.
9. *Ibid.*, pp. 19, 90, 91, 104.
10. Lewis, *Theory of Economic Growth*, pp. 51, 102.
11. *Ibid.*, pp. 78, 94, 95, 99.
12. *Ibid.*, pp. 150, 154, 182, 196, 420.
13. Ben W. Lewis, *British Planning and Nationalization* (New York: The Twentieth Century Fund, 1952).
14. *Ibid.*, p. 222.
15. *Ibid.*, pp. 47, 282, 284.
16. A. A. Berle, Jr., *Economic Power and the Free Society* (New York: Fund for the Republic, pamphlet, 1957).
17. John Wellens, *Technical Education: Shortage of Scientists, Technologists, and Technicians* (Oldham, Lancashire, England: privately printed, 1956).
18. Clark Kerr, *Unions and Union Leaders of Their Own Choosing* (New York: Fund for the Republic, pamphlet, 1957).
19. *Ibid.*, p. 15.
20. C. Wright Mills, *White Collar* (New York: Oxford University Press, 1951; paper-bound edition, 1956).
21. *Ibid.*, pp. 182–184, 340.
22. See below, Chapters 8, 12, 14.

CHAPTER 4. SOME THEORIES OF DECAY

1. H. G. Barnett, *Innovation: The Basis of Cultural Change* (New York: McGraw-Hill Book Company, 1953), p. i.

2. Arnold J. Toynbee, *A Study of History* (New York and London: Oxford University Press, 10 Vols., 1934–54), Vol. IV, pp. 14, 36.
3. *Ibid.*, Vol. II, p. 393.
4. *Ibid.*, Vol. VI, p. 177.
5. *Ibid.*, Vol. IV, pp. 5–6.
6. *Ibid.*, Vol. I, p. 169.
7. *Ibid.*, Vol. III, pp. 24, 216.
8. *Ibid.*, Vol. IV, pp. 127–128.
9. *Ibid.*, Vol. IX, p. 587.
10. *Ibid.*, Vol. VI, p. 322; Vol. IX, p. 605; C. Wright Mills, *White Collar* (New York: Oxford University Press, 1956), pp. 228, 347.
11. Toynbee, *op. cit.*, Vol. V, p. 44.
12. See below, Chapter 15.
13. *Ibid.*, Vol. IV, p. 34.
14. I am indebted to Professor Stephen Bailey of Princeton University for making this point so clearly in conversation. On the larger question, see my article, "Executive Development After Ten Years," in *Public Administration Review*, Spring, 1958.
15. Chris Argyris, *Personality and Organization* (New York: Harper & Brothers, 1957), pp. 25–27, 239.
16. Toynbee, *op. cit.*, Vol. IX, pp. 169, 170.
17. *Ibid.*, Vol. IV, p. 131.
18. *Ibid.*, Vol. IV, p. 57.
19. *Ibid.*, Vol. VIII, pp. 502, 530–533.
20. Below, Chapter 11.

CHAPTER 5. BRITISH ELECTRICITY

1. *Report of the Committee of Inquiry into Electricity Supply Industry* (London: Cmd. 9672, H.M.S.O. Presented by the Minister of Fuel and Supply to Parliament by Command of Her Majesty, January, 1956). The study was made by an independent nonpolitical staff. The scope and methods of the inquiry are dealt with in Parts I and II of the report.
2. Interview with Ronald Edwards, Deputy Chairman, Electricity Council, June 26, 1958.
3. *Report of the Committee of Inquiry into Electricity Supply Industry*, pp. 140–141.
4. *Ibid.*, p. 25.
5. *Ibid.*, pp. 64–65.

6. *Ibid.*, p. 139.
7. *Ibid.*, p. 139.
8. *Ibid.*, p. 73.
9. *Ibid.*, p. 86.
10. *Ibid.*, p. 116.
11. *Report from the Select Committee on Nationalised Industries (Reports and Accounts)*, (London: H.M.S.O., 1957).
12. *Report of the Committee of Inquiry into Electricity Supply Industry*, p. 151.
13. *Report of the Advisory Committee on Organization* (London: National Coal Board, February, 1955).
14. Acton Society Trust, *Hospitals and the State* (London: Acton Society Trust, 1955), Vol. I, p. 42; Vol. II, pp. 36–37, 42 (italics added).
15. Ben W. Lewis, *British Planning and Nationalization* (New York: The Twentieth Century Fund; London: George Allen & Unwin, 1952).
16. *Ibid.*, pp. 89, 214, 278.
17. *Ibid.*, p. 282.

CHAPTER 6. THE TRADITIONAL CASE FOR BUREAUCRACY

1. William H. Whyte, Jr., *The Organization Man* (New York: Simon & Schuster, 1956).
2. Joseph A. Schumpeter, *Capitalism, Socialism, and Democracy* (New York: Harper & Brothers, 1942, 1946), pp. 205 ff.
3. See, for example, Herbert A. Simon, *Administrative Behavior* (New York: The Macmillan Company, 2nd ed., 1957), especially Appendix, "What is an Administrative Science?"
4. For the influence of Max Weber on sociologists, see Robert K. Merton (ed.), *Reader in Bureaucracy* (Glencoe, Ill.: The Free Press, 1952).
5. Max Weber, *The Protestant Ethic and the Spirit of Capitalism*, translated by Talcott Parsons (London: George Allen & Unwin, 1930, 1948).
6. Weber, *Wirtschaft und Gesellschaft* (Tübingen, 1925). English translations of sections dealing with bureaucracy are by A. M. Henderson and Talcott Parsons, in Talcott Parsons (ed.), *The Theory of Social and Economic Organization* (New York: Oxford University Press, 1947), and H. H. Gerth and C. Wright Mills (eds.), *From*

Max Weber: Essays in Sociology (New York: Oxford University Press, 1946).
7. James Burnham, *The Managerial Revolution* (New York: The John Day Company, 1941); A. A. Berle, Jr., *The 20th Century Capitalist Revolution* (New York: Harcourt, Brace and Company, 1954); White, *op. cit.*
8. Merton (ed.), *op. cit.*, pp. 24–26.
9. Gerth and Mills (eds.), *op. cit.*, p. 220.
10. Frederic S. Burin, "Bureaucracy and National Socialism: A Reconsideration of the Weberian Theory," in Merton (ed.), *op. cit.*, pp. 33–47.
11. Gerth and Mills (eds.), *op. cit.*, p. 234.
12. Carl J. Friedrich, "Some Observations on Weber's Analysis of Bureaucracy," in Merton (ed.), *op. cit.*, p. 33.
13. Schumpeter, *op. cit.*, pp. 190 ff.
14. Merton (ed.), *op. cit.*, pp. 12, 17.

CHAPTER 7. A NEW LOOK AT BUREAUCRACY

1. Chester I. Barnard, *The Functions of the Executive* (Cambridge, Mass.: Harvard University Press, 1938), Appendix, "Mind in Everyday Life."
2. More fully developed by the present author in *A Philosophy of Administration* (New York: Harper & Brothers, 1958).
3. General Robert E. Wood in an interview, November 22, 1937.
4. John Dickinson, General Counsel, Pennsylvania Railroad, in an interview, May 17, 1937.
5. Kemal Karpat, "The Transition of Turkey's Political Regime to a Multi-Party System" (unpublished doctoral dissertation, New York University, 1957).
6. Dealt with further by the present author in *Business and Government* (3rd ed.; New York: Henry Holt and Company, 1957).
7. Cultural influences and their control are discussed in Chapter 15.
8. For this insight I am indebted to Mr. John Goormaghtigh, Executive Director of the International Political Science Association and a close student of the European market.
9. Acton Society Trust, *Hospitals and the State* (London: 1956), Vol. III, p. 11. The balance of time is occupied by "discussions and interviews," 32 per cent; "committee work," 18 per cent; and "other," 5 per cent.

Notes 280

10. *Report of the Advisory Committee on Organization* (Fleck Committee), (London: National Coal Board, February, 1955), p. 2.
11. Eli Ginsberg and Ewing W. Reilley, *Effecting Changes in Large Organizations* (New York: Columbia University Press, 1957).
12. Robert K. Merton, "Bureaucratic Structure and Personality," in Merton (ed.), *Reader in Bureaucracy* (Glencoe, Ill.: The Free Press, 1952), pp. 361–371.
13. From an unpublished case entitled "Inter-Planetary Research Establishment, File B," H.M. Treasury Training and Education Division, in consultation with Z. M. T. Tarkowski, undated.
14. Acton Society Trust, *op. cit.*, Vol. II, pp. 20–21.
15. *Ibid.*, Vol. I, p. 17; Vol. II, pp. 20, 39, 52.
16. Sir Wilfrid Neden, "Human Relations as a Positive Factor," in *Vitality in Administration* (London: George Allen & Unwin, 1957), p. 54.
17. Peter M. Blau, *The Dynamics of Bureaucracy* (Chicago: University of Chicago Press, 1955).
18. Roy G. Francis and Robert C. Stone, *Service and Procedure in Bureaucracy* (Minneapolis: University of Minnesota Press, 1956).
19. *Ibid.*, pp. 126–127.
20. *Ibid.*, p. 135.

CHAPTER 8. THE PATHOLOGIES OF BUREAUCRACY

1. The simplest definition of efficiency is the ratio between input and output, a view that applies well enough to combustion engines, for example, but which, if applied to administration, creates a distortion and leads to the excesses of bureaucracy. Another definition has it that efficiency maximizes results with limited resources, but this also implies a niggardliness which is self-defeating. On this whole subject, see Herbert A. Simon, *Administrative Behavior* (2nd ed.; New York: The Macmillan Company, 1957), Chapter IX. Harrington Emerson is quoted on p. 181.
2. The best discussion of this point is by Arthur K. Davis, "Bureaucratic Patterns in the Navy Officer Corps," *Social Forces*, XXVII (1948), 143–153; reprinted in Robert K. Merton (ed.), *Reader in Bureaucracy* (Glencoe, Ill.: The Free Press, 1952), pp. 380–395.
3. On this point, see Robert K. Merton, "Bureaucratic Structure and Personality," in *Reader in Bureaucracy*, pp. 361–371.

4. Ordway Tead, *The Art of Administration* (New York: McGraw-Hill Book Company, 1951), pp. 45 ff.
5. Chris Argyris, *Personality and Organization* (New York: Harper & Brothers, 1957), pp. 229–239.
6. *Ibid.*, p. 230.
7. Joseph M. Juran, *Bureaucracy: A Challenge to Better Management* (New York: Harper & Brothers, 1944).
8. National Coal Board, *Report of the Advisory Committee on Organization* (London: February, 1955), p. 13.
9. Carl J. Friedrich, "Some Reservations on Weber's Analysis of Bureaucracy," in Merton (ed.), *op. cit.*, p. 29. The other five factors are hierarchical aspects, differentiation of functions, qualification for office, objectivity, and precision and continuity.
10. Juran, *op. cit.*, Chapter V.
11. Interview, May 18, 1937. The ideas expressed to the author are more fully developed in *Fortune*, "Owen D. Young and General Electric," in the issues of January, February, and March, 1931.
12. Interview with Lucius Eastman, President of Hills Brothers Company, December 9, 1937.
13. V. Dudintsev, *Not By Bread Alone*, translated by Dr. Edith Bone (New York: E. P. Dutton & Company, 1957), pp. 50, 137, 197, 235, 240.
14. E. O. Learned, D. N. Ulrich, and D. R. Booz, *Executive Action* (Boston: Harvard Graduate School of Business, 1951), pp. 38, 41, 163, 177.
15. Davis, *op. cit.*, p. 383.
16. M. E. Dimock, *The Executive in Action* (New York: Harper & Brothers, 1945), p. 240.
17. C. Wright Mills, *White Collar* (New York: Oxford University Press, 1956), p. xvii.
18. A. Northcote Parkinson, *Parkinson's Law* (Boston: Houghton Mifflin Company, 1957), pp. 60, 61.
19. Davis, *op. cit.*, pp. 384–385.
20. Simon, *op. cit.*, p. 102.
21. *Ibid.*, p. 88.
22. Parkinson, *op. cit.*, p. 24.
23. Dudintsev, *op. cit.*, pp. 24, 93.
24. G. E. Eades, *The London We Love* (London: Evans Brothers, 1946), p. 165.

25. Dudintsev, *op. cit.*, p. 181.
26. *Ibid.*, pp. 173, 174.
27. Peter F. Drucker, *The Practice of Management* (New York: Harper & Brothers, 1954), London: Chapter 12.
28. A good specimen is John H. Crider, *The Bureaucrat: A Natural History of the Bureaucrat, His Habitat, Feeding Habits, Protective Coloration, Ubiquitous Activities, and Probable Future* (New York and Philadelphia: J. B. Lippincott Company, 1944).
29. Carl J. Friedrich and Taylor Cole, *Responsible Bureaucracy* (Cambridge, Mass.: Harvard University Press, 1932), p. 86.
30. Carl Dreyfuss, "Prestige Grading: A Mechanism of Control," in Merton (ed.), *op. cit.*, p. 260.
31. Davis, *op. cit.*, pp. 389, 392.
32. Learned, Ulrich, and Booz, *op. cit.*, pp. 188, 212.
33. Sir Alexander Fleeck, "The Pressure of Technical Change," in the symposium *Vitality in Administration* (London: George Allen & Unwin, 1957), pp. 30–31.
34. A. A. Berle, Jr., *The 20th Century Capitalist Revolution* (New York: Harcourt Brace & Company, 1954), p. 180.
35. Robert Michels, "The Bureaucratic Tendency of Political Parties," in Merton (ed.), *op. cit.*, p. 89.
36. Mills, *op. cit.*, p. 210.
37. Parkinson, *op. cit.*, pp. 33–36.
38. British Museum, Papyrus 752, presented by the Egypt Exploration Society.

CHAPTER 9. THE INCENTIVE AND THE IDEA

1. This summary derives largely from the writings of Professor David C. McClelland of Harvard University and his associates. See especially McClelland, *Community Development and the Nature of Human Motivation* (Cambridge, Mass.: Associates for International Research, Inc., mimeographed, 1957), constituting part of the background papers for the Conference on Community Development sponsored by the Center for International Studies, Endicott House, December 13–15, 1957; David C. McClelland, J. W. Atkinson, Russell A. Clark, and Edgar L. Lowell, *The Achievement Motive* (New York: Appleton-Century-Crofts, 1953); and David C. McClelland (ed.), *Studies in Motivation* (New York: Appleton-Century-Croft,

1955). I was privileged to attend the conference where the first of these studies was discussed.
2. In McClelland (ed.), *Studies in Motivation*.
3. McClelland, *Community Development and the Nature of Human Motivation*, pp. 25–26.
4. *Ibid.*, p. 42. See also McClelland and others, *The Achievement Motive*, pp. 78, 328.
5. From a paper entitled "The Use of Measures of Human Motivation in the Study of Society," to be published in J. W. Atkinson (ed.), *Motives In Fantasy, Action, and Society* (Princeton: D. Van Nostrand Company, 1958).
6. Tests conducted by Freda Milstein and reported by David R. Miller in "Defense Mechanisms and Personality," *Conference on Cross-Cultural Research on Personality* (New York: Social Science Research Council, mimeographed, 1955), pp. 43–58.
7. McClelland and others, "Religious and Other Sources of Parental Attitudes Toward Independence Training," in *Studies in Motivation*, pp. 395–396.
8. Bernard C. Rosen, "The Achievement Syndrome: A Psychocultural Dimension of Social Stratification," *American Sociological Review*, XXL (1956), 210–211.
9. McClelland, "Interest in Risky Occupations with High Achievement Motivation" (Cambridge, Mass.: Harvard University, unpublished, mimeographed, 1956).
10. D. Berlew, "The Achievement Motive and the Growth of Greek Civilization" (unpublished A.B. thesis, Wesleyan University, 1956), quoted in McClelland, *The Use of Measures of Human Motivation in the Study of Society*, to be published in Atkinson (ed.), *op. cit.*
11. McClelland, *Community Development and the Nature of Human Motivation*, p. 41.
12. Joseph A. Schumpeter, *Capitalism, Socialism, and Democracy* (3rd ed.; New York: Harper & Brothers, 1947), pp. 141, 156.
13. *Ibid.*, p. 141.
14. Sir Alexander Fleck, Chairman, Imperial Chemicals Industries, "The Pressure of Technical Change," in *Vitality in Administration* (London: George Allen & Unwin, 1957), pp. 38, 41.
15. John Jewkes, David Sawers, and Richard Stillerman, *The Sources of Invention* (London and New York: The Macmillan Company, 1958).

16. *Scientific Research and Development in American Industry* (Washington, D.C.: United States Department of Labor, Bulletin 1148, 1953), p. 6.
17. William H. Whyte, Jr., *The Organization Man* (New York: Simon & Schuster, 1956), p. 403.
18. W. I. B. Beveridge, *The Art of Scientific Investigation* (2nd ed.; London: William Heinemann, Ltd., 1953), pp. 2, 3, 130.
19. Jewkes and others, *op. cit.*, p. 121.

CHAPTER 10. PERSON AND PROCESS

1. This analysis is based on my own fourfold classification of the problems that recurred in discussions reported in a part of the course at the Administrative Staff College at Henley-on-Thames, in a part entitled "Maintaining Administrative Vitality."
2. Joseph A. Schumpeter, *Capitalism, Socialism, and Democracy* (3rd ed.; New York: Harper & Brothers, 1947), pp. 131–134, 140.
3. Arthur H. Cole (ed.), *Change and the Entrepreneur* (Cambridge, Mass.: Harvard University Press, 1949). These are the conference proceedings of the Research Center in Entrepreneurial History. Definitions are by Chester Barnard, W. T. Easterbrook, Joseph A. Schumpeter, and Clarence H. Danhof, respectively.
4. Joseph A. Schumpeter, "Economic Theory and Entrepreneurial History," in Cole, *op. cit.*, pp. 63–84.
5. Schumpeter, *Capitalism, Socialism, and Democracy*, p. 132.
6. Reported in Cole, *op. cit.*, pp. 19–20.
7. W. Arthur Lewis, *The Theory of Economic Growth* (London: George Allen & Unwin, 1955), pp. 51, 196.
8. Cole, *op. cit.*
9. *Ibid.*, p. 104.
10. *Ibid.*, p. 88.
11. Basil Smallpcice, "The Challenge of Competition," in *Vitality in Administration* (London: George Allen & Unwin, 1957), pp. 28–29.
12. See, for example, William H. Newman and James P. Logan, *Management of Expanding Enterprises* (New York: Columbia University Press, 1955); and Eli Ginzberg and Ewing W. Reilley, *Effecting Change in Large Organizations* (New York: Columbia University Press, 1957).
13. Peter H. Drucker, *The Practice of Management* (New York: Harper & Brothers, 1954), pp. 30–39, 58–59, 75–80, 90.

14. *Report of the Advisory Committee on Organization* (Fleck Committee) (London: National Coal Board, February, 1955), p. 3.
15. *Ibid.*, pp. 16, 19, 20, 22.

CHAPTER 11. MARKS AND SPENCER

1. Speech by Sir (then Mr.) Simon Marks, as reported in *The Times*, London, May 17, 1935.
2. Stated at the annual meeting in 1929, as reported in *The Times*, London, June 12, 1929.
3. Interview with Mr. Norman Laski, Director, Marks and Spencer, April 15, 1958.
4. Statement of the Chairman, annual meeting, 1932, reported in *The Times*, London, May 11, 1932.
5. Annual meeting, reported in *The Times*, London, June 18, 1930.
6. Interview with Mr. Norman Laski, Director, April 22, 1958.
7. Sir Simon (then Mr.) Marks, annual meeting, 1933, reported in *The Times*, London, May 18, 1933.
8. Mr. I. M. Sieff, Vice-Chairman, reported in *The Times*, London, May 18, 1934.
9. Interview with Marks and Spencer technicians, April 22, 1958.
10. Annual meeting, 1937, reported in *The Times*, London, May 29, 1937.
11. Interview with Mr. B. W. Goodman, Director and Secretary, May 22, 1958.

CHAPTER 12. INTEGRATIVE LEADERSHIP

1. National Coal Board, *Report of the Advisory Committee on Organisation* (Fleck Committee) (London: National Coal Board, February, 1955), p. 8.
2. See Frederick W. Taylor, *The Principles of Scientific Management* (New York: Harper & Brothers, last printed in 1947); and Taylor Society, *Scientific Management in American Industry* (New York: Harper & Brothers, 1929).
3. H. P. Kendall, "Modernizing an Old Business by Simple Methods," *Factory and Industrial Management*, LXXVII (February, 1929), 272–274.
4. Percival White, *Business Management—An Introduction to Business* (New York: Henry Holt and Company, 1926), p. 79.

5. L. Urwick, "Executive Decentralisation with Functional Coordination," *Public Administration*, XIII (1935), 344–358.
6. John Lee, "The Parallels Between Industrial Administration and Public Administration," *Public Administration*, IV (1926), 216–222.
7. Edmund P. Learned, David N. Ulrich, and Donald R. Booz, *Executive Action* (Boston: Harvard University Press, 1951), pp. 138, 191.
8. *Ibid.*, pp. 146–147.
9. Ralph C. Davis, *Industrial Organization and Management* (New York: Harper & Brothers, 1940).
10. C. F. Carter and B. R. Williams, *Industry and Technical Progress* (London: Oxford University Press, 1957); this report is summarized and discussed by R. D. Young in "Technical Progress in British Industry," *The Listener*, July 14, 1957, pp. 11–12 (italics added).
11. Bosworth Monck, "How to Make a Captain of Industry," *The Listener*, January 13, 1955, pp. 57–58 (italics added).
12. Sir Alexander Fleck, "The Pressure of Technical Change," in *Vitality in Administration* (London: George Allen & Unwin, 1957), pp. 34–35.
13. E. N. Gladden, *Civil Service or Bureaucracy?* (London: Staples, 1956), pp. 174–175.
14. *Ibid.*, pp. 182, 191, 192.
15. *Ibid.*, p. 192 (italics added).
16. C. Wright Mills, *White Collar* (New York: Oxford University Press, 1956), pp. 310, 340.
17. Gladden, *op. cit.*, p. 201 and Chapter XIII, *passim*.
18. Sir Wilfred Neden, "Human Relations as a Positive Factor," in *Vitality in Administration*, pp. 43, 52.
19. For a fuller statement of this plan, see Ordway Tead, *The Art of Administration* (New York: McGraw-Hill Book Company, 1951); Peter Drucker, *The Practice of Management* (New York: Harper & Brothers, 1954); or Marshall E. Dimock, *A Philosophy of Administration* (New York: Harper & Brothers, 1958).
20. Drucker, *op. cit.*, Chapter 19, "The IBM Story."
21. Ordway Tead, "Democracy in Administration," *Social Frontiers*, III (1937), 105–107.
22. See especially his essay, "Mind in Everyday Affairs," which is an appendix to *The Functions of the Executive* (Boston: Harvard University Press, 1938).

23. John Jewkes and others, *The Sources of Invention* (New York and London: The Macmillan Company, 1958), pp. 115, 223.
24. V. Dudintsev, *Not By Bread Alone* (New York: E. P. Dutton & Company, 1957), pp. 35–36.
25. Learned, Ulrich, and Booz, *op. cit.*, p. 35.
26. Chris Argyris, *Personality and Organization* (New York: Harper & Brothers, 1957), pp. 130, 232.

CHAPTER 13. DECENTRALIZATION

1. Arthur Pound, *The Turning Wheel* (New York: Doubleday, Doran & Company, 1934), *passim;* also author's interviews in 1937 with Donaldson Brown, Vice-President; Steve DeBruhl, Chief Economist; Merle Hale, Assistant to the President, all of General Motors Corporation.
2. My field study of the American Telegraph and Telephone Company, with Howard K. Hyde as my principal assistant, was made in the late 1930's, and the interviews and observations reported here relate largely to that period. However, the decentralization policy remains unchanged and only the personalities and some of the applications differ today.
3. Noobar R. Danielian, *A T & T: The Story of Industrial Conquest* (New York: The Vanguard Press, 1939), p. 272. Among others, there are interesting chapters in this study on "The Politics of Profit," "Molding the Public Mind," "Selling the System," "Regulating the Bell System," and "Reflections on Political Economics."
4. Chester I. Barnard, *Collectivism and Individualism in Industrial Management* (pamphlet, undated).
5. American Telephone & Telegraph Company, Annual Report, 1957; Frederick R. Kappel, President of A. T. & T., *Design for Service in a Growing Nation*, a series of articles reprinted from *The Christian Science Monitor*, January, 1955, p. 2.
6. *Ibid.*, pp. 17, 20, 25. See also *A T & T—Your Business* (printed by the company, undated).
7. Interview with C. P. Cooper, Operating Vice-President, A. T. & T., December 3, 1936.
8. Interview with Arthur W. Page, Vice-President, A. T. & T., May 22, 1936.
9. According to an article in *Fortune* ("A T & T's Board of Directors,"

Notes   288

in the issue of September 1930), the corporation had then eleven vice-presidents as against eighteen outside directors, but deliberately restricted its management directorate so as not to confuse the board's position as an advisory body with that of a superexecutive committee. In an interview on March 2, 1936, with Walter Gifford, president of the company, he remarked that the company had no chairman, only an executive committee on which the president also served. He criticized the more common dual system of independent board chairman plus an elected president as unsound because "nothing will ruin a concern sooner than not knowing who runs it."

10. "A T & T's Board of Directors," *Fortune*, September, 1930, p. 41.
11. Interview with Bancroft Gherardi, Vice-President, A. T. & T., May 21, 1936.
12. Interview with C. P. Cooper, Vice-President, A. T. & T., December 3, 1936.
13. From an address by E. K. Hall, "The Personnel Job: What It Is and What It Is Not" (unpublished, 195 Broadway, New York, 1925).
14. Interview with Chester I. Barnard, December 3, 1936.
15. Interview with K. W. Waterson, Vice-President, A. T. & T., May 20, 1936.
16. Interview with E. H. Winkleman, R. H. Brooks, and J. E. Halligan, Illinois Bell, April, 1937.
17. Interview with Bancroft Gherardi, Vice-President, A. T. & T., May 20, 1936.
18. Interview with G. L. Seaton, J. W. Fisher, Jr., and F. B. Kennedy, Illinois Bell, April 16, 1936.
19. *Ibid.*
20. Interview with Winkleman, Brooks, and Halligan.
21. Interview with Seaton, Fisher, and Kennedy.
22. Interview with Traffic Results Supervisor, Chicago Area, Illinois Bell, March 3, 1936.
23. Interview with Cyrus Hill, Federal Communications Commission Engineer in Charge of Telephone Investigation, March 10, 1939.
24. Interview with H. H. Veerhusen, Management Consultant, U.S. Steel, February 20, 1936.
25. A. T. & T. Stockholders' Prospectus, January 17, 1958, p. 14.
26. Interview with E. F. Carter, Vice-President, A. T. & T., March 4, 1936.

27. Interview with Mr. Bracelen, Vice-President, Legal Department, A. T. & T., December 3, 1936; testimony of same before the Federal Communications Commission investigation, Docket No. 1, Vol. I, p. 7.
28. Interview with Fred Kleinman, Illinois Commerce Commission, June 3, 1937.
29. Interview of Howard K. Hyde, research assistant, with Paul A. Walker, member of the Federal Communications Commission, March 9, 1939.
30. Interview with Mr. McCorkle, Vice-President, Illinois Bell, January 28, 1936.
31. On this question, see my chapter, "The Limits of Decentralization," in *Free Enterprise and the Administrative State* (Tuscaloosa, Ala.: University of Alabama Press, 1951).

CHAPTER 14. RESPONSIBILITY AND RESPONSE

1. David Cushman Coyle, "The Big Cannot Be Free," *Atlantic Monthly*, Vol. 179 (June, 1947).
2. See my articles on the principles underlying public corporations in the October and December, 1949, issues of the *American Political Science Review*, XLIII, 899–921, 1145–1164; also articles by Sir Josiah Stamp, Sir Henry Bunbury, and others in *Public Administration* (London: circa 1928–36).
3. The best statement of principle is found in *Report of the Committee of Inquiry into the Electricity Supply Industry* (Herbert Committee) (London: H.M.S.O., Cmd. 9672, 1956); and National Coal Board, *Report of the Advisory Committee on Organization* (Fleck Committee) (London: National Coal Board, February, 1955).
4. See Chapter 11.
5. Russell Baker, "Lexicon of Gobbledygookese," *The New York Times Magazine*, January 26, 1958.
6. J. Donald Kingsley, *Representative Bureaucracy* (Yellow Springs, Ohio: Antioch Press, 1944); E. N. Gladden, *Civil Service or Bureaucracy?* (London: Staples, 1956); Philip Selznick, "Co-optation: A Mechanism for Organizational Stability," in Robert K. Merton (ed.), *Reader in Bureaucracy* (Glencoe, Ill.: The Free Press, 1952), pp. 135–143; and Charles S. Hyneman, *Bureaucracy in a Democracy* (New York: Harper & Brothers, 1950).

7. See Chapter 13.
8. *Report of the Advisory Committee on Organisation* (Fleck Committee), p. 42; see also section entitled "Standards of Performance," pp. 62–63.
9. Webster Robinson, *Fundamentals of Business Organization* (New York: McGraw-Hill Book Company, 1925), p. 36.
10. Edmund P. Learned, David N. Ulrich, and Donald R. Booz, *Executive Action* (Boston: Harvard University Press, 1951), p. 37.
11. See Alexander Leighton, *The Governing of Men* (Princeton: Princeton University Press, 1946), pp. 304–352; Eli Ginsberg and Ewing W. Reilley, *Effecting Change in Large Organizations* (New York: Columbia University Press, 1957), p. 148; and Ronald Lippitt, Jeanne Watson, and Bruce Westley, *The Dynamics of Planned Change* (New York: Harcourt Brace and Company, 1958).

CHAPTER 15. POWER AND SECURITY

1. This point is developed admirably in A. D. Bonham-Carter's article, "The Motive Power of Higher Management," in *Vitality in Administration* (London: George Allen & Unwin, 1957), Chapter V.
2. Chris Argyris, *Personality and Organization* (New York: Harper & Brothers, 1957), pp. 37–44. Argyris points out that the deeper the psychological need, the more important it is to release potential energy.
3. Edmund P. Learned, David N. Ulrich, and Donald R. Booz, *Executive Action* (Boston: Harvard University Press, 1951), pp. 108, 198, 208.
4. Alexander H. Leighton, *The Governing of Men* (Princeton: Princeton University Press, 1946), p. 339.
5. *Ibid.*, p. 350 (italics added).
6. See Chapter 11.
7. Sir Oliver S. Franks, *Britain and the Tide of World Affairs* (London: Oxford University Press, 1955), pp. 69–70.
8. W. Arthur Lewis, *The Theory of Economic Growth* (London: George Allen & Unwin, 1955), pp. 70–77.
9. For an interesting discussion of this issue, see James D. Thompson and Frederick L. Bates, *Technology, Organization, and Administration* (Administrative Science Center, University of Pittsburgh, printed pamphlet, Reprint No. 1, 1957).

10. Peter Drucker, "The IBM Story," in *The Practice of Management* (New York: Harper & Brothers, 1954), Chapter 19.
11. William H. Whyte, Jr., *The Organization Man* (New York: Simon & Schuster, 1956), p. 401.
12. *Ibid.*, pp. 394, 396.
13. Drew Middleton, *These are the British* (New York: Alfred A. Knopf, 1957), Chapter X, pp. 197 ff.
14. *Ibid.*, p. 199.
15. David Nicolson, "Demarcation: A Problem in Industry," *The Listener*, May 2, 1957, pp. 699–701.
16. Middleton, *op. cit.*, p. 204.
17. *Ibid.*, p. 205.
18. This program is sponsored by the Trades Union Congress and is said to be highly successful. Interview with the Right Honorable John Edwards, M.P., London, March 18, 1958.
19. Clark Kerr, *Unions and Union Leaders of Their Own Choosing* (New York: The Fund for the Republic, 1957) (italics added).
20. Robert N. McMurry, "Manhunt for Top Executives," *Harvard Business Review*, Vol. 32 (January-February, 1954), p. 46.
21. Drucker, *op. cit.*, pp. 205–206.
22. Harry A. Hopf, book review in *Georgetown Law Review*, XXIV (1936), 1066.
23. John H. Williams, "Is There an Optimum Size of Organization?" *Bulletin of the Taylor Society*, XV (February, 1930), 22.
24. Acton Society Trust, *Size and Morale* (London: pamphlets, two parts, 1953 and 1957), a study of attendance at work in large and small units.
25. Acton Society Trust, *Hospitals and the State* (London: 1956), Vol. II, p. 23 (italics added).
26. H. P. Barker, "Have Large Firms an Advantage in Industry?" *The Listener*, May 30, 1957, pp. 872–874.
27. Learned, Ulrich, and Booz, *op. cit.*, pp. 210, 212.

CHAPTER 16. A VITAL ECONOMY

1. "A Suggestion for Mobility," *The Economist*, June 23, 1956, pp. 1164–1166.
2. Dealt with and refuted in John Jewkes, David Sawers, Richard Stillerman, *The Sources of Invention* (London and New York: The Macmillan Company, 1958), Chapter IX.

3. See, for example, Edward Crankshaw, *Russia Without Stalin: The Emerging Pattern* (London: Joseph Michael, 1956); also Harry Schwartz, "The Organization Man, Soviet Style," *The New York Times Magazine*, June 2, 1957.

Index

Accountability, and managerial freedom, 70ff, 220ff
Achievement motivation, in administration, 125ff, 188
Acton Society Trust, 74, 91n, 96n, 97n, 257
Adaptation, to change, 236ff
and specialization, 33, 66ff
Adjustment, *see also* Response
to administrative reorganization, 151-152
to change, 236ff
examples of, 147ff
a process, 144ff
Advisory Committee on Organization, *see* Fleck Committee
Administration, achievement motive in, 125ff
decentralization of, 199ff, 206ff, 210ff
and mobility, 146-147
by objectives, 189ff
sources of bureaucracy, 87ff
Administrative federalism, 199-200; *see also* Decentralization
Administrative Staff College, xi-xii, 136-137
Alfred P. Sloan Foundation, xi, xiii
American Telephone & Telegraph Company, xi, 234
as case history, 200ff
Aquinas, Thomas, 53
Archbold, John D., 15
Argyris, Chris, 54, 105-106, 197n, 242n
Atkinson, J. W., 123n, 126n

Bailey, Stephen, 54n
Baker, Russell, 232n
Barker, H. P., 257-258
Barnard, Chester, 87, 123, 134, 139n, 168-169, 193-194, 200, 207
Barnett, H. G., 49
Bates, Frederick L., 246n
Bell Laboratories, 132, 200, 212
Bell System, *see* American Telephone & Telegraph Company
Berle, A. A., Jr., 17, 21n, 40ff, 77, 114
Berlew, D., 127n
Beveridge, W. I. B., 133-134
Big business, *see also* Size
pioneering in, 11ff
Blau, Peter M., 98, 99
Bone, Edith, 108n
Bonham-Carter, A. D., 27n, 242n
Bonner, J. T., 33n, 34
Booz, D. R., 108, 114, 179-180, 197, 237n, 242n, 260
Brandeis, Louis, 188-189, 257
British Electricity Industry, as case history, 61ff
British hospital administration, 39-40, 73-74, 95-96, 97
British Overseas Airways, 147
Brooks, R. H., 208n, 211n
Brown, Donaldson, 199n
Budgeting, influence on bureaucracy, 91
Bunbury, Sir Henry, xiii, 223n
Bureaucracy, advantages claimed, 80ff
American, 98ff, 227
behavior in, 104ff
blended with enterprise, 173ff, 267ff

British, 227
defined, 3–4, 59–60
and the economy, 89, 261ff
and education, 89
elements of, 1–2
external sources, 87ff
French, 226
German, 226–227
and hierarchy, 95–96
and impersonality, 79, 82, 98–99
incentives needed, 187–188
independent life of, 82, 96
inefficiencies of, 102–103
influence of budgeting, 91
　of control function, 91
　of directing function, 91
　of family, 89, 126–127
　of government, 89
　of labor unions, 89, 91
　of organization, 90–91
　of personal factor, 93ff
　of planning, 90
　of position classification, 91
　of professionalization, 91
　of public policy, 89
　of size, 92–93
　of specialization, 91
　of supervisory function, 91
internal sources, 90
and legalism, 88–89
and the military, 88, 108–109, 114
and organization, 179–180, 199
pathologies of, 102ff
personality in, 94–95
and power, 241ff
power and status, 113ff
re-examined, 86ff
and religion, 88
responsibility avoided, 110ff
in Roman Egypt, 115–116
self-centeredness and stratification, 106ff
sources of, 87ff
theory of, 264–265
traditional case for, 76ff
a universal phenomenon, 1ff
Weber's thesis evaluated, 83ff
Burin, Frederic S., 82n
Burnham, James, 77, 243

Carter, C. F., 182n
Carter, E. F., 214n
Change, see also Adaptation and Adjustment
　effecting, 238–239
　response to, 6–7, 236ff
Chester, D. N., 12n
Clarey, Northrup, 21n
Clark, Russell A., 123n
Cochran, Thomas C., 12n
Cole, Arthur, 139n, 141n, 142ff
Cole, Taylor, 113
Committee of Inquiry into Electricity Supply Industry, see Herbert Committee
Competition, as incentive, 128–129, 211–212
Control, administrative, influence on bureaucracy, 91
Cooper, C. P., 203n, 205n
Coordination, and hierarchy, 65–66
　through leadership, 191–192, 248–249
　and organization, 34
　and specialization, 32ff
Corporations, large, 40–41, see also Size
　responsibility of, 201–202, 222
Coyle, David Cushman, 220
Crankshaw, Edward, 267n
Creative minority, influence of, 50–51, 53
Crider, John H., 113n

Danhof, Clarence H., 139n
Danielson, Noobar R., 200
Dante, 55
Davis, Arthur K., 104, 108–109, 110n, 114
Davis, Ralph C., 181n
De Bruhl, Steve, 199n
Decay, elements of, 46ff
　nature of, 48ff
　prevention, 57–58
　symptoms, 45ff
　theories of, 45ff
Decentralization, in administration, 199ff, 206ff, 210ff
Dickinson, John, 88

Index 295

Directing function, 91, 191–192
Dimock, M. E., 87n, 89n, 109n, 190n, 217n, 223n
Dreyfuss, Carl, 113–114
Drucker, Peter F., 112–113, 150–151, 190, 190n, 246, 255
Dudintsev, Vladimir, xii, 108, 111, 112, 196
Du Pont Co., 24, 259

Eades, G. E., 111n
Easterbrook, W. T., 139n
Eastman, Lucius, 107–108
Economy, the, and bureaucracy, 89
vitality of, 261ff
Education, and bureaucracy, 89
for leadership, 194ff
Edwards, John, 252n
Edwards, Ronald, 65n
Efficiency, defined, 102, 102n
effect of bureaucracy, 102–103
and people, 191
Weber's thesis, 80
Emerson, Harrington, 102
Enders, Robert K., 33, 34n
Energy, in administration, 191–192
forms of, 54–55
and power, 241
Enterprise, *see also* Entrepreneur
blended with bureaucracy, 173ff, 267ff
defined, 5, 119–120
effort and reward, 128
elements of, 2, 121–122, 143
ideas in, 130ff
incentive, 122ff
and opportunism, 147ff
person and process, 136ff
personal qualities needed, 142
process in, 142ff
profit as a motive, 128ff
responsibility and response, 218ff
role of the person, 137ff
theory of, 265ff
Weber's thesis, 81
Enterpriser, *see* Entrepreneur
Entrepreneur, defined, 124–125, 138–139
qualities of, 144

Entrepreneurship, elements of, 143
Equilibrium, and size, 51ff

Family, and bureaucracy, 89, 126–127
Fisher, J. W., Jr., 209n, 210n, 211n
Fleck, Sir Alexander, 7n, 29n, 114n, 131n, 183
Fleck Committee, 73, 93, 106, 151–152, 176, 224n, 235n
Flexibility, *see* Adjustment *and* Mobility
Ford, Henry, 192
Francis, Roy G., 99–100
Franks, Sir Oliver, 244–245
Friedrich, Carl J., 84, 107, 113
Functionalism, limitations of, 236

General Electric Company, 20, 106
General Mills, as case history, 21ff
General Motors, xi, 42, 93, 96, 199, 200
Gerth, H. H., 77n, 81n, 82n
Gherardi, Bancroft, 205–206, 208
Gibb, George S., 12n, 13, 18ff
Gifford, Walter, 203n, 205, 214
Ginzberg, Eli, 7n, 93n, 147n, 239n
Gladden, E. N., xii, 185–186, 233n
Goodman, B. W., 166n
Goormaghtigh, John, 90n
Gordon, Robert, 141
Government, economic role of, 42, 89, 266–267
Gray, James, 12n, 21ff
Groups, in administration, 142
and individuals, 144
social, 35–36
Growth, *see also* Size
biological theory of, 32ff
and bureaucracy, 40ff
economic theory of, 37ff
institutional, 9ff, 30–31
and mobility, 145
social theory of, 34ff
and vitality, 43–44

Hale, Merle, 199n
Hale, E. K., 206n
Hall, Sir Noel, xiii
Halligan, J. E., 208n, 211n

Index 296

Harvard Research Center in Entrepreneurial History, xii, 12n, 139n
Hayworth, Sir Geoffrey, 24, 26ff
Hegel, Georg Wilhelm Friedrich, 48
Henderson, A. M., 77n
Herbert Committee, 61ff, 65ff, 72, 224
Hidy, Ralph W., and Muriel E., 12n, 13ff, 19
Hierarchy, *see also* Stratification
 influence of, 95–96
Hill, Cyrus, 212n
Hobson, J. A., 129
Holmes, Oliver Wendell, 209
Homogeneity, in administration, 55ff
Hopf, Harry A., 255–256
Hospital administration, British, *see* British hospital administration
Hyde, Howard K., 200n, 216n
Hyneman, Charles S., 233n
Human relations, in administration, 180–181, 184ff

Ideas, in enterprise, 130ff
Imperial Chemicals Industries Limited, 25, 114
 as case history, 28ff
Incentives, in a bureacracy, 186ff
 in enterprise, 69–70, 122ff
Individuals, in a bureaucracy, 117, 185ff
 bureaucratic behavior of, 94–95, 104ff, 242ff
 and the group, 142, 144
 influence on bureaucracy, 93ff
 in large institutions, 42–43, 81–82
 role in enterprise, 137ff
Innovation, *see also* Ideas *and* Invention
 and entrepreneurship, 150–151
 and growth, 38–39
International Business Machines, 190, 246
Invention, *see also* Ideas *and* Innovation
 in enterprise, 130ff

Jewkes, John, and others, 131–132, 133, 134n, 195, 196n, 267n
Juran, Joseph M., 106, 107

Kappel, Frederick R., 201n, 202n
Karpat, Kemal, 89n
Kendall, Henry, 177
Kennedy, F. B., 209n, 210n, 211n
Kerr, Clark, 41–42, 252
Kingsley, J. Donald, 233n
Kleinman, Fred, 216n
Knowlton, Evelyn H., 12n, 13, 18ff
Kopac, M. J., 33n

Labor unions, and bureaucracy, 42, 89, 91
 vested interests of, 249ff
Laski, Harold J., 110
Laski, Norman, 160n, 162n
Lasswell, Harold, 243
Laura Spelman Rockefeller Foundation, xi, xiii
Leadership, and authority, 197–198
 education for, 194ff
 mitigating rules, 99
 role of, 53ff, 175ff, 242, 248–249
Learned, E. O., 108, 114, 179–180, 197, 237n, 242n, 260
Lee, John, 179
Legalism, and bureaucracy, 88–89
 excessive reliance on, 225ff, 228ff
Leighton, Alexander, 239n, 243
Lever Brothers & Unilever Limited, 93
 as case history, 23ff
Leverhulme, Lord, 24
Lewis, Ben W., 39–40, 74–75
Lewis, W. Arthur, xii, 1, 37ff, 141, 245
Lippitt, Ronald, 239n
Logan, James P., 147n
Lowell, Edgar L., 123n
Lynex, R. A., 28n

Management, and technology, 181ff
Managerial freedom, and accountability, 70ff, 220ff
Managers, influence of, 95
 remoteness of, 192–193
Marks, Michael, 154
Marks, Sir Simon, 157, 158, 159n, 161, 162, 166, 170, 192, 231

Index

Marks & Spencer, 56, 190, 245
  as case history, 153ff
Marx, Karl, 48
Mayo, Elton, 123
McClelland, David, 123n, 124–125, 127, 129, 137
McClelland, Robert G., 12n
McMurry, Robert M., 253
Means, Gardiner, 17
Melchett, Lord, 28
Merton, Robert K., xii, 77n, 80n, 82n, 85, 94n, 104n, 114n, 233n
Michels, Robert, 114
Middleton, Drew, 249ff
Military administration, and bureaucracy, 88, 108–109, 114
Miller, David R., 126n
Mills, C. Wright, xii, 42–43, 52, 77n, 81n, 82n, 109, 114–115, 186
Milstein, Freda, 126n
Milward, G. E., 12n, 24n, 28n
Mobility, administrative implications, 146–147
  economic implications, 145–146
Monck, Bosworth, 182
Murray, Henry A., 123–124, 129

Neden, Sir Wilfrid, 98n, 187n
New York University, xiii
Newman, William H., 147n
Nicholson, David, 250, 251n
Nuffield, Lord, 192

Objectives, administration by, 189ff
Organization, influence on bureaucracy, 90–91, 199
  in enterprise, 179–180
  and size, 61ff

Page, Arthur W., xiii, 203–204, 215
Parkinson, C. Northcote, xii–xiii, 110, 111, 115
Parsons, Talcott, 77n
Pennsylvania Railroad, xi
Planning, and growth, 38
  influence on bureaucracy, 90
  and strategy, 149–150
Plato, 48
Policy, centralized, 202ff

Policy, public, see Public policy
Pope, Alexander, 4
Position classification, 91, 180
Pound, Arthur, 199n
Power, bureaucratic, 113ff
  and security, 241ff
Process, of adjustment, 144ff
  in enterprise, 142ff
Professional exclusiveness, 243ff
Professionalization, influence on bureaucracy, 91
  and specialization, 66ff
Profit, as incentive, 128ff
Psychology, and enterprise theory, 127–128
Public policy, and bureaucracy, 89
  and responsibility, 220ff

Reilly, Ewing W., 7n, 93n, 147n, 239n
Religion, influence on bureaucracy, 88
Resistance, bureaucratic, 237ff
Response, to change, 236ff
  obstacles to, 231ff
Responsibility, avoidance of, 110ff
  and response, 218ff
  securing, 220–221, 223–224
Robinson, Webster, 236
Rockefeller, John D., 14, 15, 21
Rosen, Bernard C., 127n
Routine, remedy for, 246
Royal Institute of Public Administration, The, xii, 12n
Rules, influence of, 100
  and leadership, 99
  Weber's thesis, 79–80

Sawers, David, 121–132, 133, 134n, 195, 196n, 267n
Schumpeter, Joseph A., xii, 48, 76–77, 84, 129, 130, 138, 139n, 139–140, 141, 142
Schwartz, Harry, 267n
Scientific management, elements of, 177ff
  and human relations, 180–181
  at Marks & Spencer, 162ff
Sears, Roebuck, xi, 88

Seaton, G. L., 209n, 210n, 211n
Security, and power, 241ff
Select Committee on Nationalized Industries, 72
Self-centeredness, in a bureaucracy, 106ff, 233ff
Selznick, Philip, 233n
Shakespeare, William, 56, 188
Sieff, I. M., 157, 163n
Simon, Herbert A., 77n, 102n, 110–111
Size, *see also* Growth
  and communication, 37
  effect of, 104ff, 252ff
  and the family firm, 259
  influence on bureaucracy, 92–93
  at Marks & Spencer, 166
  optimum, 255ff
  and organization, 61ff
  pitfalls of, 72–73
  and the profit motive, 129–130
  and social distance, 114
  a symptom of weakness, 52–53
Skill groups, exclusiveness of, 243ff
Sloan, Alfred P., Jr., 199
Smallpiece, Basil, 147n
Specialization, and adaptation, 33
  and coordination, 32–33
  influence on bureaucracy, 91
  and professionalization, 66ff
Spencer, Thomas, 154
Spengler, Oswald, 48
Staff function, 212ff
Stamp, Sir Josiah, 223n
Standard Oil, 25, 26–27, 29
  as case history, 13ff
Standards of performance, 210ff, 234–235
Status, as bureaucratic pathology, 113ff
Stillerman, Richard, 131–132, 133, 134n, 195, 196, 267n
Stone, Robert C., 99–100
Stratification, *see also* Hierarchy
  bureaucratic, 96, 106ff
  causes of, 109–110
Supervision, influence on bureaucracy, 91

Tarbell, Ida, 18

Tarkowski, Z. M. T., 94n
Tawney, R. H., 129
Taylor, Frederick W., 177, 181
Tead, Ordway, 104–105, 190n, 191, 247
Technology, and management, 181ff
Thompson, James D., 246n
Toynbee, Arnold, 49ff, 55–56, 123, 219, 263
Trusteeship, at A T & T, 201–202

Ulrich, D. N., 108, 114, 179–180, 197, 237n, 242n, 260
Unions, *see* Labor unions
United States Steel, 42, 96, 213
University of Chicago, xi, xiii
Urwick, L., 179

Variation, and organization, 33–34
Veerhusen, H. H., 213n
Vitality, and competition, 5ff
  conditions needed for, 2
  contributions of bureaucracy and enterprise, 267ff
  defined, 5
  economic, 261ff
  environment for, 270–271
  paradox of, x

Washburn, Cadwallader, 21ff
Waterson, K. W., 207n
Watson, Jeanne, 239n
Weber, Max, 48, 74, 77ff, 88, 96ff, 226, 227, 264
Wellens, John, 41n
Wells, H. G., 129
Western Electric Company, 200, 212
Westley, Bruce, 239n
White, Percival, 177
Whyte, William H., Jr., x, xii, 76, 77, 133, 138, 246–247, 248
Wilson, F. M. G., 12n
Williams, B. R., 182n
Williams, John H., 256–257
Winkleman, E. H., 208n, 211n
Wood, Robert E., 88n
Worth, C. Brooks, 33, 34n

Young, Owen D., 107
Young, R. D., 182n